Jerry & Regina Greenberg

The Sacraments and Social Progress

BY THE SAME AUTHOR

A Igreja em estado de dialogo. Manhumirim, Brazil: 0 Lutador, 1965.

Le Coeur de Marie, Coeur de l'Eglise. Paris: Lethielleux, 1967.

Padres Profetas e Mistagogos. São Paulo, Brazil: Ed. Paulinas, 1968.

Reinhold Niebuhr, théologien de la communauté mondiale. Paris-Brussels: Desclée de Brouwer, 1969.

Christ for the World. Chicago: Franciscan Herald Press, 1974.

La Trinite' Chretienne dans l'Histoire, Paris; Beauchesne, 1974.

The publishers express their gratitude to the International Institute of the Heart of Jesus for its generous cooperation in the publication of this book.

This is I I H J Publication No. 2.

The Sacraments and Social Progress

BY BERTRAND DE MARGERIE S.J.

Translated by Malachy Carroll

FRANCISCAN HERALD PRESS

1434 WEST 51st STREET • CHICAGO, 60609

The Sacraments and Social Progress, by Bertrand de Margerie S.J., translated by Malachy Carroll. 1434 West 51st Street, Chicago, Illinois 60609.

Library of Congress Cataloging in Publication Data:

Library of Congress Cataloging in Publication Data

Margerie, Bertrand de.
The sacraments and social progress.

Bibliography: p.
1. Sacraments—Catholic Church. 2. Sociology, Christian (Catholic)
I. Title. BX2203.M3713 261.8 74-1451 ISBN 0-8199-0499-6

Imprimi Potest:
Daniel L. Flaherty S.J.
Provincial, Chicago Province of the Society of Jesus

Imprimatur:
Msgr. Richard A, Rosemeyer, J.C.D.
Vicar General, Archdiocese of Chicago

April 17, 1974

"The Nihil Obstat and Imprimatur are official declarations that a book or pamphlet is free of doctrinal or moral error. No indication is contained therein that those who have granted the Nihil Obstat and Imprimatur agree with the contents, opinions, or statements expressed."

MADE IN THE UNITED STATES OF AMERICA

Contents

Abbreviations

AAS — *Acta Apostolicae Sedis*, Rome, 1909 ff.

Abbott — W. M. Abbott, ed., *The Documents of Vatican II*. New York: America Press, and London: Geoffrey Chapman, 1966.

AG — *Ad Gentes*, Decree of Vatican II on the Church's Missionary Activity.

DBS — *Dictionnaire de la Bible Supplement*, Paris, 1928 ff.

DC — *Documentation Catholique*, Paris.

DV — *Dei Verbum*, Dogmatic Constitution of Vatican II on Divine Revelation.

DSAM — *Dictionnaire de Spiritualité Ascétique et Mystique*, Paris, 1923.

DTC — *Dictionnaire de Théologie Catholique*, Paris, 1903, ff.

ES — *Ecclesiam Suam*, Encyclical of Paul VI on Council Themes of Vatican II, August 6, 1964.

GS — *Gaudium et Spes*, Pastoral Constitution of Vatican II on the Church in the Modern World.

HV — *Humanae Vitae*, Encyclical of Paul VI on Birth Control, July 25, 1968.

LG — *Lumen Gentium*, Dogmatic Constitution of Vatican II on the Church.

MG J. P. Migne, *Patrologia Graeca*, Paris, 1857-1866.

ML J. P. Migne, *Patrologia Latina*, Paris, 1878-1890.

MM *Mater et Magistra*, Encyclical of John XXIII on Christianity and Social Progress, May 15, 1961.

NRT *Nouvelle Revue Théologique*, Louvain, 1879 ff.

OT *Optatam Totius*, Decree of Vatican II on Priestly Formation.

PG *Patrologia Graeca* (J. P. Migne), Paris, 1857-1866.

PL *Patrologia Latina* (J. P. Migne), Paris, 1879-1890.

PO *Presbyterorum Ordinis*, Decree of Vatican II on the Ministry and Life of Priests.

PP *Populorum Progressio*, Encyclical of Paul VI on the Development of Peoples, March 26, 1967.

PT *Pacem in* Terris, Encyclical of John XXIII on Peace in the World, April 11, 1963.

QA *Quadragesimo Anno*, Encyclical of Pius XI on Social Reconstruction, May 15, 1931.

RUO *Revue de l'Université d'Ottawa.*

SC *Sacrosanctum Concilium*, Constitution of Vatican II on the Sacred Liturgy.

ST *Summa Theologica* of St. Thomas Aquinas.

STS *Summa Theologica, Supplement*, of St. Thomas Aquinas.

UR *Unitatis Redintegratio*, Decree of Vatican II on Ecumenism.

Introduction

THE idea of a liberating development of the human person and of human society is one of principal foci of contemporary thought. It is also the ambition which inspires the action and shapes the projects of modern man.

In his encyclical, "Populorum Progressio," Pope Paul VI has formally committed the Church to devote herself to the development of the world. We have presented, in another context,[1] the basic elements of the idea of development as this pope synthesized them:

"Development cannot be limited to mere economic growth. In order to be authentic, it must be complete, integral; that is, it has to promote the good of every man and of the whole man. . . . In the design of God, every man is called upon to develop and fulfil himself, for every life is a vocation. . . . Endowed with intelligence and freedom, he is responsible for his fulfilment as he is for his salvation. . . . By the unaided[2] effort of his own intelligence and will, each man can grow in humanity, can enhance his personal worth, can become more a person".[3]

Human development, as understood in the light of what Pope Paul says, has therefore a meaning which is inseparably personal and social. It is concerned with developing, on the one hand, man's faculties, his mind and his will, his whole psychic dynamism, and, on the other, his social action, his power to make nature serve man, his earning ability. It is growth towards freedom from all the chains that bind and enslave man and society.

In this book, we propose to examine the indispensable and unique contribution made by the sacramental life of the Catholic Church to the personal, economic, and social development of man and of society. Does not Vatican II exhort us to react against the "false opposition between professional and social activities on the one hand, and religious life on the other"?[4] Now, is not the sacramental life the religious life *par excellence?* It would be inconceivable that each and all of the seven sacraments instituted by Christ should not influence the human, professional, economic, and social life of those who receive them.

If the sacraments are to presented in a manner acceptable to modern man, they must be seen by him to be at the very heart of his vision of the universe. Now, as Father Calvez tells us, "man's center of interest has shifted. It is no longer the social or mental situation in which man is and ought to be, for this center of interest is no longer even man.[5] It is now the process of development, in which he is caught up, a process which is not, however, outside himself. It is his development, something achieved by himself and first of all on himself. It is also, therefore, his future, and is concerned with creating something different from his present."[6]

What can the sacramental life within the Church contribute to the future of man? Of what value for this future are the seven sacraments instituted by Christ, Himself the sacrament *par excellence* and the absolute future of man — if one may combine the expressions of Saint Augustine and of Karl Rahner?

By and large, therefore, what we are seeking to outline here, though sketchily of course, is a theology of the interpersonal and socio-economic radiating influence of the sacraments inasmuch as they transform the future of man and society. We hold, with Moltmann, that "in the dynamic movement out-of-the-past-into-the-future which is man, the future projected on the basis of the past is of critical importance. The hoped-for future makes history; it makes our history today by evoking our decisions today: it made the history of the past, for past decisions were also made on the basis of what was then regarded as the future to be hoped for in the real possibilities the then-present moment."[7]

This amounts to saying, in modern terms, that man acts for a variety of purposes, all inter-related and all polarized by the eschatological dynamism of his final purpose. He acts in order to achieve self-fulfilment, and thus to come to the vision of Him who, through the sacraments, develops man. If the sacraments are the "structures" of the Covenant of the Lord and of His "being-with-men,"[8] they are and should be also the structures of human action, of an "acting-with-and-in Christ the Savior." In short, the sacraments are the structures of the supernatural development to which man aspires in his desire to see and to enjoy the God who is Light, Love, devouring Fire.

This book contains numerous texts of Scripture used in a variety of ways. Sometimes a text is used in its literal sense (the meaning the inspired writer intended) and in its full sense (the meaning God intended),[9] but not without thought for historic context or literary genre. So, for example, a fresh interpretation of Gn. 1, 28, is offered, in the light of Jr. 29, 6. In chapter VI especially, I cite numerous modern exegetes to justify my views.

In other instances, I cite Biblical texts designed to clarify and illustrate my idea, but without claiming to establish their literal sense (what the hagiographer wanted to say). At times, I follow the practice of the Fathers of the Church, who investigate the Old Testament in the light of the New Testament and *vice versa*. My purpose, like theirs, is to seek out the full meaning. Such a method is often the only way to meet the wish expressed by Vatican II in a work not specifically intended for professional exegetes, among whom I do not number myself: "The exploration and exposition of the divine writings should be done in such a way that as many ministers of the divine word as possible will be able effectively to provide the nourishment of the Scriptures for the People of God, thereby enlightening their minds, strengthening their wills, and setting men's hearts on fire with the love of God."[10]

Sometimes, I use a Biblical text simply as an extension of what I have been saying. Thus, in citing Gn. 11, 7, concerning the multiplicity of human languages, I do not pretend (nor would the hagiographer) to give a technical explanation valid at the level of secondary causes, but rather to proceed as does Vatican II, which uses this text following the Fathers of the Church[11] and thus marking the relationship between this phenomenon and the divine plan of salvation. The reader is not to conclude from this that I contemn modern research, notably of the philosophical kind, into the diversity of languages. I have made an extended analysis of some of this research in my book: *Reinhold Niebuhr, théologien de la communauté mondiale* (Brussels, 1969, pp. 143-150 and 383-390).

Aquinas Institute of Theology
Dubuque, Iowa Bertrand de Margerie S.J.

NOTES

[1] See our Book: *Le Christ pour le Monde* (Paris: Beauchesne, 1971). chapter 16, p. 414. English translation, *Christ for the World* (chicago: Franciscan Hearld Press, 1974).

[2] "Unaided" must be understood here as referring to the absence of aid from social influences, as the context clearly show. There is, of course, no suggestion of the absence of divine aid.

[3] PP, par. 20, 14, 15.

[4] GS, par. 43. 1.

[5] No doubt, the author means human nature, if one can think of it as distinct from its dynamism—which anyhow is impossible.

[6] J. Y. Calvez S.J., "Eglise et Développement," *Gregorianum,* 49 (1968), 627.

[7] Christopher Kiesling O.P., "Theology of Hope: Moltmann's contribution to catechetics," *The Living Light,* 5 (1968), 82. Similar ideas can be found in J.B. Metz, *Theology of the World,* N.Y., 1969, chap. 3, theses 1 and 2, pp. 83-93.

[8] Y. M. J. Congar O.P., *Sacerdoce et Laicat,* Paris, 1962, p. 130.

[9] cf. DV, par 12.

[10] DV, par 33.

[11] AG, par. 4

Translator's Note

For most of the Vatican II documents cited in this book the translation is that given in Walter M. Abbott S.J., General Editor, *The Documents of Vatican II* (London: Geoffrey Chapman, and New York: Guild Press, America Press, Association Press, 1966—abbreviated Abbott. Other papal documents and encyclicals are quoted from English translations published by the Catholic Truth Society (England). Translations are also found in *The Pope Speaks* (U.S.A.).

I wish to thank my colleague, Rev. Michael Downey, Ph. L., S.T.L., of the Department of Divinity, University of London Institute of Education, Coloma College, West Wickham, Kent, England, who acted as theological advisor throughout this translation.

Malachy Carroll

chapter one

Baptism and Confirmation: Sacraments of the Pledge to Foster Human Development

THE desire to see God, to see Him forever and to see Him in the company of other men, by escaping from corruption and death, is one of the constituents of human nature, and therefore an integral part of the human person. Man—a social, metaphysical and religious animal—is designed to see His Creator and to love Him with all the power of a fully developed activity of body and soul, of personal and social being.[1]

That this desire fails to become consciously explicit in an adult person, is an anomaly due to his particular circumstances and in no way destroys the natural character of such a design. It is the desire of every developing person, and it is implicit in all his particular desires as their presupposition and their horizon. It can be explaned by the dynamisms of man's natural personality, without any recourse to supernatural assistance; and this to such an extent that it subsists even in one who has chosen, against God and against himself, the disintegration of a false happiness, and even in the damned with whom this evil choice is definitive. However, this desire encounters and receives exterior and interior invitations from divine grace which seeks to divinize it and to satisfy it, at least inchoatively.

It is to this mysterious and basic desire, springing up in every man from the depths of his psychic dynamism, that Vatican II alludes in the following extracts:

"It is in the face of death that the riddle of human existence becomes most acute. Not only is man tormented by pain and by the advancing deterioration of his body, but even more so by a dread of perpetual extinction. He rightly follows the intuition of his heart when he abhors and repudiates the absolute ruin and total disappearance of his own person. Man rebels against death because he bears in himself an eternal seed which cannot be reduced to sheer matter.... For a prolongation of biological life is unable to satisfy that desire for a higher life which is inescapably lodged in his breast.[2]"

It is the grace of Christ the Redeemer which comes to save him by divinizing him and by beginning to fill him, through the gift of a supernatural love of God and of men, with this desire which, thanks to this grace, is not in vain. In and through this grace, the Blood of Christ ransoms, saves, and divinizes a desire of which He is, as God, the incessant Creator; and He does so by inserting into the mystery of His own paschal and sacrificial decision, this natural desire for full development which, as the Word inseparable from His Father and from Their Spirit, He ceaselessly causes to spring up in every human heart.

The decision to die and to rise from the dead for the salvation of the world and for the glory of the Father, is the decision of the personal development of Jesus in His individual human nature and of His development in all mankind. This decision of sacrificial development was solemnly manifested at His last Jewish Supper, followed by the first Supper of the Kingdom of the Son of Man. The Cross and the Resurrection, the Pasch of the only Son, constitutes at once His kenosis and His definitive growth. Through baptism, the Christian is grafted in this sacrificial decison of growth and fulfilment.

Thus the purely human design of development, a design which springs necessarily from the depths of every man concerned to fulfil himself, is washed and baptized in the blood which flows from the pierced Heart of Christ, in the life-giving water of the Spirit of Jesus. By incorporating himself with Christ through baptism, the adult integrates his basic design to be himself and to be all things[3] with the paschal choice of Christ the Redeemer, with the twofold decision of the human will and the divine will of the Savior to complete Himself and to consummate the universe (cf. Rm. 8, 19/f.; Ph. 3, 21; Jn. 19, 30) in passing from this world to the Father (Jn. 13, 1). In the case of an adult baptism, the baptismal action of the glorious Christ is an integration of the neophyte's decision with the decision of His divine-human activity. Let us clarify this point, so that by its light we may gain a better understanding of the significance of infant baptism and of the renewal of the baptismal vows, in the context of personal and social development.

The grace of baptism is the justification of the impious,[4] of the lost and hateful unbeliever.[5] Such justification is the remission of sins, the freely given and freely accepted passage from injustice to justice, that is, from being the enemy of God to being His friend with a friendship of faith and of hope.

The infusion of baptismal grace, therefore, divinizes and saves the human design of development which the adult person was pursuing. At the same time, the baptismal character, by deeply immersing the whole mind of the adult person in the Mystery of the Church, integrates this design with the complete design of the whole People of God, which is none other than the divine-human design of Christ deployed in time and space.

For the grace of justification and the baptismal character have important inter-personal and social implications for each baptized person and for the whole body of the baptized. As we have said elsewhere,[6] no one can be justified without receiving the supernatural love which inspires the desire to labor even for the temporal betterment of others. The freely given justification necessarily includes at least implicit faith in God's historical design for the salvation of all mankind, and the will to contribute to this design by building up, not only the Church, but also the temporal world community, in history. Reinhold Niebuhr saw this very clearly, even if he did not grasp all the implications of his intuition: justification through the gift of faith and of charity, justification which is the grace proper to baptism, has social and political aspects,[7] and, in the final analysis, envisages the consecration, the supernaturalization and the divinization of the developmental design of all mankind and of the whole People of God (although this justification immediately transforms only the personal choice for development).

In effect, if already, at the natural level, a person's design of self-fulfilment is inseparable from that of all other people, the baptismal consecration and divinization of the choice for development implies the integration of this choice with the whole design of the entire People of God. It is the whole People of God that the baptismal grace of insertion into Christ's passage from this world to the Father, causes to pass from social injustice to social justice, from enmity towards men to a sacrificial friendship concerned to promote their temporal and eternal salvation. The grace of baptism commits the whole Church to the service of the health and happiness of the whole world. The state of grace, the justice which justifies, cannot be received and retained unless one is disposed to be just towards men by fostering their personal development and their development together.

There is, of course, the person who has freely rejected the design of personal and social integration written in his very being; who, on the contrary, has freely made his choice for disintegration. If baptism is received with these dispositions, how can it be denied that, however valid, it will remain sterile? Marked with the baptismal character, and therefore a member of the Church, such a baptized adult is neither justified nor divinized, because his choice against authentic development could not be assumed by Christ the Redeemer. On the other hand, the adult who prior to baptism had accepted the desire for self-fulfilment stamped in his psychic dynamism, will be able, after baptism, to persue this purpose with the help of the baptismal grace proper to baptism. It is by dying to himself and living for God and Christ, that he will bring all his energies to bear on the development of the world and of the Church. Through him, Christ will continue to be the architect of the world community and of the universal Church.

In conferring baptism on a person, in order through him to secure her own "building up," the Church incorporates in her own design of development, intended to foster the growth of the world, this person's project of self-fulfilment. She shows herself to be the sign of the God-who-is-coming, of the God to come. She is the sacrament of this coming of a God who wills to take up man's design of self-fulfilment into the design of His own pleroma. She is the sign of the frelly given redemptive divinization of man's choice for development.

At baptism, God anticipates His eschatological coming. The Christ of the Johannine Revelation says: "I will come to you... I will come to you soon... I am coming soon... Lo, I am coming like a thief!" (2, 5; 2, 16; 3, 11; 16, 15).

In the Johannine Revelation, as Father Comblin emphasizes, "God is He who will come. Saint John even introduces this attribute into the name of God, as though it belonged to the essence of Yahweh. God is called 'He who is and who was and who is to come' (1, 4. 8; 4, 8), a designation which one recognizes as an amplification of the name of God, Yahweh, according to Ex. 3, 14—the name revealed to Moses, the true divine name.... According to the author of Revelation and in accordance with the inspiration which the Holy Spirit gave to that author, God is, therefore, He who is absolute existence. But, seen in its relationship to mankind, this absolute existence presents itself as an absolutely certain future coming. As surely as God exists, He will come."[0]

If the final coming of God is designed to consummate and to fix immutably in Him man's contingent aspiration to full development, the baptismal anticipation of this final coming is already designed to rectify and to divinize this aspiration in an incomplete way.

The anticipated coming of the Son of Man, through the

Church, in baptism, signifies that He continues to proclaim, as at the Last Supper, His decision of sacrificial development in adopting as His own the purely human[9] designs of complete temporal and eschatological development. The choice of Christ the Redeemer for development, a development of which the Eucharist is the constant renewal, is a divine-human choice which assumes in baptism the purely human choices of His new members, in order to extend Himself in them to the building up of His Mystical Body.

To adopt the terminology of Karl Rahner,[10] Jesus, the absolute Future of man and of all men, Himself becomes a reality in man through baptizing men in His redemptive Blood (cf. Jn. 4, 1-2; Rom. 6, 3). The only Son of the Father comes to insert Himself in man, in order that man may be able to make good his own definition: a being capable of attaining to the absolute Future. The absolute fullness of God the Son is the supreme basis and the ultimate goal of all human striving. It is Christ Jesus who sets in motion the dynamism of developments, by giving Himself as its goal. The true point of departure, therefore, for the proper understanding of the being and activity of Man, is, therefore, the future and the light it casts on the beginnings. Man is in growth towards the Parousia of Jesus, towards the fullness of His Presence.

The baptismal grace causes the Christian to tend towards the epiphany and towards the perfect manifestation of this Presence of Jesus which, using Saint Paul's term, we call His Parousia. This Presence comes to strengthen man who finds such difficulty in becoming himself. It divinizes the fulfilment of his preeminent duty, the duty of development, so well described by Karl Rahner:

"Every construction of the future which involves man's reason and creative mind; every effort made to free man as fully as possible from slavery to nature; the whole process of the socialization of existence which aims at producing for each and every person the maximum of liberty—all this represents for Christianity a task written in the very nature of man such as God has willed it to be. Christianity sees all this as an obligation which is an integral part of its religious behavior, properly so called, the latter being in effect simply human freedom opening itself, in faith and hope, to the absolute Future. It is Christian faith in an absolute Future promised to everyone, which constitutes the only foundation for the absolute value of each and every person. It therefore engenders a conviction calculated to give to secular efforts themselves, whose purpose is to inaugurate the best possible social order, their deepest and most assured foundation."[11]

Baptism is, therefore, at once the Presence of the absolute Future of man, and the redemptive divinization of his fundamental design to be himself and to be all things.

This is what is signified and effected for the adult person by his reception of the sacrament of initiation. Now, it is not in the faith of their parents, which is often deficient, but in the faith of the Church, according to Saint Augustine and Saint Thomas Aquinas,[12] that infants are baptized. They are thus inserted into the choice of the whole People of God for the development of the world; or more accurately, they are thus integrated with Christ's own choice for the paschal and sacrificial development of His Body which is the Church. For these infants, the grace of their baptism is a grace of growth which tends towards its own fullness.

In this light, the renewal of the baptismal promises on Holy Saturday night, takes on a social and personalist dimension often unperceived by those who take part in the ceremony. Does not the renouncing of Satan with all his works and pomps in order to cleave to Christ, imply the rejection of all social injustice and personal non-fulfilment?

For a Christian, to renew his baptismal promises is to bind himself anew to combat misery, disease, ignorance, death. To renounce Satan and his works is to refuse to have any truck with all the fruits of sin inspired by him. For, is it not to pledge oneself to fight against the activity of Satan, in a world of which he is the dethroned prince and in which he is "a murderer from the beginning" (Jn. 8, 44)?

Would it be possible for the Church to add to the existing

formula of the renewal of the baptismal vows, and explicit pledge concerning the personal and social development of each and every man? At all events, there is nothing to prevent the Christian on Holy Saturday night from adding his own private pledge, sealed in the blood of Christ the Developer, concerning the development of the world. In re-affirming his faith in the Father-Creator, in the Son-Redeemer, and in the Spirit-Sanctifier of the Church, the Christian renews his promise to labor for the perfecting of the creation, to collaborate in its redemption (cf. Rm. 8) and in its sanctification. He manifests anew, before the Church and the world, his decision to save himself by helping his brethren to fulfil themselves, to save themselves and to sanctify themselves.

To renew his baptismal promise, is for the Christian to will to build up the world and the universal Church, for the love of Christ, Savior of the world and Head of the Church. It is to will to be himself fully and immutably one with the immutable Word, for love of the Spirit who is the eternal communion between the Father and the Son.

And yet, the baptized Christian who aspires, in renewing his baptismal promises, to fix himself immutably, by the supreme act of death, in the Word, is strengthened by a new gift of the Spirit of the Son in the sacrament of confirmation.

In confirming the Christian's baptism, the Spirit-Paraclete bears testimony to Christ the Redeemer and makes this Christian a solemn and public witness to Christ's salvific work. The Spirit sends the confirmed Christian to proclaim before the world that the Eucharistic Christ is his mighty "developer."

The new consecration of confirmation makes the Christian the representative and the witness of the Church to the whole world; the witness to the involvement of the whole People of God in promoting the growth and the earthly development of the world for the greater glory of the Father and of the Son. The Christian is confirmed by the Spirit in order to bear public witness to the choice of the whole

Church for the social and personal progress of each and every man.

In this personal Pentecost, the Spirit of the Father and of the Son, the Breath of Their common love for Their divine lovability, gives Himself anew to the Christian and sends him into the world to bear witness to the Pasch of the Son, passing from this world to the Father, thanks to the development of His glorious Ressurection with a view to the growth of mankind.

This Spirit, sent to confirm the Christian's baptism, also confirms in him the paschal and baptismal resolution to contribute to the development of the world. The Holy Spirit gives to the person whom He consecrates by His chrism, the rich outpouring of His gifts and charisms, in order to make him the witness, the prophet and the promoter of human development, in the fullness of the joy of the Lord—and to be so with ease and perseverance.

But there can be no development without heroism: neither can there be any without humility and the spirit of poverty. At first sight, these appear to be paradoxes. Would it not be easier, first and foremost, to develop one's personality? In reality, however, nothing is more difficult. Far from promoting personal and social development, pride with all the passions it infects suffocates such development. It prevents a man, and even a Christian, from being sensitive and responsive to the suffering, misery, ignorance, and disease of his brethren. It makes one want to be served rather than to serve. It indicates a man to accumulate the goods of this world, even by unjust methods, and this feeds his will to domination. The Holy Spirit, Confirmer of baptism, kindles in the Christian the desire to practice at least spiritual poverty in order to enrich others; to humble himself in order to honor them; and to be humbled by them in order to find occasion for abasing himself before men and, above all, before God. For otherwise how could one abase himself before God, if one did not do so before men, who are all superior and inferior to one another in various respects?[13]

Like many other saints, Saint Ignatius Loyola has urged

these dispositions in his "Spiritual Exercises,"[14] In this respect, as Pius XI has already sensed,[15] the Ignatian retreat, lived in the light and in the climate of the authentic doctrinal ideas of Vatican II, could and should be, in our age, a powerful stimulus to this personal and socio-economic development, which is impossible without humility and the spirit of poverty. Today, as in the sixteenth century, Christ wills, through these Exercises and by numerous other means, "to urge His servants and friends to devote themselves to helping all men, by attracting them to a complete spirit of poverty and to the desire to be belittled and despised, because it is from these two that humility is born. . . . From these three degrees, they will lead men to all the other virtues."[16]

Notice the forcefulness of the Ignatian expression, in this extract from the celebrated meditation on "the Two Standards." It is *all* men whom the friends of Christ must endeavor to attract to a *complete* spirit of poverty, to the desire for belittlement and scorn, as to the condition indispensable for personal and social development.

At first sight, this statement might well cause surprise. Would it not be better to urge men to try to increase their personal and collective possessions, to seek to be a name among men, and to cultivate the awareness of personal worth which is essential to nobility of soul? Do not these latter two qualities, praised by Saint Thomas Aquinas,[17] contribute more effectually to personal development than do those recommended by Saint Ignatius?

However, it is easy to see that there is no real conflict within the mind of a virtuous person, between these two series of qualities. They complete and strengthen one another. Classic theology would speak here of a "connection of virtues." In the power of His Gifts whose purpose is the public witness which is the mission of the confirmed person, the Holy Spirit effects this harmonious synthesis of contraries. A perfect spirit of poverty seeks both to avoid those possessions which positively impede the practice of the virtues, and to seek an abundance of those which assist this practice. The Christian wishes to see his sins despised, his nothingness recognized, while at the same time he holds in high esteem the gifts freely bestowed on him by God for the good of the whole Church and of the whole world. Finally, while he learns from men's scorn to despise himself even more than they despise him, he also has such trust in the natural and supernatural resources given him by God that he enters courageously upon great undertakings with a view to his personal and social development for the glory of his Creator.

Furthermore, would not this quest for creature comforts and esteem and this awareness of personal worth be inevitably perverted by inordinate self-love, were they not accompanied by detachment and the despising of self?

The Spirit of Christ has always urged the saints to decrease themselves so that Christ may be increased (Jn. 3, 30). The spirituality of human development is a spirituality of seeming decrease and of real increase. It is precisely by despising themselves in the sight of God and of men, that the saints became and become more worthy of esteem; and it is by depriving themselves that they enrich others.

In short, human development, like the Pasch of the Lord, is a mystery of death and of life. The Holy Spirit effects this paschal development of the Christian by leading him to distrust the devil's advice to *have* more, and to listen to God's call *to be* more.[18] This Spirit often urges him to have less by giving more, and in this way *to be* more.

Seeking to free love more completely from the shackles which earthly passions could place upon its exercise, the Spirit of the poor and virginal Jesus calls some of the baptized and confirmed to a life of full poverty and of celibacy for the Kingdom of Heaven's sake.

Vatican II reminds us that "the special consecration (of the religious life) is deeply rooted in their baptismal consecration and provides a more ample manifestation of it."[19] It could be added that the religious life is rooted in that of confirmation and manifests it. Here again, therefore, we have a design of personal, social, and ecclesial development,—a design elaborated under the action of grace, which the religious life consecrates. The choice of poverty and celibacy is a decision, confirmed by vow, to be more in having less, and this so that all men may have more in order to be more.

If already in virtue of their baptism, "the faithful must confess before men the faith which they have received from Christ through the Church,"[20] are not members of religious orders and congregations, as a result of their past confirmation, "endowed by the Holy Spirit with special strength" through which they are more strictly obliged to spread and defend the Faith both by word and by deed as true witnesses of Christ"?[21]

And is not the Faith which both layman and religious should confess, that which recognizes the divine will in the duty *par excellence* of every human person—namely, the duty of growth?[22] Is it not also the Faith which affirms, often against all seemingly palpable evidence to the contrary, that the Church never ceases to grow in love?[23]

Through the prophets and prophetesses (cf. Acts 2, 17) whom He has consecrated for this purpose by confirming their baptism, the Holy Spirit continues to speak to men and women about their growth and development. Among all these consecrated people, some have chosen, not only to pledge themselves to be the witnesses and the fulfillers of the divine design of human development, but also to renounce that particular type of growth offered by marriage and property, in order that through their sacrifice all may grow more effectively. The confirming Spirit has made these chosen people the prophets and prophetesses *par excellence* of the mystery of human development, which the sacramental grace helps them to live, to proclaim, and to realize in the sight of the world. Through them, the Spirit bears witness to Christ (Jn., 15,26;16,14). The constant action of the Eucharistic Christ for the spiritual growth and, indirectly but really, for the socio-economic growth of mankind, is surely a special purpose of this witness of the Holy Spirit. Through confirmation, has not this Paraclete-Spirit given to the witnesses of the Christophany of development, tongues of fire in order to manifest it to the world and in order to make it tend towards its own fullness? Are not these tongues of fire orientated towards the Eucharistic Communion of the confirmed? Do they not symbolize, in effect, their mission to proclaim the teaching and the love of Christ the Developer, present and active in the Eucharist?[24]

Confirmed as we have been by the Spirit to bear witness to the action of the Eucharistic Christ in favor of the spiritual and temporal growth of mankind, and thus to share more intensely in it, it is right that we should celebrate, in thanksgiving and prayer, each anniversary of the day of our confirmation which marked such an important stage of our personal development within the Church. In order to intensify our commitment to growth, let us renew, at each anniversary of our personal Pentecost, our individual consecration to the Spirit of the Promise[25] who has sealed us with an indelible seal for the praise and glory of the Father and of the Son. Let us consecrate our energies anew to this other Paraclete (Jn. 14, 16) sent by the Father in answer to the prayer of the Son, to be the soul of the Church, the soul of the Church's growth, and therefore the soul of the growth of a world distinct from but irrevocably linked with the Church. Let us become with increasing effect, the instrument of the Spirit in His work of development.[26]

And may this not very well provide an easier solution, in the light of personal and social development to the pastoral problems connected with confirmation?

NOTES

[1] Cf. B. de Margerie S.J., *R. Niebuhr, théologien de la communauté mondiale,* Paris-Bruges, 1969, p. 376, where there are some bibliographical details.

[2] GS, 18. 1.

[3] Here we presuppose some knowledge of the doctrine of Saint Thomas Aquinas, such as it has been presented in our day by Fathers J. de Finance and A. Marc.

[4] Cf. B. de Margerie S.J., *op.cit.* (see note 1), p. 409 (using the Council of Trent).

[5] *Ibid.*: in the strict sense, the impious one or the unbeliever is one who has rejected faith, hope, and charity.

[6] *Ibid.*, p. 279, note 12.

[7] *Ibid.*

[8] J. Comblin, *Le Christ dans l'Apocalypse,* Paris, 1965, p. 52.

[9] That is, the designs of a mere creature, as distinct from those of Jesus Christ, the Creator become a creature.

[10] Cf. K. Rahner S.J., *Est-il possible aujourd'hui de croire,* Tours, 1966. p. 55: "the expression, absolute Future, simply designates what we mean when we use the word God."

[11] *Ibid.,* p. 160-161.

[12] Cf. Saint Augustine, *De peccatorum meritis et remissione,* 1, 25 (ML 44, 131); epist. 98 (ML, 33, 362); Saint Thomas Aquinas, ST, III. 68. 9, art. 1 and 2.

[13] Saint Thomas Aquinas, ST, II. II. 161. 6. 1; 3 c.

[14] Saint Ignatius Loyola, *Spiritual Exercises,* mediation on "The Two Standards."

[15] Pius, XI QA, sub fine: AAS, 23 (1931), 226: "pretiossissimum socialis instaurationis instrumentum."

[16] Saint Ignatius, *op.cit.* (note 14), par. 146.

[17] Saint Thomas Aquinas, ST, II. II. 129. 3 and 6.

[18] In this connection see Paul VI, PP (1967), par. 18 and 19: "The desire for necessities is legitimate ... but the acquiring of temporal goods can lead to greed, to the insatiable desire for more, and can make increased power a tempting objective. Individuals, families, and nations can be overcome by avarice, be they poor or rich, and all can fall victim to a stifling materialism. Increased possessions is not the ultimate goal of nations or of individuals. All growth is ambivalent. It is essential if man is to develop as a man, but in a way it imprisons man if he considers it the supreme good, and it restricts his vision .... The exclusive pursuit of possessions becomes an obstacle to individual fulfilment and to man's true greatness. Both for nations and for individual men, avarice is the most evident form of moral under-development" (English trans.: C.T.S., pp. 11-12).

[19] PC, 5. 1 (Abbott, p. 470).

[20] LG, 11. 1 (Abbott, p. 28).

[21] *Ibid.* Although the text cited applies to all Christians, i.e. to all who have received the sacrament of confirmation, we think it legitimate, in the light of Saint Thomas Aquinas's doctrine on the religious life, to apply it more especially to those whom the Spirit has freed from the obstacles and limitations to the universal announcing of the Word, represented by family life, private property, and autonomy in the exercise of freedom.

[22] Cf. Paul VI, *PP*, par 16: "human fulfilment constitutes, as it were, a summary of our duties" (English trans.: C.T.S., p. 11).

[23] LG, 65.

[24] It is a traditional view (traditional in the best sense of the word) that the Christian should preferably be confirmed before he receives Holy Communion, because it is above all by receiving this sacrament that he bears public witness to his faith. His faith, rendered more intense by confirmation, normally develops the desire for the most perfect possible union with Jesus Christ, realized here on earth in the Eucharistic Communion.

[25] Cf. Eph. 1, 13-14; 4, 30. For the growth of the world and of the Church, confirmed Christians are sent by the Church on a mission

to spread the Gospel, and are sent, through the Church, by the Son and by the Spirit, who are the invisible missionaries of the Father in human souls. Reciprocally, in order to serve these invisible missions of the illuminating Word and of the enfolding Spirit, they become the collaborators of the "presbyterium" in intimate union with the Vicar of the Two Paracletes (cf. Jn. 14, 16; LG, 33. 2; Saint Thomas Aquinas, ST, 1. 43. 5. 3).

[26] In this connection, see Guy Limousin, "Pour eclairer le problème de la confirmation," in *Catéchèse,* 9 (1969), 349 ff.

chapter two

Marriage: Development: World Population

Many people think that the Church's doctrine about birth control, far from being a help, is an obstacle to the proper and harmonious development of couples, of families and of mankind. One often hears it said that the greatest problem of our day is that concerning the planned growth of world population. Mankind it would seem, is like a group of shipwrecked people marooned on an island with severely limited food supplies. In due course, a second and large group, without any supplies, attempt to come ashore. And what, the critics of the Church ask, is the only solution some people would offer? That all die of starvation!

Meantime, they go on, the Church is breaking up homes or filling them with anxiety, by imposing a norm of behavior which is actually an impracticable ideal. In fact, they claim, the encyclical on human life, published by Paul VI on 25 July 1968, is the negation of the one he had published at Easter of the previous year on the progress of nations.

Such accusations arise from ignorance of the data of the problem, and from ignorance of the spirit, sometimes even of the letter, of the Church's doctrine. In the light of the conciliar Constitution on the Church in the Modern World, complemented by the encyclical of Paul VI we shall show how and in what sense Christian marriage sacramentalizes the personal and interpersonal development of the couples, as well as the development of mankind as a whole. It is the grace of marriage which promotes the sexual dialogue of the couples and their dialogue with God with a view to responsible parenthood. On the contrary, secularization, in desacralizing marriage, leads to the twofold abortion of human life and of matrimonial life.

A. *The inter-personal development of the couple is the meaning and purpose of marriage and of the conjugal act.*

More clearly than any previous document of the Church's magisterium, the encyclical of Paul VI on human life[1] states that the *raison d'être* of marriage is the inter-personal development of the couple; and it does so in the context of emphasizing that this inter-personal development itself finds its meaning and purpose in a generative and educative collaboration of the married couple with the Creator:

"Husband and wife, through that mutual gift of themselves, which is specific and exclusive to them alone, seek to develop that kind of personal union in which they complement one another in order to co-operate with God in the generation and education of new lives."

In other words, the conjugal act is presented as a sign and means of a growing inter-personal communion in the service of the creation (and of the personal education) of new human beings brought into existence by the Three Divine Persons.

A little further on, Paul VI clarifies this point yet more: "The marriage act, because of its fundamental structure, while it unites husband and wife in the closest intimacy, also brings into operation laws written into the actual nature of man and woman for the generation of new life."[2]

In other words, the marriage act visibly signifies another reality already present — namely, the intimate personal communion of husband and wife orientated towards the generating of new human beings. Signification presupposes the positing of an external sign of an already present reality; whereas the terms "meaning" and "purpose" allude to a reality not yet present towards which one tends with a view to securing it.[3] Thus it can be said beyond any contradiction, that the marriage act, if it is truly an act of complete and inter personal love, always signifies orientation towards the procreation for which it remains instrinsically and essentially destined,[4] but does not always signify procreation itself, which often does not result from it even though it remains its meaning and its purpose. For, this act simply makes the couples *opt* for procreation, whereas actual generation of a new life depends on other conditions which are not always simultaneously present. That is what the pope means by the phrase: "laws written into the actual nature of man and woman." In short, the signification of orientation towards procreation is always present in every true conjugal act, even though its purpose or procreative meaning is not always effectively secured. The signification is, therefore, distinct from the purpose (or meaning) towards which it is orientated; the meaning transcends the signification, in which it is potentially but not necessarly present.

Conjugal love thus presents itself as an open communion, as a communion not closed on itself. The internal ethical law which specifies its purpose could not insert itself in a closed morality; it fits much more easily into an open morality. Contraception limits and perverts the gift of themselves made by husband and wife, since it tears them one from the other at the very moment of their (abortive) attempt to secure full intimacy. And it is thus that it tears them away from the design of their communion as willed by God, by a God who is a Society of Persons.

"The God who gives human life clearly performs an act of love, whose object is he who receives it. God's will to associate human creatures with this act of giving human life, rather than Himself alone doing so, is also an act of love towards them. In effect, God has willed to call upon the husband and wife to offer their cooperation with Him in the transmission of human life, but only through a total reciprocal giving, capable of creating and expressing an intimate and stable union between them."[5]

It is therefore by the same and indivisible movement, in a single aspiration, that conjugal love tends, by means of its specific conjugal act,[6] not only "to endure and grow through the joys and sorrows of daily life . . . so that husband and wife attain their human fulfilment,"[7] but also "to bring new life into being."[8] What this signifies is that their procreation of children together, and their shared task of rearing and educating them, nourish the parents' love for one another. Their children are the personal and autonomous signs of their inter-personal love, as well as the occasion and the source of its growth. As Vatican II put it: "Children contribute very substantially to the welfare of their parents."[9]

And if one wishes to grasp more profoundly, at the level of being itself, how the complete and reciprocal giving of husband and wife necessarily tends to strengthen their inter-personal bond in their child (even though this giving does not always result in conception), it suffices to recall that the Father and the Son, in a single, eternal and shared act of love — an act of love by which They love, as a single principle, the unique object of Their common divine lovableness — produce Their Breath, the Person of Their Spirit, the Bond of Love between Them![10]

The unicity of this eternal Act of the love of the Father and of the Son is analogically manifested in the multiplicity of the marital acts, just as the unique Person of the unique Spirit of the Father and of the Son is manifested in the plurality of the children.

It thus emerges that marital love is ecstatic in the sense that its continuance and its growth demand that it tend towards what actually transcends it but is potentially part of it — namely, the child, not only generated, but also educated, by this reciprocal love of the parents. The mutual love of husband and wife can fully personalize them only if it is not exhausted in their reciprocal communion: any shared egotism would kill that love by reducing their relationship to the encounter of two "solitudes" incapable of a real merging together. Their dialogue would degenerate into two monologues. The eyes of husband and wife would no longer steadily and confidingly meet, if their bodies refused to one another the completeness of reciprocal giving, by rejecting together the child who is nevertheless the pledge written into their act.

In other words, the development of the human species, like that of the married couples, is written into the dynamism of the conjugal act. The latter links husband and wife together with all the strength of their being, while at the same time it associates them with God. This act involves not the bodies only, but the soul as well; not only the imagination and the affectivity or passions, but also the intelligence and the will, the whole higher psyche.

An eminently inter-personal act, the marriage act is the "personalizing" instrument of the persons of husband and wife; but, extrinsically, it is this too when it results, through an immediate action of the divine Persons, in the generating of a new person, member of the whole human family. At this level, and we shall later examine this point, it is the relationship of the husband and wife with the whole human race that it deepens. Through the mediation of the child who is its fruit, conjugal love serves to give a new dimension to the mysterious bond which unites husband and wife to all other people. It is, therefore, a love which opens into a universal interpersonal friendship, and so is a factor of universal development.

Furthermore, it must even be said, that the conjugal act, in cases where it does not result in pregnancy but where no obstacle was put to its doing so, does in fact share in this quality of the fecund conjugal act, and has the significance of universal communion: it is with all mankind that it links the married couple who accept the possibility of enriching the human race with a new person.[11]

Signifying, as it does, universal communion in different degrees, the conjugal act is, by being intended to result in pregnancy, the agent of the creative work of the Holy Trinity, with which work it intimately associates the married couple. By refusing to separate the two significations, procreative and unitive, of their act, married couples acknowledge "that one is not the master of the sources of life but rather the minister of the design established by the Creator," and "does not have unlimited dominion . . . over the specifically sexual faculties, for these are concerned with the generation of life, of which

God is the source."[12] The conjugal act thus accomplished becomes in effect an act of adoration by husband and wife as two in one flesh; for, is not adoration the recognition of the sovereign rights of God the Creator? And, as long as it remains open to the transmission of life, the conjugal act is the concrete recognition of God's dominion over the couple's generative faculties, which have been created by Him for the creation of new life. One understands, therefore, how Paul VI could describe the conjugal act, as regards its procreative consequences, as "an activity in which . . . man is so closely associated with his Creator."[13] If one can say this about human work inasmuch as it transforms and completes the world, with what greater justification still cannot one say it with reference to the act which peoples the earth?

It emerges, then, that the matrimonial act and the whole conjugal life which it symbolically sums up, constitute a dialogue of the married couple with one another, with their children, with the whole of mankind, and with the creative Trinity. The matrimonial act which is truly a total giving, is a reciprocal *yes* of husband and wife, as well as the *yes* spoken together to God and to the humanity they will to conserve and to enrich. On the other hand, when the married couple refuse in practice to recognize this act as essentially destined for the transmission of life, the act becomes a refusal of the *otherness* of husband and wife in relation to one another, as well as a *no* uttered against mankind and against the creative love of God. In the first case, it is a factor of personal and social integration; in the second, it becomes a factor of disintegration.

In other words, and this again is what the Church emphasizes, the natural law forbids contraception only because contraception is "repugnant to the nature of man and of woman and strikes at the heart of their relationship."[14] The contraceptive act is one in which the person violates himself or herself by violating his or her nature, while at the same time it is a mutual violation effected by husband and wife (who may in no way feel it to be such). The divine law condemns contraception only because the latter hinders the authentic full communion of husband and wife inasmuch as it prevents them from being fully themselves in the perfection of their mutual giving. Vatican II emphasizes this truth: "Man . . . cannot fully find himself except through a sincere giving of himself."[15] By claiming the right to separate the inseparable unitive signification and procreative signification of their marriage and of their conjugal relations, married couples renounce not only procreation, but also the authentic love that binds them together. Because they are thinking only "of their own interests,"[16] they can no longer reach God or the whole of mankind or even one another; and hence it can be said that, at least objectively, they lose one another in what is no longer a genuine act of love.[17] The contraceptive act is no longer an act of union but an act of mutual separation and of rebellion against the Creator of human sexuality.

Equally, however — and for the first time in the history of the Church's magisterium, Paul VI has emphasized the immorality of the conjugal act forced "on one's partner without regard to his or her condition or personal and reasonable wishes in the matter."[18] This is "no true act of love," nor does it even deserve to be called a conjugal act; much rather should it be called marital rape, absolutely counter to the conjugal love which constitutes the right and the duty of husband and wife. In these conditions, the duty to accept procreation ceases to exist,[19] for the matrimonial contract implies a mutual giving in love of free wills and not merely of bodies. Neither of the marriage partners, in placing his or her sexuality at the service of the other partner, intends to become the slave of passions uncontrolled by reason. The marriage contract is not one of slavery, but of mutual liberation. Because husband and wife are endowed with free will, they cannot serve one another except in respecting one another's inalienable dignity.

The conjugal act is therefore the sign of a "creative vow" of the married couple — of this creative vow considered in its fullness. Their carnal union signifies the shared will of each to secure the full development of the other partner in the procreative act destined to engender the child to be the bond of their love. In giving himself or herself without reserve to the other partner, each spouse manifests the intention to become the instrument of the divine plan; for does not God will to give each fully to himself or herself, so that he or she may be able to make a total gift of self to Him? The conjugal act fulfills the mystery of the perfect and inalienable identity of the human person within a complete yielding up of his or her person; or, more precisely, it tends towards this perfect identity, it is the instrument of the process of self-identification which in turn is a stage in the genesis of perfect identity. Through it, God the Creator of this identity, makes the latter develop towards its fullness. And the yielding of the body which the conjugal act implies, is made not only to the body of the other partner, but also to that of the infant. The communion of the couple is not closed, but open.

B. *The development and complete fulfilment of all human persons is the meaning and purpose signified by the conjugal act.*

We think that classic theology is far from having developed all the potentialities of the principles it has formulated. On the one hand, it acknowledges that, in a sense, man is all things — i.e., that, through knowledge and love, each person wills to become all the others in order to be fully himself; and, on the other hand, it recognizes that the conjugal act is orientated to the common good of the human species, this common good being the conservation of the human race. Before we deal with the meaning which such an expression still carries in the current context of the rapid growth of world population, let us here develop the above two propositions and show the ways in which they are inter-related.

In the first place, Saint Thomas, commentating on Aristotle,[20] says that, in a sense, the human person, through knowladge and love, becomes all things. This idea has frequently been investigated by modern Thomists,[21] but perhaps they have not sufficiently emphasized the potentialities in regard to the human person that are implied in this principle. The statement that, through knowledge and love, man becomes all things, means that through knowledge he takes the whole universe into himself in order to enfold it in the ecstasy of a voluntary love; but it also and especially means that he becomes the other human persons known and loved, since "the person is what is most excellent in the universe."[22]

This "becoming universal" of the human person signifies that he needs to take into himself, in some manner, the whole of reality, in order to be fully and distinctly himself. This aspiring to fully developed personal identity deepens into the natural desire to see God and to live, beyond death, in society with other human persons; and such a natural desire could not be in vain, even if its realization did not depend on human nature.[23]

Louis Lochet has very well expressed this basic aspiration of every human person:

"The human person is called to direct towards God a nature which that person does not possess entirely for himself. He is, so to speak, deficient in his very condition of *person* — or rather, he needs others in order to realize fully his own personality.

To accomplish his full vocation, it is not enough, therefore, that a man should lift up to God the praise and offering of his individual nature. As a spiritual person, he carries in himself the desire to draw together into a single all-embracing act all the activities of his nature in time;[24] but he also carries the secret desire to offer to his Creator the total image of all mankind. He needs all mankind in order to be able to give himself wholly to God: he needs all his human brethren in order to say to God, 'I love You.' "[25]

In short, man, a naturally social animal, a person within a species, tends, through the communion of an activity of intellect and will, towards the perfect inter-personal community without which he cannot be fully himself. Of this perfect and universal community, the marriage community in its spiritual aspect is an image in time and space, a dynamic first sketch, a partial and limited anticipation: "the body enters in a transitory way in the conjugal act, whereas love and reason, when they express themselves, aspire to the eternity of the bond that they form."[26] However strong the physical union between husband and wife, their souls remain, here on earth, opaque to one another. The limited transparency existing on earth between husband and wife, is still only a remote image of the perfect eschatological translucency which the elect will have in relation to one another.[27]

Furthermore, the matrimonial relationship should not be limited to symbolizing and incompletely achieving in a limited way the universal interpersonal relationship beyond death; it should also contribute in a unique and decisive way to its own universality. Marriage, Saint Thomas Aquinas writes,[28] "is directed to the common good of the species that is, to the conservation of the human race." This is a view which, though just and proper, represents an imperfect integration, within Christian thought, of the Aristotelian idea of the relationships between species and individual. Let us try to integrate it more fully, in the light of Saint Augustine.

Aristotle's ideas are within the framework of a universe at once closed, indefinite, and cyclic. For the Stagyrite, better understood by Saint Bonaventure than by Saint Thomas,[29] only the common intellect is immortal. We can see this as somewhat like an anticipation of Hegel's idea of absolute Knowledge.[30] Souls are mortal, and procreation is therefore the only possible survival for a man (apart from his reputation), since he is in a sense continued through his children. The conservation of the species becomes, therefore, the means *par excellence* of personal survival, the latter being impossible in itself.

Divorced from its materialist connotations, Aristotle's intuition links up with a basic Christian truth — namely, that, at the natural level, mankind may not interrupt its history by ceasing to reproduce itself. Awareness of its spiritual immortality in no way authorizes it to interrupt the temporal and mortal course of carnal generation.[31] Pius XII could therefore write:

"Both nature and the Creator impose on husbands and wives, in the specific act of their state (of marriage), the function of providing for the conservation of the human race. This is the special commitment which creates the value proper to their state — the "bonum prolis," the children. The people and the State, the Church herself, depend for their existence, in the order established by God, on fruitful marriage."[32]

Now, the context of this passage, or more exactly the phrase immediately preceding it, in presenting the human race at the "plaintiff" *vis-à-vis* the married couple, shows what is meant by the words: "Both *nature* and the Creator impose . . . the function of providing for the conservation of the human race." What is clearly involved is an identification between "nature" and "human race": the *nature* mentioned here is human nature as possessed by the totality of human persons existing here and now. The text signifies, therefore, that God our Creator, through the totality of human persons, demands that married couples should see to the conservation of this temporal and mortal humanity of whom they form a part. This is what the human race demands of these couples in the name of God, and it does so as a "claimant" who demands justice in the name of a strict right.

Pius XII, therefore, expressed the idea that the marriage contract, in linking the couple together for the conservation of the human race, thereby constitutes a new link between the couple singly or together, and the totality of mankind. Marriage takes a man and a woman away from the families into which they were born, but does so only in order to insert them more profoundly, as a couple, into the great human family and, through the act of generation, to unite them vitally to God the Creator. The mutual contract of husband and wife is extended into a quasi-contract with the human race, with all the members of the human family.

Let us now view this profound idea within the great intellectual current of Augustinian and Biblical thought. The conservation of the human race would more aptly be called its propagation[33] until it reaches the number fixed by God in His eternal wisdom. Needless to say, such a statement does not mean a return to the thesis which would make the eventual number of the elect equal to that of the fallen angels. With Saint Thomas Aquinas (ST, 1. 23. 7), we reject this view and we affirm that a transcendent Providence, infinitely superior to all number pertaining to the world of matter, has predestined to salvation a fixed number of people. Does not this view anticipate the legitimate demands strongly made today, of a Christian personalism? In effect, had not God fixed the number of His elect, could each and every person regard himself as the object of an infinite and eternal knowledge and love? This is so true that one could not point to a single Catholic theologian, ancient or modern, who denies the existence of a fixed number of the elect. The beginning must therefore be understood in the light of the end: the command "increase and multiply and fill the earth and subdue it" of Genesis (1, 28) in the light of the other text, "then they were told to rest a little longer, until the number of their fellow servants and their brethren should be complete," of the Johannine Revelation (6, 11). Marriage is the nursery of the City of God,[34] designed to introduce into the heavenly Church its predestined members. In this respect, the "plaintiff" of whom Pius XII speaks, grows in size: it comprises men present, past, and to come, the already dead and the not yet born. All demand of married couples that they contribute to their eternal happiness by completing their number, until the figure is reached that has been eternally fixed by the divine Love: *all*, that is, except for those who separate themselves from the community by refusing to accept, however implicitly, the grace of Christ the Redeemer. For, as Pius XII says, the Church depends on married couples for her existence. [35]

In other words, and this must be emphasized, the conjugal duty, in placing husband and wife under an obligation to one another, also obligates them to the human race. Equally, the fulfilment of this duty places all mankind under an obligation to them. Their actually or potentially procreative action redounds on all mankind.

In the Thomist synthesis, the Aristotelian perspective (primacy of the common good, identified with the conservation of the human race) and the Augustinian perspective, join and fuse together. Procreation is also directed, says Saint Thomas, towards the worship of God.[36] Saint Thomas would have had no difficulty in accepting the Augustinian perspective presented by Louis Lochet:

"Marriage creates love not only between man and woman, but also within mankind as a whole. The love of husband and wife very naturally extends to their two families. It is precisely this which rules out consanguineous marriages, because marriage should extend the social bonds of one family with the other, and ultimately, from family to family, with the whole human community. It is these multiple bonds that should make all mankind one single family, issued from the same parents and living in the same intimacy. What an admirable institution is marriage! Through the links which it forges between man and woman . . . it ensures both the multiplication and the unity of mankind."[37]

This could not be better put. We thus see more clearly that the command "increase and multiply" of Genesis (1,28) must lead, in the divine plan, to the prayer "that they may be one, even as you, Father, are in me, and I in you, that they may be one in us" (Jn. 17, 21), in the unity of our Spirit (*ibid.*), of the Eucharistic prayer of Jesus shortly before is death. Is not marriage orientated towards the Eucharist? The sacrament of the multiplication of the elect is thus completely polarized by that of their unification. Human development tends towards the unity of a universal mutuality, in the Kingdom of God. The many tend towards the One.

And it is at this point that the Augustinian philosophy of number enters to clarify an eschatological theology of marriage. In the perspective of Saint Augustine, Louis Lochet again writes:

"Number is readily regarded as constitutive of nature; so the number of the elect as foreseen by God is constitutive of the City of God and mysteriously defines it. Each of the elect forms a new element of the edifice, takes it that much nearer to completion, reveals its true appearance. When the number of the elect is complete then will occur the inauguration of the definitive reign of Christ. In completing the number of the elect, marriage hastens the coming of Christ, and opens the way to the consummation of time in eternity."[38]

By having children, married couples anticipate and prepare this consummation of the world and of the Church. The act of generation is the physical expression of the longing "Come, Lord Jesus!" which the Spirit ceaselessly inspires, throughout time, in the Church, Spouse of Christ (cf. Rev. 22, 17-20). The procreative act of the married couple, sacramentally linked with the image of Christ and of the Church, becomes the physical representation of their perfect eschatological reunion, and the sign of the proximity of the second coming of Christ ("Surely I am coming soon": Rev. 22, 20). For the life-span of the sacrament of marriage is the life-span of the Church on earth, and the conjugal act is situated, therefore, in "the last hour" (1 Jn. 2, 18). The eschatological reach of Christian marriage touches even the flesh itself to transfigure it. The conjugal act is a "form of this world" (1 Cor. 7, 41; cf. verses 29-30), a passing form of "this world that is passing away," a form that signifies the world to come with the completion of the number of the elect who, like the angels of God, will neither marry nor be given in marriage (Lk.22,34-36).[39]

In the light of this matrimonial eschatology, we can see more clearly, therefore, in what sense marriage and the conjugal act form a particular means of initially realizing the basic commitment of the human person: to be himself in being all things, to be fully himself by intentionally being, through knowledge and love, all other persons in an immortal society. But the originality of this particular means lies in the fact that, in this case and in this case only, human persons are the medium, in the most direct way possible, of the presuppositions which are indispensable to a person's very existence, instead of limiting itself to being the medium of his development.[40]

Thus the couple are simultaneously the medium of the quantitative completion of mankind in some of its members (those whom they engender and all their descendants), and the medium of the qualitative completion of all human persons, impossible without the former. For here the quality does depend on the quantity! No one can be fully himself if he does not know and love all those whom God knows and loves (cf. 1 Cor. 8, 3: "If one loves God, one is known by him"; Mt. 25, 12: "Truly, I say to you, I do not know you."). In bringing a child into the world, the couple make a unique contribution to the good and the happiness of each human person and therefore to the happiness and good of all mankind. They thus savor a unique joy: thanks to them, a man has been born into the world (cf. Jn. 16, 21), that is, into the human world, into the world of human persons. In the image of God the Father, they have so loved the world that they have given to it a son or daughter in bringing a child into the world (cf. Jn. 3, 16). The world thus loved and enriched is no longer the same as before. Each new-born person makes of this world a new world, of this humanity a new humanity qualified and modified by a new existential relationship.

Suffice it to say that the procreative act of Christian husband and wife in a state of grace is one of mutual human and supernatural love. It should be added that it is for love of all men, in virtue of their universal infused charity, that the couple wills to give them a new brother. Supernatural love is indivisible: it is universal under pain of not existing at all. In this connection, the conjugal act, which we have just seen to be an aspiring towards the glorious Parousia of the Redeemer of the universe, reveals itself to be in addition a completive love as regards each and every one of us.

In grasping the universal import of the conjugal act, we are better able to face up to the problem posed by mankind today — the problem of responsible parenthood. We cannot see the possibility of viewing the demand for a rationalizing of conjugal intimacy, otherwise than within the full significance of the conjugal act, as something required by the human race in the name of God.

C. *Sacramental grace, responsible parenthood, and world population.*

An increasing number of demographers and moralists, as well as politicians, even in the under-developed countries,[41] are convinced that the present growth of world population, in geometric rather than arithmetic progression,[42] constitutes a serious danger for the future of mankind. Sauvy, a known specialist, talks of "impossible continuation."[43] Fears are expressed, not only about population-subsistence, imbalance, but above all about the "massification of mankind."[44] The encyclical *Humanae Vitae* echoes some of these fears.[45] A serious problem is thus raised for the Christian and the human conscience.

Other dangers have also been sternly pointed out. Recently, the "heart of the drama of world destiny at the present time" in terms "equally heavy with menace" has been summed up as follows: "to seek a rhythm of expansion one aims at ever increasing betterment at the risk of being soon stifled under the numerical excess which conditions it, or to restore the demographic balance at the risk of thereby returning to a situation of stagnation at the level of life itself." [46] But, it is immediately added, "the danger in world terms clearly leans towards numerical excess."[47]

Until a very recent period, it was the survival itself of mankind on the earth that seemed more or less constantly threatened. One cannot rule out that the command to "increase and multiply" of Genesis 1, 28, was colored by the situation in which the writer found himself: the book was written in an era of disaster for the Jewish people, whose partial emigration to Babylon could have seemed to certain people a threat to the very survival of the nation. Perhaps the Genesis text should be interpreted, at least to some extent, in the light of the famous letter of the Prophet Jeremiah to the exiles in Babylon: "Be you multiplied there, and be not few in number" (Jer. 29, 6). It is quite possible that the command to multiply signified in particular, "be not few in number."[48]

We shall therefore list various solutions offered by different theologians who have considered the consequences of the population explosion; and we shall attempt to show how the idea of "responsible parenthood," adopted by Vatican II, opens new horizons, especially if it is clarified by the idea of an intrinsic relationship between the conjugal act and the human race, such as Pius XII presents it.

But we must first briefly recall some data of the Church's magisterium which often lie behind the statements of these theologians.

In 1958, Pius XII extolled the Providence of God that governs the evolution of world population. No one can usurp the place of this creative Providence. The Church encourages large families. Local overpopulation is due, not to any failure on the part of Providence, but to a lack of generosity and of wisdom among men.[49]

The pope hints that the remedy may lie in eventual interplanetary emigration.[50]

In 1963, John XXIII recognized the existence of a problem which could, through mankind's fault, become insoluble:

"Besides, the resources which God in His Goodness and wisdom has implanted in Nature are wellnigh inexhaustible, and He has at the same time given man the intelligence to discover ways and means of exploiting these resources for his own advantage and his own livelihood. Hence, the real solution of the problem is not to be found in expedients which offend against the divinely established moral order and which attack human life at its very source, but in a renewed scientific and technical effort on man's part to deepen and extend his dominion over Nature. The progress of science and technology that has already been achieved opens up limitless horizons in this field. . . .

"A provident God grants sufficient means to the human race to find a dignified solution to the problems attendant upon the transmission of human life. But these problems can become difficult of solution, or even insoluble, if man, led astray in mind and perverted in will, turns to such means as are opposed to right reason, and seeks ends that are contrary to his social nature and the intentions of Providence"[51]

In other words, it is within men's power to reject God's providential plan for them, since the Providence of God is not exercised without the cooperation of man's own foresight. When some men prefer voluntarily to ignore this fact, their problem can become insoluble at the temporal level: (at the spiritual level, God will always give to every person the means to save himself). Certain people may die through their fellow men's fault. But scientific and technical progress, in opening up "limitless horizons," rules out any forecasts of limits to our earth's capacity to feed a ceaselessly growing population.

In 1965, in *Gaudium et Spes*, Vatican II made a pronouncement on this matter. Here is the most important section of it:

"In view of the inalienable human right to marry and beget children, the question of how many children should be born belongs to the honest judgement of parents. The question can in no way be committed to the decision of government."[52]

It is true that this text, while asserting that the domain of the transmission of life does not belong to the sovereignty of the State, does not say that the Church cannot in some way advise couples in this domain. Neither does it deny the State's right and even duty to educate couples in methods of birth regulation when "the reliability of these methods" has been proved and "their harmony with the moral order" made clear.[53] We might add that it is also the State's duty to keep the married couples informed about developments in the demographic situation. [54]

The couples, therefore, are not answerable to the State or to public opinion, but to God, for their decision about having children. The Council provides them with a basis for such an important decision:

"With docile reverence towards God, parents will come to the right decision by common counsel and effort. They will thoughtfully take into account both their own welfare and that of their children, those already born and those who may be foreseen. For this accounting they will reckon with both the material and the spiritual conditions of the times as well as of their state in life. Finally, they will consult the interests of the family group, of temporal society, and of the Church herself."[55]

It will be noted that Vatican II does not impose on married couples the duty explicitly to take into account the repercussion on world population of their decision to have children, but neither does it exclude such a consideration. The object of the decision of which it speaks not only concerns the number of children, but also, as emerges from a previous text of Pius XII,[56] the fact of having or not having children, although normally procreation corresponds to the couple's obligation to the human race. This is so evident that the Council explicitly praises large families: "Among the couples who fulfil their God-given task in this way, those merit special praise who, with wise and common deliberation, and with a brave heart, undertake to bring up suitably even a relatively large family."[57] Such praise would have been impossible if the Council had intended to make it a duty to proclaim the limitation of births because of a dangerous population explosion.

However, the Council does not rule out the possible emergence of such a duty at some time in the future. And while it stresses that "the parents themselves should ultimately (*ultimatim*) make this judgement, in the sight of God,"[58] the use of this adverb (*ultimatim*) implies that others may advise and counsel the parents, both those of the world at large or those of a particular nation, to plan the number of their children. But the greater danger, in the Council's opinion, is clearly not the possibility that the State will abstain from interference, but that it will unduly interfere and try to impose regulations concerning procreation, strengthening these regulations with economic sanctions.[59]

The two main points, on which (after *Populorum Progressio*, which adds nothing new to this matter) the encyclical *Humanae Vitae* completes the conciliar teaching, relate to the idea of responsible parenthood and to the very value of demographic considerations.

On the one hand, Paul VI clearly embodies in the idea itself of responsible parenthood, the recognition of the relationship between the conjugal act and the whole of human society: "The commitment to responsible parenthood requires that husband and wife, keeping a right order of priorities, recognize their own duties towards God, themselves, their families, and human society (*erga humanam societatem*)."[60] The phrase "human society" implies no space-time limitations, and is more precise than is the other phrase, "temporal society," used by Vatican II in an analogous context and to designate the same obligation.[61] The whole of mankind is therefore at the heart of the ethical dimension of each and every conjugal act.

On the other hand, the pope integrates the demographic viewpoint, which is an incomplete one, into the whole vision of man. "The question of the birth of children, like every other question which touches on human life, is too large to be resolved by limited criteria, such as are provided by biology, psychology, demography, or sociology. It is the whole man and the whole complex of his responsibilities that must be considered, not only what is limited to this earth, but also what is supernatural and eternal."[62] This is a particularly opportune statement, for do we not often find that, despite its incompleteness, the demographic viewpoint is taken to cover the whole field of human consciousness? Many people become so obsessed with the question of population growth that they lose their sense of proportion. Letting the imagination do the work of the reason (and not just that of reflections in faith), they overlooked the fact that even the highest figures never suppress either the finite nature of created humanity or the omnipotence of the loving Wisdom that governs it. How can one fail to direct upon this problem, or rather upon this mystery, of world population, the light of these Pauline statements: "For this slight momentary affliction is preparing for us an external weight of glory beyond all comparison, because we look not to the things that are seen but to the things that are unseen; for the things that are seen are transient, but the things that are unseen are eternal" (2 Cor. 4, 17-18)? Should one not conclude from this that the temporal developments of the world population, its growth and its excess, are only for a time; it is the eternal weight of glory which the predestined will together constitute, and whose fullness, now invisible, will become eternally visible to each and every one of them?

In lifting us to these heights, the magisterium is inviting us to see the connection between world population and the mystery of the Church. Even when the conjugal act is contrary to reason and to the divine will, it is still integrated in the mysterious and salvific plan of divine Providence, for whom obstacles are means of action; no human being can come into the world except as object of the creative and saving love which destined him to eternal life in the new and heavenly Jerusalem. The Church's magisterium causes us, therefore, to pass from the problem to the mystery, from the problem of visible mankind to the mystery of the invisible Church. One understands, then, how Pius XII could write (20 January 1958): "Providence reserves to Itself the future destiny of the world. . . . God will not call on men to account for the general destiny of mankind, since this pertains to Himself; but He will call on them to account for their deliberate individual acts done in obedience to or in defiance of the commands of conscience."[63] Pius XII here sought to stress the limited character of the responsibility of man, compared with the infinite nature of the Creator; but he may well have been the first to recognize that, among the deliberate individual acts mentioned, the conjugal act, practiced in an atmosphere of prayer[64] and of sacramentalized prudence and foresight,[65] is a sharing in the divine plan for the human race, since this pope said in 1951 that this act is a couple's duty to the human race and has therefore a universal signification.[66]

The development of the doctrine of the Church's magisterium in the twofold direction of the mystery of world population and of responsible parenthood, leads us to seek the link which connects this responsibility with this mystery. This will prepare the way for a fuller expression of the Church's doctrine concerning her duties towards couples in demographic matters.

But straightaway one must admit how very difficult it is for the Church to give advice to couples in these matters, since the analysis of demographic phenomena and developments does not properly and directly come within the competence of the Church's magisterium.[67] Demography is concerned with a contingent and changing domain, and involves analyses and syntheses by specialists who do not agree among themselves in interpretations which anyhow never carry more than moral certitude. The view taken of over-population varies considerably, dependent on whether the demographer is a neo-Malthusian, a Marxist, or a Christian. Value judgements, existential choices, are already active in the very way in which the demographic data are regarded. A whole *Weltanschauung* is involved in the specialist's declaration. Even Christians themselves are not in agreement in their approach to demographic phenomena;[68] and, as we shall see, the same is true of the theologians. But even their differences of opinion will help us to a more synthesized view of the human and Christian obligations of married couples, and the pastoral possibilities of the Church.

We shall therefore consider three opinions whose differences are rooted in the geographical location, cultural background, and mental attitudes of those who express them: the opinions of Fathers Gorospe, Mols, and Zalba.

Gorospe writes in the Philippines and finds himself at grips with the problems of Church and State in a developing country. In his view, the Church in the Philippines should urge upon married couples the duty to limit their families, to establish parochial and diocesan study groups for this purpose, and also urge the State to fulfil its duty to inform the people about demographic matters, all this being aimed at the common good.[69] Gorospe even holds that the civic authorities should explain to them the different methods of birth control, including those condemned by the Church as contrary to the natural law, so that the freedom of the individual conscience may be respected and the possibility of a real choice offered. This view comes as no surprise when one knows this author's opinions on associated matters.[70] Anyhow, he offers no precise justification for his assertion that the Church should preach the duty of family limitation; nor does he indicate whether he thinks it possible to reconcile such a statement with that of Vatican II—namely, that in this matter the ultimate right to decide and the supreme responsibility belong to the parents. Finally, Gorospe does not say precisely what should be, in his view, the maximum number of infants which Philippine couples can bring into the world without violating the prohibition which the Church there is supposed to have an obligation to impose.[71]

On the other hand, for Father Mols—historian of Flemish

demography in the Middle Ages, as well as a specialist in present day demographic problems—"there can be no question of leaving it to some scientific bureau of demographic planning to decide what size each family should be," because this is something for the couples alone to decide.[72] However advice can, and perhaps sometimes should, be given;[73] and here Father Mols' idea goes beyond but does not contradict that of Vatican II. In his view, not only information but also advice of a precise kind should be given in order to guide the couples in their decisions. Father Mols does not specify, however, the source from which this advice should come: the State? international bodies? the local or universal Church? One point is clear, at all events: *advice* is all that is involved here, and not the declaring of an obligation.[74]

Father Zalba—Spaniard, moral theologian, member of the Congregation of the doctrine of the faith, Professor at the Gregorian University—recognizes the existence, in certain cases, of a duty to limit the size of a family, but not because of demographic indications. Such limitation as suggested by demographic indications is lawful and reasonable only in the following circumstances:

"A couple may accept demographic indications voluntarily to limit the number of their children for the sake of the common good, even if they are able to afford to have a larger family. They are not strictly obliged so to limit the size of their family, even primarily to serve the interests of society. One can therefore suggest to couples that they might consult and be guided by demographic data in the planning of their families, but not urge the matter as though such data indicated a duty.... Couples are not obliged to have children in an underpopulated country, if there are sufficient reasons for their not doing so. Neither, then, should they be obliged not to have children in an overpopulated country, if they are sufficiently well off to look after the future of their children.... It scarcely promotes the true common good to prevent the birth of human beings who could live a decent life in this world and prepare themselves for eternity, without perceptibly worsening the demographic problem in the country where they must live. . . . It is reasonable to take into account the demographic situation of the country and even of the world, since God has willed that we should all be united in one moral body".[75]

Father Zalba's position has the merit of recognizing the ethical importance, for the couple, of a consideration of the local demographic situation. But can such consideration simply be advised? If it is "reasonable" to pay attention to this demographic situation, is not its study a duty for those with sufficient intelligence to cope with it? Would it not be irrational, and therefore imprudent and inhuman, for a couple not to examine the demographic indications when they are considering together whether or not to have children, since every such decision has consequences for the whole human race? For all that, this would not turn the examination of these demographic considerations into the declaration of a duty not to have children in a situation of local or even world overpopulation. We think, therefore, that Father Zalba is not perfectly consistent with the principle he himself accepts ("It is reasonable to take into account the demographic situation"), in failing to recognize that couples, when they are intellectually able to do so, have a duty to examine this situation when they are deciding whether to have a child. But this immediately leads us to add that, in fact, many husbands and wives—through lack of the education required, and through an inability to reach a value judgment on the information laid before them—are unable to make a fruitful examination of the demographic indications, that consequently such an obligation falls down in the majority of cases. Furthermore, this statement is valid even for couples who are educated in other fields, but not in that of demography. One understands, therefore, why it is that Vatican II has not formulated such an obligation, since in most cases it would be inapplicable.

With one important qualification, we therefore accept in large measure but not purely and simply, Father Zalba's practical conclusion, which links up with that of Father Mols:

"That, in practice, the choice of a method of birth control

is most unlikely to be dictated by demographic considerations, proves scarcely anything. Economic imperatives or medical indications can perfectly well be the interpreters of a demographic situation. Nowhere is it said that parental responsibility should be consciously alerted by the problem of world population today and still less by that of the future".[76]

Mols therefore says that it is indirectly through economic and social indications, that couples take demographic indications into account when considering whether to have children.

Such a statement does not do away with the problem raised and variously answered by the three theologians we have mentioned—viz. can and should the Church give precise advice concerning birth regulation? We have seen that the couple's right to make a personal decision in this matter, is inalienable; but this does not mean that is is not hedged with conditions. The Church can help the couple by specifying the conditions for the exercise of this inalienable right. She may even be led to declare that, in certain extreme cases, this right does not exist;[77] or, more precisely, to investigate thoroughly the meaning of this right as the right of a couple as such.

It is not enough that the decision to have a child should be freely taken by one of the couple; it must be the agreed and free decision of both, since it is a conjugal decision. One of the couple may not impose it on the other, if the latter has good reason for rejecting it, just as in the case of the conjugal act itself, as we have seen.[78]

Vatican II praises large families only when they are established "with wise and shared deliberation."[79] Paul VI has denounced as immoral the unjustly imposed conjugal act. In investigating and specifying the link between these two declarations, the Church would be laying down an indispensable condition for responsible parenthood—namely, the dialogue of the couple in which a shared decision to have a child is reached, while each of the couple respects both the freedom of the other partner and their mutual obligations. She would therefore condemn even more explicitly the various forms of *irre-*

sponsible parenthood, whose sinful character would, of course, be much more patent. It must be admitted, however, that it is by no means easy to be specific about the line between responsible parenthood and irresponsible parenthood. But the insistence on the need for this dialogue, as described above, would lead to a greater humanization of conjugal life, especially among the working classes and in developing countries. And is not this insistence the greatest practical help that the Church can offer to husband and wife?

In this way, the Church would figure in the intimate life of the married couple, not only as the one who in God's name reminds the human conscience about things permitted or forbidden, but also—one is tempted to say, especially—the education of the conjugal dialogue, with a mission to save the authentic mutual love and mutual respect of husband and wife. In particular, it is her duty to remind the married couple that their shared decision to have or not have a child, should be wholly inspired by supernatural love for God and for all mankind. If it avoids the selfishness and all the forms in which sinful human pride disguises itself, it cannot fail to be a decision of all-embracing love aimed at benefiting each and every person through bringing in existence, in concurrence with God, a new member of the human race. The sacramental grace of marriage is given to Christian couples in order that their decisions for or against having children may express their obedience, not to the will of the flesh and the dictates of its instincts, but to the power of the Holy Spirit. Such a grace would have freer play in the minds and hearts of the people, within the framework of a spiritual retreat directed towards the making of a rational and supernatural decision about having or not having children, and about the size of their family.[80]

We have already impinged incidentally on the question of the action of individual and local churches. These churches can and should urge the State and the municipal bodies to fulfil their duties to provide demographic information, while respecting the moral law and the freedom of the couples. Thus these individual and local churches, in placing themselves at the spiritual service of the mission which is that of the State, would reach out, beyond the baptized, to the whole local population.

Besides, in certain cases—for instance, in cases of extreme[81] local overpopulation—these churches could advise a precise family limitation to those couples who could not or would not emigrate. Needless to say, we are referring to limitation by natural methods, not by artificial contraception.

What could the universal Church do, as distinct from the local churches?

Whereas the latter are at grips directly and immediately with problems of local overpopulation and with these alone, the universal Church is concerned directly with world population. Even if it does not come within her undisputed competence to express a judgment on the technical aspects of world demography, she can and should, as led by the Holy Spirit who fills the whole earth, attempt to discern in demographic events the true signs of the presence and of the plan[82] of God. The People of God, under the direction of their leaders, are competent to distinguish, among the signs of the times, between those of the prince of this world and those of God, though they enjoy neither an active nor a passive infallibility in doing so.[83] This discernment is, however, necessary to them if they are not to be led astray by the wiles of the father of lies, a murderer from the beginning (Jn. 8, 44).

To the extent to which the present population explosion signifies irresponsible parenthood, does it not invite certain fathers and mothers to place the accent more or less on the negative "Be not few in numbers" of Jeremiah (29, 6) and no longer on the positive "Increase and multiply" of Genesis (1, 28)?[84]

The hierarchic Church, notably the Apostolic See which presides over the universal communion in love, teaches the People of God how to read the "signs of the times." Will she consider that she has the power and the duty to advise the developing nations to practise reasonable and moderate birth regulation?

Simply to raise such questions is enough to make one realize how difficult it is to give an affirmative answer without appearing to play the political game of the already developed countries.[85] Such an answer becomes less inconceivable, however, in proportion as the countries of the Third World are turning more and more towards methods of artificial birth control.

It might be objected that these political motives are of secondary importance, and this is indeed true; but the Church must not give the impression that she is seeking to curb the growth of the weak nations and to promote that of the strong ones. She is seeking to foster and to be seen to foster the true good of all men, present and to come; she is seeking to do good not only in the sight of God, but also in the sight of men (cf. the Pauline texts relevant to this[86]). In the present circumstances, advice concerning birth control used moderately and by morally lawful methods, might more suitably come from local Hierarchies than from the universal Church or from the Holy See.

It might be objected, however, that such a suggestion is incompatible with the encouragement given by Vatican II to large families.[87] Several comments are called for here. In the first place, this praise of large families is conditional: they must be the result of a decision freely taken together by the married couples, after due reflection.[88] This is an implicit condemnation of the imprudent or one-sided decision to have a large family. Furthermore, this praise occurs in the second part of the conciliar Constitution on the Church in the Modern World, a part which, on the Council's own admission, contains contingent elements.[89] Finally, we hold that this recommendation of large families retains its value, inasmuch as it shows that the Church wishes at least to praise a special call of God addressed, not to all, but to some who are more able to respond to it—the call to have a larger, but not unreasonably large, family. The witness of large families has great significance for the building up of the world and of the Church.[90] Does not this very decidedly mean that it is not irrational to go beyond the usually accepted limits of what is regarded as "reasonable," and, in faith that transcends reason, to assist the design of Providence? While the Christian may never act against reason, his moral rule of behavior is not only or even especially the rule of reason but much more the inspiration of the Holy Spirit, an inspiration recognized as such thanks to the charism of the discerning of spirits and, sometimes at least, to the help of an experienced spiritual director.[91] It will never be possible to show that the setting up of *one* large family by *one* couple is seriously injurious to the nation or to mankind!

In recognizing the command to "increase and multiply" as signifying a command to keep the population numbers stable, the Church is thinking of the majority of married couples, without denying the existence of special cases which she continues to encourage. In giving her approval to such an interpretation, the Church could regard herself as acting for mankind, to whose general good every conjugal act should be directed. We have already said, following Saint Thomas Aquinas and Pius XII,[92] that, besides being a contract between a man and a woman, marriage is a quasi-contract with the human race concerning the survival of mankind. The human race imposes on married couples the duty to see to its own conservation, but not to its multiplying if this runs counter to common good. The Church has received from Christ the mission to protect and to interpret the natural law with a view to the temporal common good and to the eternal salvation of all men. Can she not define, therefore, in the name of the human race, the conditions for this common good? Who, better than she,[93] could do so? And do so with authority, especially as regards Christians? Could she not say, in the name of the human race, that this race does not wish to increase to such an extent as to endanger its own survival, the latter being the raison *d'être* of this very increase?

As the hierarchized People of God, the Church would thus show herself to be the mediatrix who would link the conjugal act of the married couple with the common good of the human race, as Saint Thomas Aquinas pointed out.

Her interpretations of the divine command and of its significance for our age, as well as her contingent[94] advice concerning moderate limitation of families, would place her more than ever before at the service of the world and of its harmonious development. Men of good will would recognize in these interpretations and this advice, the light of reason; and this is even more true of Christians, whom the sun of grace would enable to see more readily this light of reason. By strengthening married couples with a view to responsible parenthood, does not the sacramental grace of marriage orientate them, in very many cases, towards the decisions not to have children or to have no more children, and towards the sacrifices (periodic continence) required for the morally correct implementing of this decision?

It is useful once again to stress that, since these interpretations and this advice are of a general nature and therefore leave room for special vocations, they would show how fully the Church and the Holy See respect the freedom of decision and the ultimate responsibility of the couples themselves in the sight of God. The statement of Vatican II: "The parents should ultimately make this judgment (to have children or to have more children) in the sight of God,"[95] is a doctrinal principle independent of the changing circumstances of time and place. Just as, in the government of the Church, the pope as universal vicar of Christ is responsible to God alone, so too are couples responsible for their present decisions about children, not to the pope or to the human race, but to God alone, though later on they must render an account of these decisions, not only to the supreme Judge, but also to each and every one of the elect (cf. 1 Cor. 2, 15; 6, 2). But it must also be noted that, since this ultimate responsibility of the couple to God is a shared responsibility, it is inseparable from the responsibility of husband and wife towards one another here and now—a responsibility which links them together.

Marriage, therefore, has a certain transcendence as regards the hierarchic Church, or more precisely, the couple's decision about children has this transcendence. Their orientation towards the fulfilment of humanity and of the Church, towards a purpose which goes beyond the couple and the hierarchic Church, does not however make the family "a mere organism in the service of the social community with the purpose of creating for this community a sufficient mass of 'human material,'" as Pius XII has pointed out;[96] for the claimant is not an amorphous mass, but the human race as an organized community[97] and even as the People of God.[98]

This, then, it seems to us, is what the universal Church could do in order to cooperate with God's plan and to help His people to read the signs of the times with ever renewed discernment. In order to meet the problem of overpopulation (if it exists, and its existence at world level has not been proved to everyone's satisfaction[99]), Providence may well use the reason and faith of a certain number of couples, and for the same purpose not permit but tolerate that other couples resort to methods which do "violence to man's essential dignity" and are "based on an utterly materialistic conception of man himself and his life," as Paul VI said, quoting John XXIII.[100] The progress of a mode of contraception which in reality is very often abortifacient[101], is giving rise to fears that we are well on the way to a massacre of the innocent, unprecedented in human history, under the pretext of rationalizing human reproduction. Will Christians be as zealous in denouncing the infanticide war of contraceptive abortion, as they are in denouncing war itself?[102] Would not such denounciation be the condition governing the authentic value of the war declared against overpopulation? Have not the many millions of human persons murdered every year by the "hideous crime"[103] of abortion, a right to the perfection of their human development—a right which, however, they themselves cannot enforce?

The Church, like Rachel, mourns these children of men and refuses to be consoled, because they are no more (cf. Jer. 31, 15; Mt. 2, 18). For abortion interrupts the development of a human being called to give himself freely to God. By her doctrine and by her sacraments. the Church helps men to labor for the nourishing of the Son of God in His human brethren (cf. Mt. 25, 31-46), and thus to merit the vision of this only Son. She sustains the faith of many families in the omnipotent Providence of the Father, who continues to do wonders in favor of those who believe.[104] Would she be prepared to urge the human race to attend to the command, "Be not few in number," rather than to the command, "Increase and multiply"? Only the future will answer this. One thing is certain, however: if she does so, it will not be without having thought deeply about the difficulties of all sorts inherent in such advice, or without fully respecting the different choices open to couples in assuming their shared responsibility in the sight of God,[105] or even without expressing her admiration of those who prudently and freely choose to have a large family.

Whatever may be the demographic developments in store for us, the Church will continue to welcome and to incorporate in the little flock that has received the promise of the endless Kingdom, the ceaselessly growing number of human persons. Her greatest fear is not that they will lack the earthly bread,[106] which however she seeks to help them to produce, but much more that they will fail to take the narrow way that alone leads to the true Life.

"Civilizations are born, developed, and die. But humanity is advancing along the path of history like the waves of a rising tide encroaching gradually on the shore. We have inherited from past generations, and we have benefited from the work of our contemporaries: for this reason we have obligations towards all, and we cannot refuse to interest ourselves in those who will come after us to enlarge the human family. The reality of human solidarity, which is a benefit for us, also imposes a duty.[107]

It is necessary that we should feel the already urgent nature of the problems posed by the men of tomorrow and of the day after tomorrow, and the obligations which bind us to these men, and see in these problems our splendid chance to *already now* help mankind in *its future* pilgrimage towards the Eternal.

NOTES

In this chapter we make no pretence to answering all the objections raised against the doctrine of the Church's magisterium in relation to marriage, to the regulation of births, and to world population.

[1] *Human Vitae,* par. 8 (English translation: C.T.S.). Cf. GS, par. 50: "Marriage and conjugal love are by their nature ordained towards the begetting and educating of children" ("matrimonium et amor conjugalis indole sua ad prolem procreandam et educandam ordinantur"). This clear statement in no way authorizes one to say that Vatican II waives consideration of the purposes of marriage, or the subordination of its secondary purpose (mutual love) to the primary purpose (procreation), which it maintains while expressing it in a new way: cf. GS 50. 1 ("matrimonii finibus") and 50. 3 ("matrimonium non tantum ad procreationem institutum").

[2] HV, par. 12.

[3] L. Ciccone C.M., "L'Enciclica H.V., Analisi e Commento," *Divus Thomas* (Piacenza), 72 (1969), 275. We have derived great benefit from this remarkable commentary which systematically investigates nearly every paragraph of the encyclical of Paul VI.

[4] *Ibid.,* 279. The author points out that the part of paragraph 11 of H.V. which reads: "quilibet matrimonii usus ad vitam humanam procreandam per se destinatus permaneat," has in general been badly translated. The operative words, it is clear, are "per se." As Ciccone (op.cit., p. 278) points out, "the act remains always structured by a tendential orientation towards procreation, just as the eye is always made for seeing, even when one of the elements essential to effective vision is missing and when, consequently, the visual function of the eye remains only potential." (The English version published by C.T.S., as translated by Bishop Alan C. Clark D.D. and Rev. G. Crawford, seems to be adequate: "that in *any use whatever of marriage,* there must be no impairment of its natural capacity to procreate human life." The "per se" of the original is given its due prominence in this translation. —Translator's note).

[5] L. Ciccone, *op., p.* 150.

[6] Cf. Hv, par. 12: "conjugii actus." The Church prefers to use the term "conjugal act" rather than "sexual act," since the latter is lawful only for married couples.

[7] HV, par. 9.

[8] *Ibid.*

[9] GS. 50. 1.

[10] Cf. H. Muhlen, *Der Heilige Geist als Person,* Padernborn, 1967^2, pp. 76-81 and 136-137.

[11] Even couples advanced in age, still seek to express, through the the unreserved union of their conjugal act, their basic and permanent project of universal communion: cf. note 23.

[12] HV, par. 13.

[13] HV, par. 16

[14] HV, par. 13

[15] GS, 24. 3.

[16] HY, 9.

[17] If the unitive and procreative significations of the conjugal act are inseparable, as HV, 12 clearly says, the rejection of the one objectively entails the rejection of the other. This is logically implied a little later in the same paragraph: "And if each of these essential qualities, the unitive and the procreative, is preserved, the use of marriage fully retains its sense of true mutual love." In other words, it does not preserve this sense fully when it does not also preserve these two essential aspects. However, the encyclical does not say that there is no kind of love between a husband and wife who use artificial contraception, but that this love is not "true mutual love." The encyclical does not go as far as did Gandhi who wrote in 1936: "the use of contraceptives is mutual masturbation"; and, in 1946: "the difference between a prostitute and a wife who uses contraceptives is that the former sells her body to many men, the latter to one man only."

[18] HV,13.

[19] Cf. M. Zalba S.J., *Rassegna di Teologia,* IX (1968), 234: "Since the transmission of life should be the fruit of conjugal love, there is no demonstrably certain duty to accept procreation in the absence of a duty to accept the conjugal act—that is, when one of the partners has accepted conjugal intercourse under a compulsion which does violence to the said duty of mutual self-giving in free and truly human conjugal love. Consequently, in such a case of unjust compulsion, the innocent party can guard against the aggressor without infringing the natural order, which subordinates the function of the organs to the wellbeing of the individual." In support of this idea, Father Zalba cites three discourses of Pius XII (12 Nov. 1944; 8 Sept. 1953; 12 Sept. 1958), always presupposing the free character (explicitly affirmed) of the sexual activity which entails these responsibilities. In the connection, see also: E. Boissard, "Valeur morale d'un certain cas de stérilisation temporaire," *Angelicum,* 41 (1946), 167-209.

[20] Saint Thomas Aquinas, *De Anima,* III, lect. XIII.

[21] For example, Father A. Marc S.J. and J.B. Metz: *Christliche Anthropozentrik,* Munich, 1962. The sub-title indicates that the book deals with the thought-forms (*Denkform*) of Saint Thomas Aquinas.

[22] Saint Thomas Aquinas, ST, I. 29. 3.

[23] On the whole question of these natural desires, see B. de Margerie S.J., *Reinhold Niebuhr, théologien de la communauté mondiale,* Bruges, 1969, pp. 374-379.

[24] This is an allusion to the final act, meritorious or unmeritorious, of the human free will, in the presence of death.

[25] L. Lochet, "Les fins du mariage," NRT, 73 (1951), 453.

[26] Andre Marc S.J., "L'Homme et la Femme", *Année Théologique,* 1946, pp. 424-444.

[27] Cf. 1 Cor. 15, 44; Mt. 13, 43: "Then the righteous will shine like the sun in the kingdom of their Father"; like mutually luminous suns; the spiritualized body of the resurrected person will reveal his soul in a pure and total transparency.

[28] Saint Thomas Aquinas, *De Malo,* 15, 2. 12: "Actus generationis

ordinatur ad bonum speciei, quod est bonum commune"; ST, II. II. 153. 3: "bonum commune quod est conservatio generis humani."

[29] As Mandonnet recognizes; cf. G. Jacquemet, *Catholicisme,* 1 (1948), 1121, art. "Averroes"; M. D. Chenu O.P. also accepts the opinion that the Averroist interpretation of Aristotle was "more homogeneous with his thought and with his text" (*Pour une théologie du travail,* Paris, 1955, p. 69).

[30] A comparative study of the thesis of Latin Averroism on the unity of the intellect, and of those of Hegel, would yield some interesting surprises.

[31] Saint Augustine (*De bono conjugali,* VIII, 8) brackets both knowledge and marriage as destined to destruction (cf. 1 Cor. 13, 8; Lk. 22, 34-36) and, in contrast charity and virginity, as not passing away.

[32] Pius XII *Vegliare con Sollecitudine* (Address to the Congress of the Italian Association of Catholic Midwives on 29 October 1951): *ASS,* 43 (1951), 845-846.

[33] Cf. Saint Augustine, *De bono conjugali,* IX, 9: "Hinc (nuptiae) subsistit propagatio generis humani."

[34] "Quoddam seminarium civitatis," says Saint Augustine in "The City of God": PL, 42, 450.

[35] When we speak of the demand made by men as yet unborn, we are of course alluding to an ideal anticipation of an eschatological reality. Saint Thomas Aquinas speaks in a similar way when dealing with Jn. 1, 3-4: "res, prout sic (sc. sicut in cognoscente) in Eo sunt, sunt essentia divina" (ST. I. 18. 4).

[36] Saint Thomas Aquinas, *Summa contra Gentiles,* IV. 78, where he analyses the different purposes of the act of generation: the good of the species, of the "civitas," and of the Church.

[37] Lochet, *art.cit.* (note 23), p. 563; cf. Saint Augustine, *De bono conjugi,* IX, 9: "hinc enim (sc. nuptiae) subsistit propagatio generis humani, in quo *societas amicalis* magnum bonum est."

[38] Lochet, *art.cit.,* p. 562.

[39] Thus it can be said that marriage and virginity both evoke, in different and complementary ways, the Kingdom of Heaven: marriage, in an indirect and extrinsic manner, because it is orientated to the procreation of the elect; virginity, in a direct and intrinsic manner, inasmuch as virgins live here on earth the life of abstention from all use of their sexual faculties, such as the elect will live eternally.

[40] Cf. B. de Margerie S.J., *Reinhold Niebuhr, théologien de la communauté mondiale,* Bruges, 1969, p. 357: strictly speaking, it is not *life* that the parents give, but the body, animated by the soul, the latter being immediately created by God.

[41] Cf. P. Beltrao S.J.: "Problemi attuali della Planificazione familiare", *Civitas Cattolica,* no. 287 (1970). This article (p. 237, note 35) also contains a bibliography concerning the various reactions of the Catholic Hierarchy toward the projects to legalize contraception.

[42] Cf. R. Mols S.J., "Démographie et Paternité responsible," NRT, 91 (1969), 399: "Imagine a world population capable of doubling every 33 years. . . . This is far from being in any way an outlandish suggestion. . . . At that rate, the population should double three times per century. The present figure of 3,363 million would rise to 6,000

million by the year 2000. And this 6,000 million would become: c. 50 thousand million in 2100; c. 400 thousand million in 2200; c. 300 thousand million in 2300; c. 2400 thousand million in 2400; c. 100,000 thousand million in 2469. Now, what is a span of five centuries in the history of mankind? Merely the time that separates us now from the date of the discovery of America." But these are hypothetical figures, and experience shows how often such calculations made in the past have not been borne out by events.

[43] Mols, *art.cit.* (note 37), p. 401, citing A. Sauvy, *De Malthus a Mao-Tse-Toung,* Paris, 1958, p. 85.

[44] Mols, *art.cit.,* p. 401. But if one had said to the majority of the 200 million who were peopling the earth at the time of Christ, that two thousand years later world population would have risen to some 5 thousand million, would they too not have had the impression of an "inhuman massification," inhuman to the point of being "monstrous"?

[45] HV, par. 2: "Many fear that world population is going to grow faster than available resources"; in other words, that a certain number of people will die of starvation.

[46] Mols, *art.cit.,* p. 298.

[47] *Ibid.,* p. 404. But is this so certain? Must not one foresee, even if one condemns it, an intensive use of contraception in the developing countries (see note 36 of this *art.cit.*)? Besides, the idea of overpopulation remains vague, as is shown by G. Cottier O.P.: *Régulation des naissances et développement démographique,* Bruges-Paris, 1969, pp. 85-86: "The yardstick for measuring subsistance is not furnished immediately by nature. Factors of the economic and political order, such as the type of property, or technique, such as productivity and invention, are determinants."

[48] Must not a distinction be drawn between the divine will for the survival of the human race at the temporal level, until the end of history, and the divine will for the geometric and limitless multiplication of the human race? The first, which is centainly confirmed by Biblical revelation, in no way signifies the same thing as the second. The very concept, which comes from revelation, of an end to human history, a concept inseparable from that of a beginning of that history, itself rules out an indefinite multiplication of the human race.

[49] Pius XII, ASS, 50 (1958), 90-96. It is not at all certain that, in this discourse, Pius XII intended to address the whole Church in order to settle a controversy (cf. DS, 3885). We think, however, that this discourse expresses in current terms the traditional doctrine of the Church's ordinary magisterium on divine Providence. A reference to this passage of Pius XII is in GS, 50. 2.

[50] Pius XII, *ibid.,* 94. Notice however, with Father Mols (*art.cit.,* p. 408): "As for massive emigration to other worlds, it is to be feared that this remains at the stage of an idea. It is not in tens but in tens of millions every year that people would have to be transported to some other planet, and guaranteed the possibility of normal development there."

[51] John XXIII, *Mater et Magister,* ASS, 43 (1961), 446-448.

[52] GS, 87. 3. We have here, however, a conditional right, as is shown

by this extract from a discourse of Pius XII: "When the carrier of an hereditary blemish is unable to act in a fully human way and consequently to contract marriage, or when later on he has become incapable of claiming by a free act the right acquired by a valid marriage, he can be licitly prevented from begetting a child. Apart from these cases, the prohibiting of marriage and marital relations for biological, genetic, and eugenic reasons, is unjust, whether the prohibition emanates from an individual person or from a public ministry." Text of 1953: ASS, 45 (1953), 606.

[53] GS 87. 3.

[54] See a document published in 1954 by the *Union internationale d'Etudes Sociales,* of Malines. DC, 51 (1954), 1453-1454.

[55] GS, 50. 2.

[56] Pius XII, *Vegliare con Sollecitudine,* ASS, 43 (1951), 845-846: "Serious reasons, often put forward on medical, eugenic, and social grounds, can exempt from this obligatory duty even for a considerable time, even for the entire duration of the marriage" (English translation, C.T.S., par. 36). M. Zalba S.J. comments as follows on this text: "Some claim that Pius XII was thinking about the 'social' question in the address to Italian midwives, and take what he said in this sense. But the context seems to rule this out. Elsewhere, Pius XI had already dealt with the same social question, and clearly this was done solely at the family level" (*art.cit.* in note 69: *Doctor Communis,* 21, 1968, 164).

[57] GS, 50. 2, citing the discourse of Pius XII to which notes 49 and 50 refer.

[58] GS, 50. 2.

[59] GS, 87; HV, 17, 23.

[60] HV, 10; the term is analogous to the term "human race" used by Pius XII: cf. the text cited in note 29.

[61] GS, 50. 2.

[62] HV, 7. Cf. GS, 51. 4 (an analogous, but less precisely expressed principle).

[63] Pius XII, ASS, 50 (1958), 94.

[64] Cf. 1 Cor. 7, 5; GS, 50. 2.

[65] The sacramental grace of marriage qualifies the virtue of prudence, which includes foresight.

[66] In effect, the two distinct teachings of Saint Thomas Aquinas must be brought together. On the one hand, the conjugal act is directed to the conservation of the human race (cf. notes 25 and 32); on the other hand, "per orationem, nos ipsos trahamus, mutabiles existentes, ad divinae Providentiae participationem" (Lectio prima, *De divinis Nominibus,* III): cf. B. Margerie S.J., *Niebuhr, théologien de la communauté mondiale,* Bruges, 1969, pp. 329-333. Prayer and the conjugal act constitute two modes, one somatic, the other spiritual, and each in its own way psycho-somatic, of man's sharing with Providence in the ruling of the universe.

[67] Cf. Pius XI, *Quadragesimo Anno,* ASS, 23 (1931), 190: the magisterium is not competent in questions of economic and social technique, but keeps the right and the duty to pass judgement, with the

fullest authortiy, on the moral aspects of economic and social questions.

[68] Notably in terms of the cultural and political situation of the country to which they belong. Thus Colin Clark contests what the FAO holds: that more than two thirds of mankind are suffering from hunger and under-nourishment (*Population Growth and Land Use,* London, 1968, pp. 124 ff.).

[69] Cf. PP, 37.

[70] In the same review (cf. note 71), Gorospe devotes a long article to attacking the concept of natural law made current by HV.

[71] V. R. Gorospe S.J., "The Catholic Hierarchy and the Population Problem," *Philippine Studies,* 17 (1961), 806-811.

[72] R. Mols. *art.cit.* (note 42), p. 414.

[73] *Ibid.*

[74] Except in the case we discussed in note 52.

[75] Zalba S.J., "Sens et portée de la fin première du mariage," *Doctor Communis,* 21 (1968), 164-166.

[76] Mols, *art.cit.,* p. 413.

[77] Cf. notes 52 and 74; 18 and 19.

[78] *Ibid.*

[79] GS, 50. 2; shortly before, in the same paragraph, the Council, when describing the decision about responsible parenthood, regards it as something which the couple work out together ("communi consilio atque conatu rectum judicium sibi efformabunt").

[80] The Ignatian "Spiritual Exercises," orientated as they are towards the choice of a state in life or towards choices which lead to a reformation of life, would be especially useful in the reaching of such a decision.

[81] We use this restrictive adjective because of the vagueness (cf. note 42) and the subjective assessments of the phenomenon called "overpopulation," even when studied at local level. On the possible help that local churches or national episcopal conferences can give in regard to the regulation of births, see Chauchard, *Volonté et Sexualité,* Paris, 1969, pp. 258-264; the document of the bishops of the Philippines (1969) to which V. Gorospe refers (see his note 65). In this document, the bishops urged the government to take some indirect measures ("macro-measures"), such as the putting back of the mihimum legal age for marriage (which proposal itself raised a problem, since a natural and inalienable right is involved here), the establishment of an old age pensions' scheme, and the direction of internal movements of the population.

[82] GS, 4, 11.

[83] Cf. LG. 12, relative to the infallibility of adherence and consent in faith to the formulation of revelation as presented by the Church's magisterium.

[84] Cf. the text of Saint Thomas Aquinas cited in note 28: he was not speaking about the multiplying, but only about the conservation of the human race.

[85] Cf. Colin Clark, "World Power and Population," *National Review,* 1969, pp. 481-484, which can be complemented with the follow

ing by A. M. Henry O.P., *La Croix* (6 December 1969): "Did not a Cardinal-Archbishop of a large city of the Third World say recently: The strength of the 'have-nots' is their size through which they can strike fear into the 'haves' of the population, and they know this." Father Henry rightly added: "The advanced countries, because of their high standard of education, do particular service to mankind by having children. The latter when educated will be able to educate others. Even in a rich country, it is estimated that one additional engineer or technician sometimes means thousands of additional jobs for others." This shows that it is proper to encourage a high birth rate in the already developed countries, both for the benefit of these countries themselves and for that of the world in general. But is it not difficult for the universal Church to encourage it in one area and discourage it in another?

[86] Especialy in the Second Epistle to the Corinthians.

[87] Cf. the text cited in note 79.

[88] *Ibid.*s "communi consilio atque conatu."

[89] GS 1, note.

[90] Pius XII, Address of 20 January 1958 to large families, ASS, 50 (1958), 92 and 95: large families are more easily brought up well, and are a special expression of faith in Providence.

[91] Cf. Saint Thcmas Aquinas ST, II II. 8. 3. 3: "Regula humanorum actuum est et ratio humana et lex aeterna. . . . Lex autem aeterna excedit rationem naturalem, et indiget supernaturali lumine doni Spiritus Sancti" (cf. I. II. 71. 6). In other words, no genuinely and fully authentic decision concerning the regulation of birth can be reached without the light of the gift of knowledge, in addition to the state of grace.

[92] Cf. the text to which note 32 refers. Here we quote the very useful commentary on this text, made by Fathers J. C. Ford and G. Kelly S.J.: "It would hardly have been the thought of Pius XII that his claimant, in this case the human race, had a right in legal justice to insist that the married couples procreate, and to punish those who failed to make their obligatory prestation. Much less would he have been likely to attribute to the state or to society or to some future world government the legal right, in a case where the common good of the race required fewer children rather than more, to demand that married couples not procreate, and to punish those considered too prolific. But if strict legal justice is involved, then rights on the part of the society should correspond to duties on the part of the citizen, and if the common good can ordinarily demand procreation of them, the common good might at other times require a limit to be put on procreation. . . . But the race seems to have sufficient natural unity of general destiny under God to become a subject of rights of legal justice, somewhat as nations are. . . .

While not denying that legal justice is somehow involved, we suggest that the virtue of piety (pietas) may be even more closely and appropriately associated with this duty. . . . Why can there not be a piety towards the human race which emphasizes the unity of the whole human family? Procreation to conserve this human family would then be an act not only of legal justice in some sense, but also of piety." (*Contemporary Moral Theology,* Westminster, Maryland, USA, 1963 vol. II, pp. 411-413).

It is in order to avoid the difficulties pointed out in this article that we speak, not about a contract, but about a quasi-contract between the couple and the human race. We note, in passing, that the authors cite the opinion of F. Zimmermann: "Catholic Viewpoint on Overpopulation," Garden City, N. Y., 1961. Zimmermann holds that, in a situation of "absolute overpopulation," the State could sanction a duty of the natural law (declared such by the Church) not to procreate. We ourselves would say rather that the Church cannot go beyond the giving of advice: cf. Ford, *op.cit.,* p. 412.

[93] In effect, on the one hand, mankind is destined, at the divine level, to become the Church; on the other hand, the Church is "a lasting and sure seed of unity, hope, and salvation for the whole human race" (LG, 9).

[94] Let us emphasize, in passing, that such advice would carry little weight in the Third World, since the educational backwardness of the masses would largely prevent their grasping what is at stake. In promoting education and development, the Church is working for a healthy limitation of birth, and is doing so more effectively than she could do by means of certain inopportune advice. When one is dealing with people of some education, such advice concerning moderate limitation becomes itself useless, and it could perhaps be the duty expressed as "be not few in numbers" on which the Church ought rather to insist. However, a situation could arise which would make such advice opportune.

[95] GS, 50. 2.

[96] Pius XII, AAS, 43 (1951), 856.

[97] Cf. the distinction between people and masses suggested by Pius XII, in his radio message on democracy (Christmas, 1944): ASS, 37 (1945), 13.

[98] While the human race requires the conjugal act for its temporal conservation, the Church requires it in order to grow "to the measure of the stature of the fullness of Christ" (Eph. 4, 13)

[99] To Colin Clark's, for instance; see notes 68 and 85.

[100] HV, 23.

[101] Cf. L. Ciccone C.M., *Divus Thomas,* 73 (1970), p. 14: the well known "pill" can cause abortion.

[102] One notices that many students, rightly vociferous in protesting against war, seem little concerned about the laws to make homicidal abortion more easily available.

[103] GS, 27 and 51.

[104] Pius XII, Address to large families; 20 January 1958: AAS, 50 (1958), 93 and 95: "God does not refuse the means to live. He gives through day-to-day assistance, and, where necessary, by special interventions, as many of you have personally experienced." Vatican II (GS, 50. 2) refers to this address.

[105] In the light of the doctrine of the magisterium of the Church (cf. GS, 51. 3); Ciccone (*op.cit.,* 1969, pp. 163-164) rightly points out that the role ascribed to the conscience of the married couple by HV

and by Vatican II is not that of mere executants as would appear to have been the opinion of Cardinal Ottaviani expressed at the conciliar session of 30 October 1964, nor is it that of sole judge of the means of birth control to be used; but one of interpreter. The couple has the right only to make a morally good choice on the basis of respect for the objective moral order.

[106] Cf. the commentary of Saint Thomas Aquinas on Jn. 6, 35: "I am the bread of life": "panis corporis est panis mortis" (*Sup. Evang. S. Joannis lectura,* Marietti, Turin, 1952, par. 914).

[107] PP, 17.

chapter three

The Twofold Priestly Consecration in the Service of Human Development

MARRIED couples, by giving birth to their children and educating them for the love of all men and especially for the glory of the Blessed Trinity, make a decisive contribution to the twofold development, temporal and spiritual, of mankind. But such couples know that they are dependent on the ministry of priests in order to accomplish their task and to ensure their own human fullness.

In the divine and sacramental plan for the full development of all men, the sacrament of holy orders has an essential place.

Such a statement, however, raises a difficulty. Is not the priest the man of the spiritual and the eternal? Will not the proper and necessary non-involvement of the priest at a personal level with a secular way of life mean therefore that he is cut off from the gigantic task of building the earthly city? What therefore can he contribute, without falling short of his spiritual mission, to the temporal development of mankind? Or, more precisely, what should he contribute in order to be faithful to his vocation?

We shall attempt to show here that the priestly consecration of holy orders obliges the priest to make a very great effort to promote the earthly development of mankind, an effort all the more efficacious and universal for being indirect; and that he has been already disposed to this new consecration[1] by a fuller consecration of his activity, through the loving commitment he has assumed to celibacy, for the sake of the kingdom of heaven.

It was by no mere accident of succession, but in accordance with a deep-seated purpose, that, in 1967, Paul VI published one after another the encyclicals *Populorum Progressio* and *Sacerdotalis Coelibatus*. The development of mankind is, in fact, partly linked, through ecclesiastical celibacy, with the sacrament of holy orders which causes this development to grow towards its perfect eschatological consummation.

A. *The priest is anointed by the Spirit in order to be the spiritual animator of man's temporal development.*

Vatican II has accustomed[2] us to regard priests of Christ as men consecrated as He was (ordination) and sent (mission) by the Father in order to share in the consecration and mission of the Son for the salvation of the world:

"Christ, whom the Father sanctified and sent into the world (Jn. 10, 36) has, through His apostles, made their successors . . . partakers of His consecration and His mission."[3]

One can understand the priest's activity only by tracing it back to his priesthood; just as it is by his specific activity that he shows his priesthood.

Now, by his Eucharistic and reconciling activity, the priest shows that by the very essence of his priesthood he is a mediator: in a certain sense, he gives God to men, and represents them in the eyes of God, offering to Him their prayers, their sacrifices, and their life. His ordination to the priesthood empowers him to pass from God to men and from men to God, and even to be the bridge connecting them (pontifex.)[4]

When one considers the life of men which the priest offers to God in their name and in union with the sacrifice of Christ, is not that life spent in laboriously building the earthly city? And is not the divine life which the priest gives to them, none other than Christ Himself without whom they could do nothing[5] worthy of the eternal praise of God?

The priest's role in the Mass symbolizes his main role in all phases of human existence. The Eucharistic liturgy, being the center of supernatural love, is the constantly renewed source of the divinization of human labor. Without Eucharistic love, of which the priest is the mediator, man's works are like withered branches which have borne no fruit and are doomed to be gathered and cast into an inextinguishable fire (cf. Jn. 15, 2-6). How would it profit a man to construct and organize completely mortal cities of gigantic size and mighty civilizations, if in the process he were to lose his own soul instead of fixing it more and more in Absolute Good through that very same work? What is not offered to God is lost, and the priest is the mediator of this love-inspired offering.

How does he do this? Not primarily and essentially by himself taking up, sometimes to the detriment of competent laymen, secular work for which by his ordination, he has no special charism; but by helping the laity to do their work with a correct attitude towards it, through the fulfilment of his own unique mission. This is the principle which Vatican II has outlined in a general way,[6] though the Council has also dealt with its particular applications. The priest's function is to be the architect of the eternal city, and it is precisely by fully discharging this function that he will make his influence most intensely felt in the earthly city.

The primary mission of the priest is to preach the gospel of salvation, and to call the People of God around the altar in order that there they may offer themselves in sacrifice.[7] Such preaching proclaims the eternal value of all the works done by men in God (cf. Jn. 3, 21) and for love of Him. It reminds the architects of the mortal cities: "Blessed are the dead who die in the Lord; henceforth, says the Spirit, they may rest from their labors, for their deeds follow them!" (Rev. 14, 13).

Conscious of this eternal worth of human work done in the state of grace, the preacher will be able, in his preaching itself, "to strive to deal with contemporary problems in the light of Christ," as Vatican II explicitly directed him to do.[8] It even says that it is the priest"s duty "to help Christians to become capable of reading in events great and small, what a situation demands of them, what God requires of them," with a view to enabling them to achieve what the Council calls "Christian maturity."[9] And that is why, in speaking about the preparation of seminarians for the priesthood, it specifically says: "Let them learn to search for solutions to human problems with the light of revelation, to apply eternal truths to the changing conditions of human affairs, and to communicate such truths in a manner suited to contemporary man."[10]

With all this in mind, how could it be denied that the priest who is faithful to his mission must necessarily be a spiritual animator of man's temporal development? Is not this development God's primary wish in order of earthly realities? Does not God will to give to the preacher the mission to preach and to urge this temporal development, notably "by persuading everyone to the discharge of the duties of his own state in life"?[11] Is it not the priest's duty to show to every person how the personal and conscientious discharge of his duty in life is the indispensable stone which each can bring to the building up of the earthly city and to its development? Thus placed in a broad and universal perspective, will not every person's task in life appear in a more attractive light?

Vatican II also points out to priests that, "united in concern and effort, under the leadership of the bishops and of the Supreme Pontiff," they have a duty "to wipe out every kind of division, so that the whole human race may be brought into the unity of the family of God."[12] It is painfully clear that divisions and wars are obstacles to the harmonious development, both temporal and spiritual, of all mankind. The priest's contribution to peace in all aspects, is simply another name for his contribution to human development. And who, more than the priest, contributes towards the creation of peaceful relationships among men?

However, it can be said that the preacher's supreme

task as regards human development lies not so much in constantly urging the eternal efficacy of the labors of divinized man, as in directing attention to the personal and social salvific efficacy of man's suffering. At first sight, does this not seem the sheer negation of progress? And yet, what individuals and society most expect and welcome from the preacher, is his proclaiming of the efficacy of the cross. "Unless a grain of wheat falls into the ground and dies, it remains alone; but if it dies, it bears much fruit. He who loves his life loses it, and he who hates his life in this world will keep it for eternal life" (Jn. 12, 24-25).

One could thus specifically detail how other functions of the priest contribute, in an indirect way, to the socio-economic and general development of mankind. Let it suffice that we have done so here[13] in connection with the priest's role as preacher. It can be summed up as follows: through the preacher, the word of Christ helps the Christian to become spiritually adult, by doing his work more conscientiously and by offering it up, in union with the Eucharistic sacrifice, for all mankind.

We may add that a priest who spiritually animates homes and families, who organizes catechetical study groups in his parish, who teaches religious knowledge in the high schools, who discusses current problems in a Christian light on radio or television, or who writes in newspapers and periodicals about these problems, shares more intensively and to greater effect in the building up of the earthly city than were he, under the pretext of "really getting among the people," to take up a secular profession. The outcome of this latter step would undoubtedly be to make the Word incarnate less present in the earthly city. For the Catholic priest, the decisive example is not that of Paul, who earned his bread by being a tent maker in his spare time, but rather that of Christ, who gave up being a carpenter in order to preach His own Gospel.[14]

In short, the work of human development, in its temporal aspect, is the vocation proper to layfolk, who normally need the spiritual assistance of the priest, minister of the word and of the sacrament, to enable them to respond adequately to their own vocation.

To fulfill this mission, the priest receives in abundance the sacramental grace of holy orders.[15] This is a treasury on which he can and should repeatedly draw. Furthermore, he can apply to himself those words of Isaiah which Jesus made his own with more sublime reason: "The Spirit of the Lord is upon me, because he has anointed me to preach good news to the poor. He has sent me to proclaim release to the captives and recovering of sight to the blind, to set at liberty those who are oppressed, to proclaim the acceptable year of the Lord" (Lk. 4, 18-19, quoting Is. 61, 1-2). This text, particularly emphasized by Vatican II,[16] wonderfully sums up and symbolizes the indirect temporal effects of the evangelizing mission of the priest in regard to the full development, physical and spiritual, of the human race.

B. *To dispose himself to priestly consecration, the future priest consecrates himself to Christ by a definitive celibacy in order to promote the growth of the world.*

At the very time when the Church of Vatican II was scrutinizing herself with a view to being more effectively able to serve the world, she investigated, more deeply than in any previous council, the law of ecclesiastical celibacy for the Latin rite. It is precisely with a view to serving all mankind more perfectly for the glory of God, that the Church will not admit married men to ordination in the Latin rite, and that she demands from candidates for the priesthood a promise of celibacy "for the kingdom of heaven." "Through celibacy observed for the sake of the kingdom of heaven, priests are consecrated to Christ in a new and distinguished way," the Council says explicitly; and immediately adds: "They are more free to devote themselves in Him and through Him to the service of God and men."[17] Vatican II presents ecclesiastical celibacy, therefore, as a new and liberating consecration, in the service of mankind, of a man already consecrated by baptism and destined to receive the supreme consecration of the priesthood.[18]

It is well known that this presentation of celibacy has not prevented widespread current of opinion from gathering strength within the Catholic Church, to the effect that the ecclesiastical law of celibacy is contrary to the natural divine law of personal development and to the positive divine law of ecclesiastical development, thereby implying that the obstacle it puts in the way of this twofold development is itself an obstacle to the twofold development, temporal and eternal, of the whole human race. Could eccesiastical celibacy therefore, hinder, personal fulfillment and the evangelizing of the world?

Let us look at the objections more closely. On the one hand, it is said: "Jesus gave a command to preach the gospel, and the gospel is not being preached because of a lack of priests as a result of this stupid barrier of celibacy."[19] So, it would seem, the law of celibacy is contrary to the supreme constitutional law of the Church, to her *raison d'être:* the salvation of souls. For it is "to the obligation of celibacy that some ascribe the disturbing fall off in the number of the clergy," says Paul VI in his encyclical of 1967.[20]

On the other hand, some would regard the law of celibacy as contrary to the inalienable right to marry dealt with in the encyclical *Populorum Progressio;*[21] according to them, it places the priest "in an unnatural physical and psychological condition, harmful to his equilibrium and maturity as a human person."[22]

Faced with such constantly repeated objections, let us formulate our own thesis as follows:

The evangelical counsel[23] *and the ecclesiastical law of priestly celibacy promotes the observance of the divine natural law of personal development for the priest himself, and of the collective development of mankind, as well as the observance of the divine positive law of the growth of the Church for the service of people and of the world.*

In other words, far from being an obstacle to human development, the law of celibacy has this very development as its purpose.

It now remains for us to justify the different elements of this thesis.

In the first place, the ecclesiastical law of celibacy assists the priest to fulfill the divine law of personal development because it simultaneously binds all the members of one and the same priestly body, one and the same "presbyterium," and is inseparable from the natural and positive law of mutual love between the members of this "presbyterium."[24] Abstention from marriage is accompanied by a sacramental brotherhood[25] among colleagues of the same "presbyterium," whose celibacy facilitates such mutual love. Celibacy is not, therefore, a law of isolation, but a law of social fellowship multiplying friendly relationships.

More profoundly, however, it expresses an ecclesial demand and a personal choice on the part of the candidate for the priesthood. It is aimed at his splendid marriage of soul with Christ the Redeemer of the world, and as an anticipation on earth of the eschatological consummation of this spiritual marriage to which baptism had designated him. Vatican II stresses this as follows: "Through celibacy observed for the sake of the kingdom of heaven, . . . priests evoke that mysterious marriage which was established by God and will be fully manifested in the future, and by which the Church has Christ as her only spouse." And of this spiritual marriage of the whole Church (of which the priest is a member) with Christ, Vatican II presents the priest as the paranymph (in the light of 2 Cor. 11, 2), a task to which his consecrated celibacy enables him more fully to dedicate himself. Or, more exactly, let us say that the priests of the Latin rite, by consecrating their sexuality to Christ through celibacy and living in this personal espousal with the Redeemer, fulfill their vocation as paranymphs of the mystery of the espousals between the Church on earth and her Lord, a mystery completely orientated towards the definitive marriage of the heavenly Church.[26]

In other words, consecrated celibacy, a stage in the priest's fulfilment of his personal vocation with regard to this eschatological spiritual marriage, cannot fail to be a developmental factor of his own human personality, in the sense that it simultaneously demands and manifests a greater love—a lover greater, not only towards God but also towards men. It is a love whose unceasing growth is nourished by the constantly renewed and joyful sacrifice of some of the noblest and most exalted among the natural aspirations of the human person: marriage and parenthood according to the flesh and according to the Spirit.[27]

More profoundly, consecrated celibacy enables the priest to live at its greatest intensity a truth which affects all men and which it is the priest's mission to preach to them—namely, that the mystery of the cross is an integral part of the development[28] to which every man is divinely called, in his soul and in his body. From this point of view, and indeed from all viewpoints, Christ—welcoming in Himself, as a gift[29] and as a call from the Father, the charism of celibacy for the salvation of mankind, and integrating this charism in the salvific work of His paschal mystery—is the type and model of the pastoral celibacy of the priest. Celibacy is an element of development of Christ's personality.[30] His body, consecrated from its beginning by the anointing of the Spirit, its activity having been consecrated to the Father by the choice of celibacy unto death, was taken over completely, at His resurrection, by all the power of the Spirit in a supreme consecration.

The mysterious law[31] of ecclesiastical celibacy is linked, therefore, with the development of the whole ecclesial body of Christ, the virginal Redeemer of sex-endowed mankind. This truth shone forth with particular radiance during the missionary era of the Church in the sixteenth century. Is it not true that, without this law, the success of the missionary effort of the post-Tridentine Church would have been drastically diminished? Can it be denied that the clerical congregations instituted between Trent and Vatican II were in very large measure conditioned, notably as to their growth in membership, by the law of celibacy—a law also binding the secular clergy? In effect, it seems a psychologically evident fact that many men would not have entered into clerical religious congregations if it had been possible for them to be both priests and married men. Now, the missionary effort of the Church between Trent and Vatican II was preeminently the work of these religious congregations, the secular clergy having contributed relatively very little. This observation is further strengthened by the fact that missionary work was of a very limited kind both in Catholic churches of the oriental rite and in the Orthodox churches (though the latter did send some missionaries to Siberia, Japan, and Alaska).[32]

The missionary fruitfulness of the law of celibacy in the history of the Church provides practical confirmation of what Vatican II says: "The practice of priestly celibacy simultaneously signifies and stimulates pastoral charity and is a special foundation of spiritual fruitfulness on earth."[33] In this respect, the law of celibacy presents itself as a charism—that is a gift freely bestowed on the Church by the Spirit for the benefit of mankind destined to be incorporated with her through baptism. This law is, therefore a charismatic law of the development of the ecclesial body; a law whose promulgation and increasingly effective application presupposes the charism of celibacy and its outpouring; the charism of the prayer of petition offered for this intention by the candidates for priesthood and by the whole People of God; finally, the charism of the pontifical primacy exercised with strength and love. This law, which some would regard as the negation of the charismatic order, is in reality the nucleus of a whole series of inter-dependent and coordinated charisms. The same Spirit is at work within the legislator that he may legislate wisely; within the candidates for the priesthood in order to stimulate them to aspire to the sacrificial dedication inherent in the choice of priestly celibacy; and finally, within the faithful to inspire them to beseech the Father, "with sighs too deep for words" (Rm. 8, 26), to give them celibate priests.[34]

Having thus shown to what extent the law of celibacy promotes the observance of the divine positive law concerning the growth of the Church, we must now briefly show how it contributes to the observance of the divine natural law concerning the development of mankind. This point does, in fact, follow from the preceding one. The Church is the sacrament of the salvation of the world, of the unity of the human race, and of man's intimate union with God.[35] In this respect, it can be said that the Church is the sacrament of the world, since it implements the salvific plan of God. What promotes the Church's growth, therefore, fosters the spiritual and social growth of all mankind. As Paul VI has pointed out, the law of celibacy gives encouragement to men of good will, whatever their religious convictions may be, in an era when so many forces are attempting to degrade both public and private morality.[36] In this respect, it is a law of freedom[37] which strengthens the free will by helping the celibate priest to free himself from slavery to the passions and from ill-considered decisions, which can snatch him away from the exclusive service of Jesus Christ and of the universal Church.

We have presented, therefore, some of the essential reasons why the law of celibacy is a law of ecclesial growth and of personal and human development. Far from being detrimental to the supreme constitutional law of the Church, namely the salvation of souls, it is an expression at once contingent and capital to this supreme law. It is not a barrier to the preaching of the Gospel; it is a beacon of shinning truth. Consecrating and even sacralizing[38] the priest's sexuality, it contributes decisively to humanizing him. The loving observance of this law of celibacy disposes the priest to receive more abundantly the inexhaustible sacramental grace of the sacrament of holy orders, with a view to his perfectly discharging his functions as minister of the gospel and architect of the social Body of Christ the Redeemer, entirely in the service of the development of mankind. At the same time, this sacramental grace urges him to be perfectly faithful to his freely accepted promise of personal celibacy. For, God does not demand the impossible; but in issuing a command He alerts a man to do what he can, to ask for what seems impossible, and He helps him to achieve it.[39]

One understands, therefore, why Vatican II, at the very time when it was promulgating anew the sublime[40] and providential[41] law of celibacy—for the love of the world towards which it was turning, and for its development—has also emphasized that the duty of fostering vocations to the priesthood is imposed upon the whole Christian community.[42] Furthermore, the Council invites all the members of the People of God to honor and love the precious gift of priestly celibacy, and to ask God to give that gift in increasing abundance to His Church.[43]

We shall now discuss how, in our opinion, such fostering of vocations to priestly celibacy could be encouraged by preaching and by prayer.

Although it is very difficult to ascertain whether a particular theme is preached in the majority of our pulpits, it seems to us that sufficient attention has not been paid to that of priestly celibacy. A considerable paradox is involved here. On the one hand, the mystery of priestly celibacy is rarely made the subject of a sermon, with the result that the faithful are largely conscious of it as a "problem"; on the other hand, the faithful would love to be instructed about it, so that they could appreciate it for what it really is. So it is that many preachers withhold from the faithful the light of revelation concerning a subject with which the press deals in an almost exclusively psychological or sociological way. They deprive young men of what could be a considerable stimulus towards considering the possibility of Christ's calling them to the priesthood.

We believe that priests ought to preach the gospel of the priestly celibacy of Christ the Redeemer.[44] The celibacy of Jesus resembles His death in several respects. Like His death, it is at once an historical fact and an unfathomable mystery, for it is the celibacy of the Son of God made man. Furthermore, like His death, it colors many other truths of the Christian faith, in the sense that, taking this celibacy as a point of departure, these truths can be almost exhaustively preached in relation to it. This is particularly true in regards to the sacrament of holy orders and the celibacy of the priest. The latter is, of course, a disciplinary law, but it has deep affinity with a whole series of revealed truths, as Vatican II has emphasized.[45]

Again, it would be possible to organize in our parish churches and in chapels of religious communities, Eucharistic hours before the Blessed Sacrament exposed,[46] in which silent prayer would be interspersed with readings from the Bible and from conciliar and pontifical documents bearing on consecrated celibacy and the law of celibacy. In this way, those truths which are synthesized in the mystery of priestly celibacy could more easily be offered to the prayerful contemplation of the People of God. The desire of Vatican II that the whole Christian people should pray humbly and earnestly to the Father to bestow the gift of celibacy on His Church,[47] could therefore be more easily satisfied. Notice in passing this finely chosen phrase of Vatican II: does not the Council mean that, when this gift is bestowed on certain members of the Church, it is always given for the benefit of the others, and that therefore, in a sense, it is bestowed on the whole Church?

With this in mind, what can one think but that the present celibacy crisis must be in part ascribed to the insufficient response of the People of God, to the explicit invitation of Pope Paul VI. Let us quote the text in question: "We therefore invite the whole People of God to unite together in response to their obligation to see to the increase of vocations to the priesthood. They can do so by earnestly beseeching the Father of all mankind, the divine Spouse of the Church, and the Holy Spirit, who is her soul, through the intercession of the Virgin Mary, Mother of Christ and Mother of the Church, that—especially in our day,—God may pour forth this divine gift, and that souls may dispose themselves to receive in it a spirit of profound faith and of generous love."[48]

This text even shown us the Trinitarian and Marian structure of this prayer for vocations to the celibate priesthood.[49] The vicar of Christ exhorts Christians to pray to each of the divine Persons for the outpouring of this charism, and thus to show greater perseverance in their prayer. Does God remain deaf to a persevering prayer?[50]

Authentic prayer is in practice inseparable from action, and *study* is a form of action. Why not avail ourselves of it, by inviting young Christians to study together[51] the Biblical texts relating to celbacy, and the documents of the Church which show the value of ecclesiastical celibacy? Why should study be only for those who attack this law?

Christian action to promote vocations will be more zealous and more methodical in proportion as such action is felt to be in harmony with, and instrumental to, the divine action itself. It is certainly by no mere chance that, in two places in the same encyclical Pius XI (in 1935) made these two pointed statements: "If God, at all times, has given holy priests, He has sent them in even greater numbers when the age and the manners of the age seemed particularly unfavorable to the recuiting of vocations to the priesthood . . . . One must not neglect any of the activities, inspired by the Holy Spirit, which are aimed at cultivating the divine seed of priestly vocation."[52]

Proper awareness of the role of the priest in transforming society will kindle yet more, in all Christians concerned about the urgency of human development, a zeal to promote vocations to the priesthood.

Our reflections on the relationship between ministerial priesthood and human development, have made it clear that the latter demands the organized action and persevering prayer of the whole People of God to secure the consecration to celibacy and the ordination of priests drawn from their midst. Is true human development separable from the consecration by the laity of the secularity itself of the world—from this transsecularization which causes the universe to pass from "this world" to "the world to come, by means of the hierarchically celebrated Eucharist"?[53] Through the sacrament of holy orders, Christ, eternal Priest and virginal Redeemer of the members of His Mystical Body, palpably show His invisible action as the Head who causes His members to tend towards their destined full beatitude, both spiritual and corporal. Priests are not, as some suppose, a pathetic rearguard doomed to be routed; they are the vanguard of mankind, moving towards the Father and the Son, in Their Spirit. Together, joined in one vast and closely linked sacramental brotherhood of "presbyteria,"[54] they constitute the priestly order which signifies, under the episcopal order, in a constantly renewed way, the salvific will of the Redeemer, the splendidly efficacious divine will for the full development of mankind. It is to this will that the priest consecrates himself, body and soul, through celibacy; and it is this divine will that sets him apart for the ministry, through ordination and through his new and supreme[55] consecration.

NOTES

[1] We say *new* consecration because the priest has already been consecrated through his baptism: LG, 10.

[2] On the connection between mission and consecration in the mind of Vatican II, see Y. M. J. Congar O.P., "Le sacerdoce du N.T.," in *Vatican II: Le Prêtre* (*Unam Sanctam,* 68), Paris, 1968, pp. 242-245; and also B. de Margerie S.J., "Le Christ, la sécularisation et la consécration du Monde," NRT, 91 (1969), 380-294.

[3] LG, 28. It will be noted that the same text of Saint John (10, 36) recurs several times in Vatican II documents (PO, 2 and 12; AG, 3) and is one of the key quotations in connection with the priesthood. In this connection, see André Wears, "Les citations scriptuaires du décret sur le ministère et la vie des prêtres": *Vatican II: Le Prêtre* (*loc. cit.*) pp. 337-338.

[4] Cf. Saint Thomas Aquinas, ST, III. 22. 1; 26. 1, ad 1 and ad 2.

[5] Cf. Jn. 14, 5 and 15, 5.

[6] Cf. LG, 30 and 31 on the respective missions of the priest and of the layman in the Church and to the world; see in this connection, B. de Margerie S.J., "Le prêtre de Vatican II," *Revue Eucharisitique du Clergé* (Montreal), 71 (1968), 346-349.

[7] PO, 6. 4 (cf. Rm. 12, 1).

[8] PO, 4.

[9] PO, 6. On the idea of maturity, cf. GS, 21 and 55, OT, 10-11, especially: ". . . a due degree of human maturity, attested to chiefly by a certain emotional stability, by an ability to make considered decisions, and by a right manner of passing judgement on events and people."

[10] OT, 16.

[11] PO, 5.

[12] LG, 28; cited by GS, 43. 5, where one also finds this invitation to bishops and priests: "Bishops, to whom is assigned the task of ruling

the Church of God, should, together with their priests, so preach the message of Christ that all the earthly activities of the faithful will be bathed in the light of the gospel."

[13] The other roles of the priest (his Eucharistic ministry and his ministry of reconciliation) will be dealt with in subsequent chapters.

[14] See our article cited in note 6.

[15] On the sacramental grace of holy orders, see LG, 28 and 41; PO, 2.4; Congar, *op.cit.* (in note 2), pp. 243-244; cf. DS, 3756 and 3857.

[16] AG, 3; PO, 2; 6; 17.

[17] PO, 16.

[18] Cf. note 1.

[19] See B. de Margerie S.J., "Population mondiale, celibat du clergé et évangelisation sacramentelle," RUO, 36 (1966) 86-106.

[20] SC, par. 8. In par. 49, Paul VI himself answers this objection: "One cannot simply admit that the abolition of ecclesiastical celibacy would automatically and notably increase the number of vocations. The present experience of churches and ecclesial communities where sacred ministers may marry seems to prove the opposite."

[21] The sophistry here is blatant. The right in question could not be suppressed by the State and, in this sense, is inalienable; equally, it could not be suppressed by any individual or group to the detriment of the person involved; but equally clear is the fact that any person is free to renounce the exercise of his inalienable right to marriage, since no one is under an obligation to marry. The Church does not impose celibacy on anyone. She simply declares that, in the Latin rite, she will not admit married men to holy orders. One could counter this by pointing to the following text in PO. 16: "In the Latin Church, celibacy has been imposed by law on all those who are to be promoted to sacred orders": *coelibatus omnibus ad Ordinem sacrum promovendis lege impositus est.* But this objection ignores the fact that no one is obliged to offer himself for sacred orders. The Church is extremely careful about the candidates' complete freedom of choice: an ordination accepted under pressure would be null and void.

[22] SC, 10. Such an objection bears on consecrated celibacy in general, and not merely on that of priests. It radically contradicts Christian revelation: cf. 1 Cor. 7, 25 ff., 38-40; DS, 1810; 3912; SC, 53-56.

[23] Notice that the expression, "evangelical counsel of priestly celibacy," presupposes the existence of a general evangelical counsel of consecrated celibacy, and that Christ did in fact more particularly counsel this consecrated celibacy to the priest. This is not the place to establish the New Testament authority for the existence of a general evangelical counsel of consecrated celibacy (but see the previous note). Nor do we say that the more special evangelical counsel of consecrated celibacy, as given to priests, is *explicitly* contained in the New Testament; but we do say that PO, 16. 2 has sufficiently shown it to be *implicitly* contained there, if one correlates the N.T. teaching concerning ministry and priesthood with that concerning celibacy. It also seems to us that Vatican II, in recommending (PO, 16. 1) ecclesiastical celibacy to future priests of the oriental rite (while not imposing it on them, and while praising "married priests of outstanding merit" in these rites), was simply ratifying and expressing

the counsel of the Risen Christ, invisible Head and Lord of the Church, to all candidates for the priesthood: "ecclesiam coelibatum commendat." In the light of all these considerations, it appears, therefore, that the Latin Church, in instituting the law of celibacy and in refusing to ordain married men, is protecting among Catholics the possibility of a better understanding and acceptance of the evangelical counsel of priestly celibacy. She thus offers the guarantee of a law of Christian freedom.

[24] Cf. L. Lecuyer C.S.Sp.: "Le presbyterium" in *Vatican II: Les Prêtres,* Paris, 1968, pp. 275-288. The author there analyzes the expression used by Saint Ignatius of Antioch and cited by Vatican II.

[25] PO, 8; cf. LG, 28.

[26] PO, 16.

[27] Cf. our book: "Le Christ pour le Monde" (Beauchesne, Paris 1971), and English translation, *Christ for the World* (Franciscan Herald Press, Chicago, 1974), Chapter XII, on the mystery of human sexuality and the priestly celibacy of Christ. The expression used here "parenthood according to the flesh and according to the Spirit," is an allusion to the sacramental grace of marriage which divinizes the conjugal act by making it meritorious, and also to the supernatural purpose of procreation — the education of children "ad cultum divinum."

[28] Cf. our book referred to in the previous note: Chapter XVI: "Le développement de l'humanité et le sacrifice consécrateur de l'Agneau de Dieu". "The development of the humanity and the consecrating sacrifice of the Lamb of God."

[29] Cf. PO, 16: the Council addresses itself to priests "who have freely accepted celibacy, following the example of Christ." It thus seems to be saying (and this is in every respect true) that Christ accepted celibacy as a gift. We have shown elsewhere (cf. note 27) that the decision for celibacy taken by the Man-Jesus is an act of adoring obedience to the mysterious and incomprehensible will of the Father, seen face to face by the human intelligence of the incarnate Son.

[30] We are here drawing on a work by Cardinal C. Journet: "The sacred humanity of the Savior can be regarded as a personality in the psychological sense of being a created intelligence, a created free will, the proximate center of attribution for activities emanating from it and from its faculties" (*Eglise du Verbe Incarné,* Bruges, 1951, vol. 2, pp. 235-236).

[31] Cf. B. de Margerie S.J., "La loi mysterieuse et charismatique du célibat sacerdotal," in *Revue Eucharistique de Clergé,* Montreal, 70 (1967), 602-606; an article reproduced in *Bulletin du Cercle Saint-Jean-Baptiste*, Paris, 8 (1968), 382-386: the law shares in the mystery of its purpose: cf. note 29.

[32] It might be objected that a very great number of Protestant missionaries who were married men have done splendid work in preaching the Gospel. We can only rejoice that they have, though incompletely, preached Christ (cf. Ph. 1, 18), and all those among them who have done so in good faith belonged, although imperfectly, to the People of God, to the universal Church (cf. B. de Margerie S.J., *Reinhold Niebuhr, théologien de la communauté mondiale,*

Bruges-Paris, 1969, p. 208, note 103). In this sense, their missionary activity is already that of the universal Church. We are not saying that married missionaries cannot preach the Gospel of the virginal Redeemer of the world. We are merely saying that, in the historical circumstances of the post-Tridentine Church, the law of celibacy greatly assisted the preaching of the whole (and not truncated) gospel which the Church has a duty to proclaim; and furthermore, that, in every period of history, celibate missionaries are better able to consecrate themselves wholly and definitively to the work of preaching the Gospel. One could, however, compare in all points the work of Catholic missionaries with that of their Protestant brethren—who, for example, are not confessors. The pastoral assistance given to Protestant missionaries by their wives is abundantly compensated by the more complete assistance, not limited by the need to bring up children according to the flesh, given to Catholic missionary priests by religious sisters and brothers.

[33] PO, 16. 1; cf. LG, 42.

[34] PO, 16. 3 (middle and end).

[35] LG, 1.

[36] Letter to Cardinal B. Alfrink, published in the *Osservatore Romano* (12 January 1970).

[37] Jn. 1, 25.

[38] Cf. B. de Margerie S.J., "Le Christ, la sécularisation et le consécration du monde", NRT, 91 (1969), 371 and 383-394.

[39] Cf. DS, 1536.

[40] Address of Paul VI to the Jesuits, 21 April 1969, DC, 66 (1969), 456.

[41] SC, 17.

[42] OT, 2.

[43] PO, 16. 3.

[44] Cf. our book: *Christ for the World,* Chapter XII (see note 27). This chapter could provide an adequate outline for such preaching.

[45] PO, 16; cf. RUO, 105: "The law of celibacy, although merely ecclesiastical, is rooted in a whole series of revealed truths (the example of Christ the Sovereign Priest, the sacrificial purpose of the ministerial priesthood, the excellence of virginity and its superiority to marriage) which concern the present and future conditions of human nature and the essence of the priestly function."

[46] Cf. the instruction on the Eucharistic mystery — AAS, 59 (1967), 571.

[47] PO, 16. 3.

[48] SC, 45.

[49] We deliberately use the phrase "vocations to the celibate priesthood," not vocations to celibacy or to the priesthood. That such is indeed the idea of Pope Paul VI on the efficacy of the prayer of the faithful and on the precise object of that prayer, is sufficiently shown by the close connection between paragraphs 44 and 45 of his encyclical on priestly celibacy.

[50] Cf. Mt. 7, 7-11: Lk. 18, 1-5.

[51] Cf. SC, 25 and 43, to be compared with 16 and 18.

[52] Pius XI, *Ad Catholici Sacerdotii Fastigium,* AAS, 28 (1936), 45.

[53] Cf. B. de Margerie S.J., *art.cit.* in note 38, pp. 391-392.

[54] Father Lécuyer (cf. note 24 of this chapter) shows that each bishop is surrounded by his "presbyterium," which does not include the regular clergy, members of religious orders and congregations, since they are not functionally in the service of the diocese, even though they live within it. It could be added, however, that these members of the regular clergy, exempt from the diocesan authority and having no precise diocesan charge, together form the huge "presbyterium" of the Roman Pontiff as the bishop of the universal Church. And it is the sum total of this presbyterium, of the presbyteria of the patriarchs of the Oriental Church and of the presbyteria of the diocesan bishops of the different rites of the Church, which constitute the presbyteral order in the service of the episcopal order for the common good of mankind. For the idea of episcopal order and presbyteral order, see PO, 7 and 8.

[55] In speaking of the supreme consecration of ordination, we are thinking both of ordination to the priesthood and, for those called to it, episcopal ordination, which respectively insert their recipients into the orders of the presbytery and of the episcopate. See preceding note, *sub fine*.

N.B.: Those who would like to have access to wider information concerning pastoral care for priestly vocations, to which we have alluded in this chapter, should consult the conclusions of the European congress on vocations—DC, 64 (1967), 649-654, and the review *Vocations*.

chapter four

Penance and Renewal in Relation to Human Development

PENITENTS and confessors are everywhere asking how they should examine their consciences, and make their confessions (and, in the case of confessors, hear those of others), in regard to matters pertaining to social justice; and what they should do to spread the light of the sacraments into the sphere of socio-economic progress. What should be done so that the confessional dialogue and the examination of conscience which precedes it may transform the professional life and the economic and social relationships of many Christians who hunger and thirst after justice, in every sense of that word? Does not the grace of baptism prompt the Christian to desire perfection in the God-centered exercise of the virtue of justice towards his fellow men? As we have already seen, the sacramental graces of the Eucharist, of marriage, and of holy orders influence the social dimension of men and the dynamism of their development. But, in their concrete effort to achieve personal and collective growth, men are hindered by the weakness which makes them victims of so many anti-social dynamisms of regression. They need the specific sacramental grace of the sacrament of socio-ecclesial reconciliation which we call the sacrament of penance, in order that the sacramental graces we have already discussed may be fully deployed and may produce all their social fruits.

We cannot but notice, in particular, that many people belonging to the ruling strata of the different classes do not allow themselves to be embarrassed in their sacramental practice by the very abundance of their material or cultural possessions, or by the scope of their responsibilities. For the most part, they are men and women who have never been properly instructed about their duties in matters of justice and of social progress. It is therefore to be feared that many of them commit objective sins against social justice and social charity, with serious consequences for the national and world community. And what about the consequences of the faults of omission or of tacit complicity on the part of their confessors?

Both have, however, their excuses. Is it not true that only in recent years have the directives and practical conclusion of the pre-conciliar social encyclicals begun to figure in the spiritual books and manuals of moral theology which provide guidelines for both confessors and penitents? And could it really be said that the majority of Christians or even of confessors have seriously read, with a view to the reform of their own conscience, the great Vatican II document, *Gaudium et Spes*, concerning the relations between the Church and the World, or the encyclical of Paul VI, *Populorum Progressio*, on human development?

Let us frankly admit that there is a pretty constant tendency to avoid these matters, on the part of penitent and confessor, in the confessional dialogue. A considerable number of penitents will no doubt hesitate to broach such delicate matters in the course of a brief sacramental conversation with an occasional or even unknown confessor, and many confessors will have the same reluctance in regard to an occasional or unknown penitent.

To assist both, we shall first review some positive and negative principles of social justice, and then go on to present the main points for the penitent's examination of his social conscience before confession, to make some suggestions to confessors about how to slant their answers towards the question of human development, and finally to deal with the sacrament of penance from the viewpoint of its purpose to foster the perfect observance of the natural and divine law of mankind's growth. Necessarily, we must be brief, and leave it to others to round out the observations we shall make.

A. *Positive and negative principles involved in the examination of the social conscience.*

Here our concern will be with basic doctrinal principles which simultaneously guide both penitent and confessor in their dialogue.

We can deal only in a very summary way with some points which are still often ignored in practice. They necessarily apply, not only to the penitent, but also to the confessor, who after all is himself periodically a penitent. To give these points greater immediacy, let us express them in the first person singular.

As Pius XII, John XXIII, and Paul VI have repeatedly told me, my right to property and possessions is a limited one. My right cannot place obstacles to the implementing of the irreversible demand that the goods of this earth, created by God for all men, should be made available to all men. The right of every man to use the goods of this world for his life and for his survival has priority even over my right to property and possessions; for my right is conditional, not absolute.[1]

Consequently, once I have what is sufficient to enable me to live according to my social condition, then either my possessions or the revenue from them should contribute to the good of others, on pain of not fulfilling the basic purpose which God assigned to them — namely, to satisfy, not only the necessities of one person, but as much as possible those of all mankind.

It is, therefore, not through charity alone, but also in virtue of social justice, that all my superfluous possessions should profit the needy; and this is, for me, a serious obligation.

My superfluous possessions can fulfil their social function in at least two ways:

One, as alms. This means, frequently the less efficacious

one, continues to be sometimes necessary. If my neighbor is in a situation of extreme material need, I am obliged to help him even at the expense of what is necessary to keeping up my own standard of living at my social level, and this under pain of grave sin.

Is it not certain that both in my country and especially in the Third World, there are many of my brothers and sisters in extreme need? They may be geographically remote from me, but they are close to me because they and I share a common origin and destiny. As Pope Paul VI reminds me: "The rule which up to now held good for the benefit of those nearest to us, must today be applied to all the needy of the world."[2]

Two, as capital investment to set up industries, hospitals, schools, and cultural institutions. "To use large sums of capital in order to provide an abundance of lucrative work, provided that the latter is doing something useful, should be regarded as an excellent act of the virtue of munificence," wrote Pius XI.[3]

This second means is preferable to the first. It is always better to provide work by means of socially useful investments, than to help by giving alms (though there will always be occasions for almsgiving, so as not to ignore personal needs which institutions cannot satisfy). In effect, the man who earns his daily bread is more inclined to pursue other productive work, and is certainly more conscious of his own human dignity. While this is true for individuals, it is equally true as regards nations: it is better to help them to industrialize themselves than to give them more social assistance, though the latter may also be necessary.

Such munificence may take two different forms: it will involve either an entirely disinterested generosity, or it may be an investment with moderate returns. At all events, the primary consideration in using spare capital resources should be social good, not further personal enrichment. Consequently, I must invest in enterprises which yield me less, but which are more useful to society at the national or world level. It is munificence itself which is a duty of national or international social justice. It transforms "liberal" capitalism, whose lack of real liberality makes it despotic, into a human and humane capitalism — that is, into a private possession and social usage of capital with a view to the good of the nation and of the world.

From this munificence in the use of capital, Christians will not exclude the support given to the formation and upkeep of the clergy and of lay Catholic Action groups. A serious obligation of socio-ecclesial justice is involved here. Pius XII has expressed it as follows: "The faithful must be made aware of their obligation to see to the needs of their priests: 'the laborer deserves his wages' (Lk. 10, 7)." He added that Christians, "each according to his resources, must be deeply aware of a duty to help the clergy."[4]

To what better use could I put my capital than to promoting the whole development, both physical and spiritual, of my brethren?[5]

These positive principles must be completed by some negative rules. What would the Old Testament prophets Amos and Osee say to us if they lived today? Let us consider this in the light of observations by certain moral theologians of our day.[6]

I would sin gravely against social justice and social charity if I did not make my possessions bear fruit, or if my grossly extravagant mode of living were an insult flung in the face of the poor; or again, if I invested my capital in ways useless to society — if, in some manner, I did not devote all my superfluous funds to socially useful investments.[7]

These observations, on which one could easily enlarge, already yield precise questions which the penitent can use in an examination of conscience.

B. *Examination of conscience about social obligations.*

We simply want to suggest a few questions of which the penitent can make good use in preparing his confession of sins, and which will make his sacramental confession the occasion, not only for the pardon of his past sins, but also for a reform of his present conscience, thereby enabling him to avoid the sins in the future.

First of all, we shall list the questions relevant to the conscience of nearly everyone, since in the advanced countries there are few to whom they would not apply:

Am I accustomed to enter into a notebook kept for the purpose, or at least to doing so periodically, an account of my personal gains and expenses? How otherwise could I render an account of my expenditures towards myself, towards others when necessary, and therefore towards God?[8]

In the course of the past year, have I given help to the poor or made contributions to organized charitable organizations?

In my investments, have I taken account of the urgent needs of underdeveloped countries or of the less developed sectors of the national economy?

Have I taken an active part, whenever I could, at the general meetings of shareholders,[9] in order to be vigilant about the activities and decisions of the administrative council, so as to defend the rights of small shareholders, of workers, and of consumers? Or do I pocket my dividends without asking whether the way they have been earned has injured the rights of a third party? In that case, would I not be under an obligation to make some form of restitution to such a third party?

Am I seeing to the social education of my children, and how do I intend to do so in the future?

Am I a member of a professional organization so that I may be able to foster the legitimate interests of my profession?

What am I doing, and what could I do, to transform my professional milieu into a true community of persons?

Have I prayed for and with my fellow-workers? Have I invited them to prayer?

Am I concerned about the formation of future priests? Do I set up burses to aid students for the priesthood, or do I contribute to such burses?

In addition, employers could ask themselves the following questions:

Do my employees, fathers and mothers of families, receive a *family* wage?

When my business shows increased profits, do I let my workers share in them? [10] In what way could I do this?

Wages, taxes, and what is needed to keep up my own social

standard of living having been taken into account, how do I invest or otherwise use what is left over? Do I not exaggerate to myself and to others how much is needed "to keep up my social position"?

Am I in the habit of consulting my workers, through a committee designed for this purpose, about business matters, so that they may have a voice and a share in my responsibilities?[11]

Furthermore, the big landed proprietor, especially in Latin America, could ask himself:

Through excessive accumulation, have I prevented workers from acquiring private property? Have I been conscious of my duty to open the way to such acquisition, especially by those who work on my estates?[12]

In this connection, have I thought about the possibility of changing my estates into a collective co-ownership by leasing land to the workers as tennants, or even of giving away some of it as "alms of the earth itself"[13] and at the same time providing the instruction and the machinery needed for its cultivation?

Finally, the worker can ask himself: "Before resorting to my right to strike, have I tried every means of industrial conciliation?"

One could, of course, extend and diversify such a questionnaire, in accordance with the variety of countries, of regions, and of social classes. We hope that other writers in this field will do so.

For our part, we prefer to emphasize here how important and advantageous it is for the penitent to tell his confessor straightaway what profession he follows. It stands to reason that without this knowledge, the confessor cannot help the penitent to view in God's light the social mission that should be his, the injustices he could commit, and the demands of social justice and charity in his professional milieu. Normally, the priest should know whether his penitent is married or single in order to be able effectively to help him; and similarly, though the need is not always so imperative, it would greatly assist the confessor if he knew whether his penitent was an employer, a storekeeper or a worker. However, it must be added that the penitent is under no obligation to give even the least hint as to who he is. In deciding, nevertheless, to tell his confessor what profession he follows, the Christian shows a willingness to allow the grace of Christ, the sacramental graces of penance and holy orders, to influence fully this very important sector of his life. It also shows that he is open to a social dialogue within and outside the confessional. At least, this is the meaning that such a revealing of his profession could have.

C. *Role of the confessor who desires to promote his penitent's orientation towards human development.*

The penitent who prepares for confession in the above way, is certainly the exception. With penitents who confess sins against chastity or religion, or against charity in its individual applications, confessors are often embarrassed about asking questions, which are precise and useful but not indiscreet, concerning the fulfilment of the duties of social justice.

Nevertheless, the confessor who wants to fulfill his duty in this respect and who knows the profession of his penitent, should not allow himself to be put off by the difficulty of the task. He should, however, use great tact, so that his intervention may not have the effect opposite to the one intended. The fact that he is only this particular penitent's occasional confessor is no excuse; for, it has become increasingly rare for the laity to have ordinary confessors. In the rush of modern city life, it is not always easy, even when desired, to confess regularly to the same priest and to be sure of finding him available. To limit the social mission of confessors to those who are their regular penitents, would to a great extent obliterate that mission, to the great detriment of society and of the Church.

It must be admitted that the implementing of this social mission is not made any easier by the dearth of literature on this subject. The works which are available[14] are more concerned with suggestions to the penitents about their examination of conscience, than with assisting confessors in their twofold and inseparable role of judges[15] and ministers of reconciliation.

Note, first of all, that the confessor may and ordinarily should ask about the penitent's profession if the penitent himself does not volunteer the information. On the basis of the answer given, the confessor could make a brief and friendly allusion to the social value of the particular profession, and thus give the penitent and opportunity to confess sins he may have committed in its exercise. If the penitent merely tells what his profession is, there is nothing to prevent the confessor from asking one or other of the questions suggested above concerning the examination which the penitent should make of his social conscience.

We are certainly not suggesting that all these questions should be asked in the course of one confession! They should be put with prudence and moderation, and with great care to avoid giving the penitent the impression that he is being arraigned for the "sin of capitalism." It is true that in developed countries, the former pattern of liberal capitalism has developed towards forms which are more humane and which seek to defend the individual against excessive encroachments on his freedom by the State. Paul VI, while holding that these liberalizing movements should be carefully studied by the Christians (*Octogesima Adveniens*, par. 35), has also emphatically reminded us to what extent the liberal ideology — the rule of free trade — still governs international commercial relations (*Populorum Progressio*, pars. 44 and 58-62). But it is quite clear that, in the Church's view, it is not a sin for either an individual or an organization to have capital and increase it. The confessor's purpose is precisely to help the penitent to rid himself of any unconscious vestiges of "liberalism" in the way he conducts his business or profession.

We use the word "liberalism" with the meaning it has in the Apostolic Exhortation *Octogesima Adveniens* (par. 26) of Paul VI: "The liberal ideology believes in exalting individual freedom by removing all curbs upon it, by stimulating it through the exclusive pursuit of interest and power, and by regarding matters of social solidarity as more or less automatic consequences of individual initiatives and not as a major purpose and a major criterion of the value of social organization."

To safeguard the aim of such questioning, the confessor should sometimes briefly explain his motives for asking this or that question, and above all he should adopt the following attitude: "Even if my penitent has committed material sins against social justice or against his duty to foster human development, it is at least partly because he is the inheritor of the iniquitous system in which he was brought up — that of liberal capitalism. He lives in an atmosphere which does not make it easy for him to take up a proper conscientious attitude, though the dynamism of supernatural love is already active within him to make him desire to do so."[16]

That is why the confessor should, when the need arises go on to impose a precise obligation to make restitution if the penitent has admitted to not paying a just wage, or has charged an excessive price, or has accepted very high dividends to the detriment of the workers' due share.

It is not out of the question that one day — and soon, we hope — the Church will consider it necessary to remind confessors throughout the world of their duty in relation to social justice, just as she has pointed out their mission as custodians of conjugal chastity. And the latter would, no doubt, profit indirectly from such a reminder concerning social justice!

Anyhow, confessors can largely if not completely apply the admonition of Pius XI to confessors concerning violation of the divine law in marriage (an admonition perhaps presented with more subtle shades by Paul VI in *Humanae Vitae*[17]), to the domain of social justice:

"Therefore, priests who hear confessions and others who have the care of souls are admonished by us, in the exercise of our sovereign care for the salvation of the souls of all, that they must not allow the souls committed to their charge to be in error concerning this most serious law of God, and, what is much more important, that they must themselves be on their guard against these doctrines and in no way connive at them. Should any confessor or pastor of souls himself —

which God forbid!! — lead into error the faithful committed to his care, or at least, by his approval or by a misleading silence, confirm them in holding such doctrines, then let him know that he will have to render unto God, the sovereign Judge, a strict account of this betrayal of his trust; and he must consider as addressed to himself the words of Christ: 'They are blind guides. And if a blind man leads a blind man, both will fall into a pit' (Mt. 15, 14)."[18]

Would not the confirming, by calculated silence, of the rich in error and, consequently, in injustice involving the social aspects of the divine law, be a serious omission on the part of the confessor, a real betrayal of his duty and his social mission? He would thus make himself an accomplice in the injustices he has not denounced; what amounts to condoning by his silence the witholding of proper wages, the oppression of widows and orphans, the violation of human rights, would be a sin crying as loudly to heaven for vengence as does that of his rich penitents. Besides, is it not true that the priest's own fear of the divine judgement on himself, would be a spur to his preaching divine justice in relation to other people?

Let no one seek a ready answer to all this in a conveniently strict interpretation of Canon 888.2: "The confessor must not ask prying and useless questions." Rather, let us read it in the light of an official clarification concerning its relevance to the sixth and ninth commandments: "Those questions are completely useless which are not required in order to complete the penitent's confession of sin or to sound the dispositions of his soul. Do not ask questions about material sins unless the penitent's own good or the common good suggests or demands that an admonition should be given."[19]

The confessor is judge of the dispositions required for absolution, and to pass judgement he must assure himself about the genuineness of these dispositions. *The good of the penitent*, whose ignorance must be regarded as vincible, especially when he belongs to the director class, and the *common good*, for which the confessor is equally responsible — since he concelebrated with the faithful the sacrament of penance for the good of the Church and for that of all mankind, and because he does so as minister of the Church — are not compatible with hasty absolutions which pass over in silence grave injustices. The priest has no right to become an accomplice in such sins.

There are employers who underpay their workers or exclude the workers from any share in the benefits of their labor; there are stockholders who pocket enormous dividends to the detriment of the underdeveloped countries; and such men, impenitent of these crimes against society, approach the altar and receive the Body of Him whom they have not yet ceased to crucify (cf. Heb. 6, 6). Such Communions are as scandalous as those of onanist husbands, if not more so.

Perhaps it might be objected that the attitude recommended here is scarcely compatible with the climate of mercy attributed to Vatican II. One can easily counter this: Vatican II certainly had not the least intention of encouraging the flouting of the divine law or complicity in its violation: "Since there are so many people in this world afflicted with hunger, this sacred Council urges all, both individuals and governments, to remember the saying of the Fathers: 'Feed the man dying of hunger, because if you have not fed him you have killed him.' "[20] And, speaking of moral theology, Vatican II says: "It would show the nobility of the Christian vocation of the faithful, and their obligation to bring forth fruit in charity for the love of the world."[21]

Furthermore, Paul VI later noted that "it is an outstanding manifestation of charity towards souls to omit nothing from the saving doctrine of Christ"[22] — and that also means towards the souls of rich penitents.

But the confessor passes judgement only that he may attempt to remedy: he is at once judge and physician. The purpose of the social dialogue which we are urging is to heal the wounds inflicted on the penitent's social conscience by original sin and by his own actual sins. This often deformed conscience needs to be set right through the sacrament of penance. Like Christ, the priest does not come among the directors and the employers to condemn them, but to save them. And how could he heal, without showing to the penitent his spiritual sickness, and helping him to fight against it?

In the confessional, the priest bears in mind the warning of Pius XII: "Let the priest not neglect those who, though rich in the goods of this world, are spiritually poor and need to be called to spiritual renewal, so that they may be able to say with Zacchaeus: 'The half of my goods I give to the poor; and if I have defrauded any one of anything, I restore it fourfold' (Lk. 19, 8). Fearlessly and zealously, he should present the Catholic principles concerning possessions, riches, social justice, and Christian charity between the classes, and be himself a clear example of their application."[23]

Why should the confessional be the only place where such a presentation of these principles does not ocur? Will it be said that the average priest is not capable of entering into such a dialogue with a penitent who is a businessman or employer? Pius XII certainly did not agree. Confessors who, as in duty bound, have seriously studied the social encyclicals and Catholic moral theology, and have reflected in their light on the problems of our era, are able to do much — with, of course, the help of the sacramental grace of holy orders and the gift of counsel. I do not say that these confessors can dictate technical solutions, for this would not be within their competence; but they can stimulate reflection, both supernatural and social, in their lay brethren who concelebrate with them the social sacrament of penance and reconciliation. Above all, they can kindle generosity, and establish or restore attitudes destroyed by selfishness. Finally, they can recall to these penitents the general principles of social morality in whose light particular problems can be solved.

The mere fact of having raised in a friendly and fraternal way the questions suggested above, or some of them, would already be valuable. It would be of great help in arousing the penitent's conscience, since it would consitute an invitation to reflect on the questions raised, even though at the actual time when they were raised the penitent was able to give only vague and inadequate answers.

At the end of this brief but meaningful dialogue which we had to deal with at some length, the confessor may, in certain cases, find himself uncertain about the penitent's dispositions. There is nothing to prevent him from then asking the penitent to pray with him for a few moments in silence. This will help to avoid the twofold danger of a precipitate decision to give or to refuse absolution.

If the confessor thinks he should give absolution, he can advise his penitent to study carefully one of the principal[24] documents of the social magisterium of the Church, and also Saint Luke's Gospel or the Epistle of Saint James, which deal more fully than do the other writings of the New Testament with the use of money and the dangers of avarice. It has even been suggested [25] that confessors might impose as a penance on directors and employers, a reading of *Mater et Magistra.* This idea seems very opportune. In certain cases, the penitents' prompt acceptance of this will be a supplementary or even a decisive sign that they have the dispositions needed for absolution.

The confessor's social mission will be fully accomplished only if priests discuss among themselves the themes dealt with here. But these themes should be studied by Catholic Action groups, and in reunions where priests and the laity are together. In these ways, unity of action among both confessors and laity could more easily be established, at the regional level and even at the level of episcopal decisions. No confessor can completely fulfil his role as judge and physician of the personal and social conscience, if he does not feel the support of other confessors associated with him in this task. There will be no growth of social awareness and a proper conscience in social matters among the faithful, unless there is a growing awareness of the social character of the priest's work in the confessional.[26]

D. *The sacrament of penance and reconciliation in the service of the supernatural and divine law of human development.*

Together, confessors and penitents, aim to observe fully and to secure the full observance of the divine law, whose purpose is the common good of mankind. The desire to become more perfect in the observance of this law, or to return to its observance, is the *raison d'être* of the encounter of priest and penitent in the confessional; and practical obedience to this holy law which is both loving[27] and worthy of love, is also the fruit of their encounter.

Now, the purpose of this law is very simple: the growth and development of the whole man and of all men, for the glory of the triune God, their Creator, Redeemer, and Judge. Sin has violated this law; grave sin has even made its author incapable of observing for long this divine law of human development, for the very reason that as long as serious sin continues, it is an obstacle to so many actual graces without which the divine law cannot be observed. The sacrament of penance intervenes, therefore, to ensure that the human will to observe the divine commandment concerning human development is given a natural and supernatural efficaciousness, by divinizing it anew if it has been weakened, or by giving it new strength if it is in a healthy condition.

The penitent's contrition signifies and implies his firm resolution, here and now renewed, to become involved directly or indirectly in mankind's effort at self-fulfilment for the glory of Christ. Without such a contrite decision, there would be no real sorrow for all the obstacles which the sinner has freely and deliberately placed to his own personal development and to that of others. In that case, there could therefore be no valid absolution.[28]

In the confessional, it is to all mankind, mysteriously and indirectly[29] represented by the priest as minister of Christ and of the Church, that the penitent confesses his sins. It is to all men that he accuses himself, for the love of Christ crucified, of having sinned against them by sinning against the Church. Sin, by putting this member of the Church at a distance from the holiness of the Church which it is his duty to actualize in the world, has also cut him away from men who, though not yet belonging to the Church, are mysteriously linked with her and are destined to be incorporated with her. It is at once and inseparably a war against personal, ecclesial, and social development.

Furthermore, all the tears of the holy and offended Church,

and indirectly all the tears of laboring mankind, mingle with and transfigure the tears of the penitent kneeling in the confessional. He would not be there, repentent and determined to repair his sin — that is, to develop himself and to help others to achieve their self-development for the increasing glory of Christ — had it not been for the tears and prayers of the People of God. One is reminded here of what Saint Ambrose said (which Saint Augustine has perhaps understood in applying it to himself), between the years 380 and 390: "The Church has obtained, in the coming of Christ, that all men should be redeemed by one Man; and Christ has commissioned His Church to redeem the individual man through all men."[30] This is a moving statement: the tears which the penitent has provoked by his sin become, through the blood of the Lamb, the spring whence springs up the inexhaustibly efficacious fountain of his repentance. The omnipotence of the Redeemer has found, even in the war against mankind's development, a new occasion for making it resolutely move forward.

The penitent's contribution thus emerges as being, as a fresh effort of natural and supernatural development, all the more efficacious because it is, so to speak, bathed in a sea of tears and in the ocean of Chirst's saving Passion.

In recalling principles concerning social justice, and in examining and setting right their consciences, penitents and confessors must not forget that their concelebration of the sacrament of penance and reconciliation unites them in a shared response to the divine call to human development, and that thereby they are already benefiting from the previous growth of the Church and of mankind.

NOTES

[1] GS, 69. 1; PP. 23; MM (DC, 58, 1961, col. 952).

[2] PP, 49.

[3] QA, AAS, 23 (1931), 101.

[4] Pius XII, *Menti Nostrae*, AAS, 42 (1950), 697. And one could add, with Saint Vincent de Paul: "It will never be possible to do anything more useful than to contribute to the formation of a priest."

[5] Cf. Saint Thomas Aquinas, S.T., II. II. 134. 2. 3.

[6] Notably: A. Quijano S.J. "Los bienes superfluos y la moral christianna," *Sal Terrae,* May 1960, pp. 264-276; Génicot, *Theologia*

Moralis, 17th edition, vol. 1, par. 226; Ter Haar C.SS.R., *Casus conscientiae de vitiis hujus aetatis,* Marietti, 1936, par. 187, 24, p. 181. One could also re-read Amos 8, 4-8.

[7] Cf. Génicot, *op.cit.* in preceding note; the author says that the obligation is very probably a serious one. See also PP, 49.

[8] Cf. Pius XI, *Divini Redemptoris,* par. 44: "the owner is a mere administrator, a manager, who must render an account to the Supreme Master."

[9] Cf. E. Delaye, in the encyclopedia *Catholicisme, I* (1948), 116-118, art. "Actionnaires (droits et devoirs des)".

[10] MM, DC, 58 (1961), col. 958; AAS, 53 (1961), 420.

[11] *Ibid.* DC, 58 (1961), 961; AAS, 53 (1961), 424; GS, 65 and 68.

[12] Cf. GS, 71. 6.

[13] Thus, since 1953, a Hindu ascetic, a disciple of Gandhi, has obtained for the proletariat from Indian landowners, the "alms" of several million hectares of arable land (a fact recorded in the review *Croissance des jeunes nations,* in 1961). One cannot see any reason why the disciples of Jesus should be less adventurous, reasonable, and generous.

[14] E.g, A. Chanson, *Pour mieux confesser,* Arras, 1958,[7] pars. 640-667; Lebret et Suavet O.P., *Pour rajeunir l'examen de conscience,* Ed. Ouvrières, Paris, 1952.

[15] DS, 1679 and 1709.

[56] Cf. Pius XI, *Divini Redemptoris,* 1937, par. 50: "Christian employers and industrialists, you have received the burdensome heritage of the sins of an unjust regime, which has wrought havoc for several generations."

[17] Paul VI, *Humanae Vitae.*

[18] Pius XI, *Casti Connubii,* AAS, 22 (1930), 560. (Eng. trans.: C.T.S., par. 57).

[19] Decision of the former Holy Office, cited in *Directoire pour la pastorale des Sacrements,* published by the French bishops in 1951: pp. 76-79.

[20] GS, 69.

[21] *Optatam totius,* par. 16. This is the Vatican II Decree on Priestly Formation.

[22] Paul VI, *Humanae Vitae,* par. 29.

[23] Pius XII, *Menti Nostrae,* AAS, 42 (1950), 697. The whole of p. 696 should be re-read.

[24] E.g., *Quadragesimo Anno* and *Divini Redemptoris* of Pius XI (1931 and 1937 respectively); but especially the encyclical of John XXIII (*Mater et Magistra, Pacem in Terris,* in 1961 and 1963 respectively) and of Paul VI (*Populorum Progressio*) and the pastoral constitution *Gaudium et Spes* promulgated by Paul VI.

[25] Father Jean Ceretti in an Italian clerical review.

[26] Such an idea was at least partly contained in the following lines of Saint Alphonsus Liguori, Doctor of the Church and patron of confessors: "Although, by reason of his office, the confessor must be concerned mainly with the good of his penitent, nevertheless, since he himself is a citizen of the State (*pars reipublicae*) and since he is charged with the good of the Christian community, he

has a duty to give preference to the public good over the private good of his penitent.... He must admonish (*admonere*) leaders and men of high estate (*gubernatores et similes*) who, through invincable ignorance, neglect their duty to give alms out of their superfluous riches.... For such ignorance is rarely innocent or rarely fails to do harm to others, who think they can do what they see their superiors doing" (*Theologia Moralis,* vol. II, par. 615). And the saint cites Pope Benedict XIV and Lugo.

[27] Inasmuch as the divine law is identical with the divine essence, with God Himself who is Love (1 Jn. 4, 8).

[28] On the relationship between the will to respect social justice and the justification of the sinner, see B. de Margerie S.J., *Reinhold Niebuhr, théologien de la communauté mondiale,* Bruges — Paris, 1969, 266-282 and 408-410.

[29] This statement can be justified in two ways. On the one hand, the priest represents the bishop (i.e. "he makes him present in a certain sense in the individual local congregations of the faithful" — LG, 28); the bishop represents his particular church and, with all the other members of the episcopal college, the universal Church (LG, 23) constituted by the People of God who, "although they do not include all men . . . are nonetheless a lasting and sure seed of unity, hope, and salvation for the whole human race" (LG, 9.2). On the other hand, the priest represents Christ and acts in His name; now, Christ offers Himself to the Father as Head of His members and, in this sense, represents them (cf. DS, 3850). In both cases, it is indirectly that the priest represents mankind. But it cannot be said that he receives his power from mankind, or that he acts in mankind's name. Mankind is orientated to the People of God, while remaining distinct from them (LG, citing Saint Thomas Aquinas, ST, III. 8. 3. 1).

[30] Saint Ambrose *De Penitentia* I, 15, 80 (ML, 16, 490; RJ, 1296). We give the very beautiful Latin text: "Velut operibus quibusdam totius populi purgatur, et plebis lacrimis abluitur, qui orationibus et fletibus plebis redimitur a peccato et in homine mundatur interiore. Donavit enim Christus ecclesiae suae ut unum per omnes redimeret, quae Domini Jesu meruit adventum, et per unum omnes redimerentur." It will be noted that in this text Saint Ambrose does not speak explicitly about the People of God, but simply about the people. However, this gives no ground to deny that the people in question are only the Christian people, since the words "totius populi . . . plebis . . . ecclesiae" clearly have this meaning. The "people" means, therefore, the visible Church.

chapter five

Extreme Unction: the Anointing of the Sick: Sacrament of Hope and of the Consummation of Human Development

In her theological thinking, the Church closely associates the anointing of the sick and the sacrament of penance. We shall see that, viewed in the perspective we are adopting here, this divinizing and salvific anointing leads to the supreme renewal in human development — the renewal which makes sickness, old age, and death a path to the glorious resurrection, the culmination and the crowning of earthly development. The anointing of the sick transforms this development into a victory over the underdevelopment par excellence which is that of human mortality, of the pilgrimage towards death.

Perhaps it is as well to remind the reader that we are using the word *development* with the meaning attached to it by Paul VI in his encyclical *Populorum Progressio* (pars. 20, 14, 15), as we have explicitly said in our introduction. The pope does not exclude old people from this "development which is for each and all the transition from less human conditions to those which are more human" (PP, par. 20). Old people do not, of course, contribute directly to the economic development of society; but it cannot be denied that their own development, their personal and social growth, is an element and not one of the least elements, of the total development of the society of which they are members and on which they continue to exert their influence, to the extent of being thus able to contribute indirectly to its economic development.

First, we shall consider, in the current context of the "old age population explosion" and in the light of Vatican II, the "therapeutic" purposes and the ecclesial mission which the Lord had in view when He instituted this anointing, this consecration of infirm old age. We shall then deal briefly with the advantages of its celebration as a community act, and consider the possibility of a collective self-consecration of those who have been anointed but have not died. We hope in this way to contribute to the pastoral renewal of this largely ignored sacrament.

A. *The anointing of the sick is the anointing of hope, the the consecration of old age.*

Let us begin by recalling the text of the Epistle of Saint James in which this sacrament is described:

"Is any among you sick? Let him call for the elders of the church, and let them pray over him, anointing him with oil in the name of the Lord; and... the Lord will raise him up; and if he has committed sins, he will be forgiven" (5, 14-15).

The Church[1] has understood this text as signifying that the Lord Jesus has instituted the anointing of the sick for the spiritual and physical healing of those in danger of death.[2] It is for this reason that Christ has chosen oil as the matter of this sacrament, since oil is a natural remedy and a tonic. The anointing of the sick is a "spiritual medicine," as Saint Thomas Aquinas said.[3]

Here, then, is this sacrament which Christ Himself[4] has willed to institute as an efficacious sign of the health, not only of the soul, but of the body as well. It must be pointed out, however, that the purpose of this sacrament as regards the health of the body, is conditional: "The patient recovers bodily health when this is conducive to the salvation of his soul," says the Council of Trent.[5] It is not, therefore, in every case that, to adapt Saint James' words, this sacrament "raises up" the sick man; but when it does so, the promise, "the prayer of faith will save the sick man" (Jas. 5, 15), is seen to be fulfilled in every sense of the word "save."

However, it is not only or even principally the bodies which the anointing of the sick "raises up." The souls are also sick, and Christ wills, through this sacramental anointing of the body, to heal the souls of the sick by cleansing them of their sins ("and if he has committed sins, he will be forgiven"), by strengthening them against temptations, and by preparing them to accept in love this separation from the body that we call death.

When the sick are in danger of death, and especially when they are at the point of death, this anointing, says the Council of Trent,[6] confers on them a threefold spiritual comfort; it kindles their trust in the divine mercy at the moment when they will have to appear before the supreme Judge; it helps them to endure their sufferings patiently and even with joy; it helps them to resist more effectually the temptations of the devil, who attacks their faith, their hope, and their charity. And the believer who writes these lines is careful to bear in mind that he too is a man, and that physical weakness with its attendant spiritual debilitation probably awaits him. It is for us, whom He has introduced into His pilgrim Church by the water of baptism that Christ, has instituted the spiritual tonic of the anointing of the sick in order to prepare us for entry into His glorious Church without blemish or wrinkle. In the divine plan, from the beginning to the end of human life, from the water of baptism to the oil of the sick and the Viaticum of the dying, immaterial souls constantly depend upon material things to effect their own development.

We can therefore say, with Saint Thomas Aquinas,[7] that Christ the Redeemer has instituted the anointing of the sick as a measure against the faults and deficiencies which make a man spiritually weak and prevent him from having the strength for acts of grace or for glorious beatitude; as a psychophysical tonic, therefore, towards the full expression of earthly and of heavenly life. Without thereby derogating from the power of the Holy Viaticum, we can say that the sacrament of the anointing of the sick is, in a sense, the consummation of the whole spiritual process of healing through which baptized man prepares himself for the glorious health of the Kingdom. In this respect, it is well named extreme unction.[8]

First and foremost, therefore, the anointing of the sick is always[9] a spiritual tonic for weak and mortal Christian man. It is the supernatural tonic of the Christian soul, a tonic which actuates or stimulates the activity of those spiritual sources of spiritual power, the theological or moral virtues. While this sacrament is always the spiritual tonic of the immortal soul, it is also, even when it does not effect physical healing here and now, the sacrament of the true and definitive physical healing which comes with the resurrection of the body which the risen Christ, through His minister, has anointed with the holy oil. For the anointing of the sick will contribute to make more glorious this healing which alone is definitive and, in this sense, the only real one. It is interesting to note, in this text, that the theologians who emphasize the effect of physical healing produced here and now by this sacrament, do not always sufficiently stress that this healing can only be temporary![10]

It is therefore important to state clearly that the "spiritual medicine" cannot definitively stave off death; but, when it is received with the right dispositions, it contributes decisively to a more effective eschatological victory over death in enabling the recipient to merit a more glorious resurrection to the life to come.

One understands, in this light, why Saint Thomas—who called baptism the sacrament of faith, and the Eucharist the sacrament of charity described the anointing of the sick as the sacrament of hope.[11] Understood properly as a physical remedy either terrestrial or eschatological, while also being a spiritual tonic, this sacrament is the efficacious sign of the hope of the sick or the infirm[12] person in the complete redemption of his soul and of his body. He who seeks this anointing shows his faith in Christ as the Resurrection and the Life, his hope in Christ as *his* resurrection and *his* life (cf. Jn. 11, 25).

Vatican II has taken this same line of reflection by extending and specifying in an original way the previous doctrine of the magisterium on two points: it has presented the anointing of the sick as effecting an assimilating participation in the Pasch of Christ the Redeemer; and it has implied that this sacrament is a consecration of old age. No other documents of the magisterium prior to Vatican II have opened up such rich horizons, notably within the area of our present reflections on the relationship between the sacraments and the full development of the Christian person.

On the one hand, Vatican II underlines that anointing of the sick involves a coredemptive mission confided to them by the Church: "By the sacred anointing of the sick and the prayer of her priests, the whole Church commends those who are ill to the suffering and glorified Lord, asking that He may lighten their suffering and save them (cf. Jas. 5: 14-16). She exhorts them, moreover, to contribute to the welfare of the whole People of God by associating themselves freely with the passion and death of Christ (cf. Rom. 8: 17; Col. 1: 24; 2 Tim. 2: 11-12; 1 Pet. 4: 13)."[13]

In other words, the Church, by this sacramental consecration of the sickness or infirmity of her members who are in danger of death, invites them to merge this death with her own ceaselessly renewed sacrifice united with that of Jesus, in the Eucharist, which is the victimal oblation of the Head and of the members. The Church, always concerned about her own development because always aware of her obligation to grow in love (cf. Eph. 4, 13, 16), relies very specially on her infirm and sick members to help her in her coredemptive mission.[14] Vatican II thus asserts that the offering up of sickness and death in union with the passion of Christ has a decisive importance for the salvation of the world, and for the full development, both temporal and spiritual, of mankind.

In a sense, the anointing of the sick sacramentalizes this

shared oblation of suffering. Whereas, by its negative dynamism, sickness would tend to induce a certain revolt of the body against the soul, the sacred anointing places the Christian's body in a relationship of likeness to the body of the Crucified, to the body of the incarnate Word, a body perfectly subject to the divine Person who has assumed it. Thus the anointing of the sick restores in part the integrity which was lost through original sin, and which consisted precisely of this ready submission of the flesh to the spirit. In this connection, it must be said, as Father Alszeghy rightly observes,[15] that this sacrament always has here on earth, for him who desires it, an effect of physical healing in the wide sense of the term. It extracts their poison from sickness and old age, which through this sacrament cease to be expressions of God's anger and become ways leading toward Him.[16] In short, this sacrament facilitates and effects the acceptance and the integration of infirmity. In conferring it, the Church says to the Lord: "Lord, he whom you love is ill," and Jesus answers: "This illness is not unto death (of the soul); it is for the glory of God, so that the Son of God may be glorified by means of it" (cf. Jn. 11, 4).

It is in connection with old age that the second notable broadening of the horizon occurs in the texts of Vatican II: "As soon as any one of the faithful begins to be in danger of death from sickness or old age, the appropriate time to receive this sacrament has certainly already arrived."[17]

No doubt, such an idea was already classic prior to Vatican II;[18] but it can scarcely be said that the magisterium had previously taught with such explicitness that old age as such already[19] signifies the danger of death which makes the reception of the anointing of the sick opportune and useful. It seems to us to be in perfect conformity with the ideas of Vatican II, to hold that this sacrament is an anointing which consecrates old age to Christ the Savior for His Body which is the Church.

It cannot be denied that such a statement implies a wide area of pastoral care. Of the whole population of France in 1968, 12 per cent (nearly 7 millions) was made up of people more than 65 years old who were registered as "the old"—or, if one prefers, as "the third age." In 1901, these represented only 8.2 per cent of the population. Parallel with this, the average expectation of life changed from 59 to 72 years between 1938 and 1964. The science of "gerontology" was born. Never before, both absolutely and relatively, has the number of "the aged" been so high in the world and in the Church.

Faced with this "old age population explosion," is it not an excellent thing that, more clearly than ever before, the Church is looking on the anointing of the sick as the sacrament of the consecration of "the third age"? Immense pastoral consequences follow from this, as we shall see.

It seems to us that Father Teilhard de Chardin would have regarded with emotion the perspectives thus opened up by the coincidence of Vatican II with this demographic explosion of the aged. Has he not written with great beauty about "the passivities of diminishment": old age, weakness, death? They aroused in him a renewed desire for Viaticum,[20] but not, it seems, for the anointing of the sick, which is undoubtedly the least noticed of the sacraments. And, like other priests, he died without receiving it (which does not mean, needless to say, that he never desired it[21]), no doubt because he never learned to regard it as the sacrament which consecrates old age; the sacrament which transforms "the passivities of diminishment" into "passivities of growth and of development," both personal and social, into means of "ecclesial growth."

Thanks to the comfort given by the anointing of the sick, the aged Christian can identify with the sentiments of Saint Paul: "So we do not lose heart. Though our outer nature is wasting away, our inner nature is being renewed every day. For this slight momentary affliction is preparing for us an eternal weight of glory beyond all comparison" (2 Cor. 4, 16-17).

Thus, the aged person who has received this sacrament can more easily live in a continual victory over the spiritual weakness which accompanies physical debility. The power of the Risen Christ is ceaselessly shown in his weakness. Such a man can say with Saint Paul: "When I am weak, then I am strong" (2 Cor. 12, 10). He feels the power of Christ the Healer who spiritually heals the inner weakness which accompanies the incurable malady of bodily age. Like every other malady of bodily age and more than most of them, old age, since it is incurable, is a sharing in death.[22] The "inner nature" watches helplessly as the "outer nature" slowly withers away. The sacrament makes no permanent change in this state of affairs. True, it can restore physical health for a time, if God wills for the good of the soul, but its more basic effect is much rather to transform the disintegrating state of old age into a salvific[23] situation which promotes personal salvation and cooperation in the salvation of others. The anointing of the sick turns physical old age into the occasion for a rejuvenescence of the soul and for its renewal in the service of the eternal youthfulness of the Church.

How does this sacrament effect such change? By increasing the virtue of hope, which is at once a desire for the vision of the Risen Christ and confidence of being admitted to this vision in the context of his own resurrection. Just as baptism bestows faith and the Eucharist increases love, so the anointing acts as a tonic to the sick by helping them to overcome the twofold despair that threatens them: the lack of any desire for death in order to see God and the lack of trust in the divine fidelity which shines forth in the grace of final perseverance. Christ who anoints pours into the soul the oil of desire and the balm of trust. This sacrament conquers in them the excessive fear of eternal loss and the excessive love of temporal life which otherwise would swamp their souls. It prevents Christians from turning too exclusively towards the past, and orientates them toward their eternal future. By strengthening himself with the holy oil, the Christian prevents old age from extinguishing in him the lamp of hope which he keeps alight as he walks to meet the Bridegroom (cf. Mt. 25, 1-13).[24]

And this lamp of hope throws a new light on the past.

Former achievements are no longer regarded with sterile regret that they can no longer be, nor are past sufferings any longer a subject for bitter brooding: in both achievements and sufferings, hope now sees only the activities and passivities which merit the eternal joy of its own absorption into the endless possession of the divine Eternity: "if we hope for what we do not see, we wait for it with patience" (Rom. 8, 25).

As a grace of hope, the sacramental grace of the anointing of the sick creates in the aged Christian the dispositions so well described by Saint Paul:

"Christ will be honored in my body, whether by life or by death. For to me to live is Christ, and to die is gain. If it is to be life in the flesh, that means fruitful labor for me. Yet which I shall choose I cannot tell. I am hard pressed between the two. My desire is to depart and be with Christ, for that is far better. But to remain in the flesh is more necessary on your account... for your progress and joy in the faith" (Phil. 1, 20-25).

One can and should also stress that, in receiving this sacrament, the aged Christian enters more deeply into the hope of the whole Church as she yearns for the return of her visibly absent Spouse. The pilgrim Church makes the recipient share as his own the eagerness with which she strives towards the Parousia of her Savior.[25] In calling "for the elders of the church" so that they may "pray over him, anointing him with oil" (Jas. 5, 14), the aged Christian identifies with the sighing of the Bride who, under the influence of the Spirit, ceaselessly says to her Lord: "Come!" (Rev. 22, 17-21), and in the words that accompany and express the sacramental anointing, he catches an echo of Christ's answer: "I am coming soon" (Rev. 22, 20).

The anointing of the sick thus accentuates the special dynamism of the theological virtue of hope, a virtue infused into the soul by baptism. This virtue had never ceased to work a continual conversion in the Christian by making him lift up his face to the heavens—"Raise up your heads, because your redemption is drawing near" (Lk. 21, 28).

Now, at the time when the face of the aging Christian would be more inclined to turn towards mortal life and towards the past, the sacramental anointing lifts it more vigorously towards the future and towards the Christian resurrection. It strengthens the Christian's mind so that he may recognize in the daily cross of the weakness attendant upon old age, a source of spiritual good both for himself and for others.

This anointing of hope inclines the aged person to see in the temporal evils of old age, a help towards eternal life, a salutary remedy;[26] and as such, the cross of old age becomes, strange as this may seem, itself the secondary object of the theological virtue of Hope.[27] Hope makes the Christian desire and expect eternal life in accordance with God's promises, but also the temporal good and evil which, in the plan of the eternal Wisdom, condition the practice of the salvific virtues. We say that both temporal good and *temporal evil* are the secondary object of the virtue of hope. This emerges from an analysis of evil undertaken with Saint Thomas Aquinas as guide.[28]

For the fears of old age, therefore, the anointing of the sick substitutes this trusting desire. In this way, it greatly assists the aged person to adapt himself to his situtation and to society. It helps, in an indirect but real manner, to place at the service of a ceaselessly developing society, all the physical and moral forces which exist within this "third age."

In consecrating old age, the anointing of the sick shows all its splendor as a sacrament of total hope, both temporal and eternal. Both time and eternity feel the light and the ardor of this holy oil of the weak and the infirm. For does it not kindle hope for the earthly completion of personal development—namely, the last meritorious act of the free will which fixes the anointed person in the mystery of the Whole Christ, and also his eschatological consummation—that is, the passively received act of the glorious resurrection of the body?

We are now in a position to see more clearly the dimensions for a renewed pastoral approach to the celebration of the anointing of the sick, an approach which could best promote the development of its sacramental grace.

B. *The communal consecration of sickness and of infirm old age to the service of human development, in response to the consecrating gift of the anointing of the sick.*

In the context of the liturgical reform inaugurated by Vatican II, Mgr. Theas, bishop of Lourdes, organized for the first time, massive communal celebrations of the anointing of the sick, during twenty successive pilgrimages in 1969.[29]

Those who on those occasions received this sacrament, were unanimous about the psychological and pastoral advantages of this, in a sense, new mode of its celebration.

Let us list some of these advantages: the opportunity such a celebration gives for real if brief catechesis concerning this largely ignored sacrament; the very solemnity of a communal ceremony more readily focuses the attention of each and all upon it; the fruits of this sacrament will therefore be greater; its celebration outside the sickroom will make this sacrament more desired by those who, while already in danger of death, are not however at the point of death.[30]

This communal celebration even seems to be more in line with the ideas of Vatican II than is its merely individual and quasi-private celebration:

"It is to be stressed that whenever rites, according to their specific nature, make provision for communal celebration involving the present and active participation of the faithful, this way of celebrating them is to be preferred, as far as possible, to a celebration that is individual and quasi-private. This rule applies with special force to ... the administration of the sacraments...."[31]

In this connection, it might also be observed that the presence of a number of priests as ministers of this anointing of the sick, although in no way necessary, is more in line with the text of Saint James: "Let him call for the *elders* of the church, and let *them* pray over him, anointing him with oil in the name of the Lord" (5, 14). Hence it is that the Greek church and the Eastern churches of the Byzantine rite in communion with Rome, normally assign seven priests to the administration of this sacrament. Without admitting concelebration as regards the properly sacramental part of the anointing, nevertheless, in situations where there are several priests present, for example a community, the new ritual of the Latin rite (1973) provides that each of them may impose hands and that they may share among them the preparatory and concluding rites.

The communal celebration of the anointing of the sick indicates clearly that it is by no means necessary to be bedridden or incapable of work to be a person in danger of death, even if such danger is as yet remote. This makes it easier for such a person to seek this supernatural and natural tonic for the body and the soul.

A recent experiment in the United States[32] also goes a long way towards the promotion of an integral and massive preaching and practice of the anointing of the sick. At the practical level, it scarcely differs from the Lourdes experiment; but its special merit is that it brings out more clearly the meaning and importance of this sacrament in the present-day context of the world (the increased and increasing population of old people) and of the Church (a greater insistence on the mission and on the socio-ecclesial role of the laity). We shall sum up here this original presentation of the anointing of the sick.

It is in the sacraments that Christ assures us that he comes to save us from our present human condition, and that He wills to give us eternal life—a life free from sickness and death. He shows this very specially in the sacrament of the anointing of the sick.

In anointing through this sacrament, Christ who is the Anointed of God provides not only things (such as oil) but also persons as salvific signs for the people whom He wills to save. These anointed people receive the mission to teach us how to accept disease, old age, and death as integral parts of the human condition. The infirm are anointed in order to teach us how the Christian should react to these conditions and to this ending of earthly life.

Neither society nor the state can conquer or suppress disease, old age, and death. Christ alone can overcome them.

That is why the Church asks her sick, her aging, her agonizing, to do this wonderful service for her. She asks them to manifest Christ's victory over old age, disease, and death, by allowing Christ to make them, for us and in our midst, living proofs and personal symbols of His triumph. It is on them that the People of God rely to teach them how to behave when faced with weakness and infirmity.

Just as the state of marriage has become a sacrament, so too the state of old age and of sickness with danger of death becomes, through the holy oil of Christ, a sacrament of the New Covenant, a sign of the redemptive action of Christ who saves and heals us.

We would like, therefore, to gather together as many as possible of the sick and the aged in order to anoint and consecrate them with the oil of the sick, so as to establish them in our parish, in our city, as a special group, as an "order"—the group of those who have a mission to prepare us to accept in a Christian spirit our personal ailments and our death. In receiving this sacrament, they have agreed to become for us, weak and mortal men, signs of Christ whose weakness is stronger than the power of men (1 Cor. 1, 25).

By accepting this consecration by Christ of their state of weakness, the sick and the aged in danger of death pledge themselves, in thanksgiving, to consecrate to God, in Christ and through the inspiration of the Holy Spirit, their sickness and their old age—and even, in advance, their death—for the growth of the whole Church in love.

Their sacrificial prayer as believers united to Christ, anointed by Him through His priests, will save the other patients (cf. Jas. 5, 15) and will obtain for them the forgiveness of their sins. For the fervent supplication of the righteous man, particularly if he also is sick, "has great power"; it brings back sinners who have strayed far from the truth. And the sick-in-Christ who " brings back a sinner from the error of his way, will save his soul from death and will cover a multitude of sins" (cf. Jas. 5, 16. 19. 20).[33]

The anointed sick or aged person takes on, therefore, a big responsibility. He does not merely say: "I am approaching the meeting with the Lord in death, and this sacrament will help me on my way to Him by filling me with hope"; he also says: "I am sick, old, on my way to death, a pilgrim on the path to eternity; I shall show how a Christian behaves when faced with disease and death. This is my mission to the world and in the Church."

These two experiments, in Lourdes and in the United States, converge in their purposes. We had hoped to see the new rite of the anointing of the sick aimed in the same direction. We hoped that it would indicate the broad outlines for a communal celebration of the sacrament of hope; that the prayers of the new rite would highlight the twofold consecration implied in this sacrament: the objective consecration by Christ of the state of illness involving danger of death; and the patient's subjective consecration to God, in Christ, by which he offers up his sufferings to God for the Church and for the world. This subjective consecration is his response to Christ the Consecrator of his sickness, and to the gift of anointing and the sacramental grace bestowed on him. We should like to see this subjective consecration orally and communally expressed by those who receive this sacrament. The liturgy of baptism includes the *promise* of the baptized; why could not the liturgy of the anointing of the sick also include an explicit engagement (publicly accepted by those who receive it) that they may unite themselves more intimately with the whole Christian community? The reform of the ritual for the anointing of the sick, in 1973, has substantially met these wishes. The new ritual provides for the inclusion of the sacrament within a more complete liturgical celebration, with, notably, a penitential act and a universal prayer. It even envisages the possibility of conferring this sacrament in the course of the Mass or at a large gathering of the faithful—pars 83 to 92—thus giving to the seriously ill the means of consecrating their condition to God.

It even seems to us that, as a practical step towards bringing this sacrament out of the shadows of neglect, the Church might well fix a minimum age after which it could and should normally be received on the grounds of advanced age. Within certain limits, the more precise fixing of this minimum age could more effectually be left to the episcopal body of the individual country, since the effects of ageing vary according to culture and country. Those whom old age does not seriously enfeeble, a minority, would not be admitted to this sacrament.[34] The age envisaged could vary between 60 years (the age at which the canonical obligation to fast ceases,[35] precisely because of physical weakness) or 65 years (the average retirement age) and 70 years.

We are, of course, aware that various objections could be made to such proposals. We shall summarize and attempt to answer these. The difficulties raised concern the description of old age as a serious illness involving danger of death; the attitude of the young; the example of the clergy themselves; and, finally and especially, the idea itself of this sacrament as a consecration of a condition of dangerous illness.

There are aged people, we are told, who are not seriously ill, and this we readily admit.[36] But can one conclude from this that, generally speaking, old age is not a serious illness? So to conclude would be to fly in the face of all the evidence to the contrary, from Cicero onwards. Ordinary common sense is enough to show that the old age implies the possibility of dying soon. This is certainly so in the vast majority of cases, and the rare exceptions do not disprove our assertion.

Then there is the first objection: Did the authors of the 1917 Code of Canon Law identify old age with "danger of death"? Besides, were there not authors, even after 1917,[37] who held that, for the conferring of this sacrament, there must be specific indications of approaching death—fainting spells, for example?

Yes, of course. But the Roman Ritual of 1925 has entered a precise qualification of this: the anointing of the sick should be administered only to old people whose state of enfeeblement is such that their death appears to be imminent ("in die morituri"). There is no longer any reference to a specific condition,[38] and this silence is certainly deliberate and significant. Such a condition was making it more difficult to administer this sacrament on grounds of advanced age than on grounds of other sicknesses. Besides, it was ignoring the seriousness of old age as an infirmity—a seriousness of which Benedict XIV had certainly been aware: "people advanced in age die easily, and old age leads to the degeneration of physical strength."[39]

Furthermore, the present Code (art. 941) provides that this sacrament should be administered conditionally in cases where there is some doubt that there is a real danger of death. This provides an excellent pastoral classification: in case of doubt, the administration of this sacrament is not only lawful, but obligatory as well. We find justification in this for our proposal that the Church fix a certain age after which the administration of this sacrament would be obligatory, except in cases where danger of death is clearly not present. This "except" qualification would be very difficult to establish practically, in the case of an old person. As a French bishop, Msgr. Theas, rightly observed: "The state of health is hard to decide. Patients who seem to be pretty healthy can, in the doctor's judgement, be gravely sick. It is impossible to be categorical about the demarcation line between the patient who certainly meets the physical conditions needed for the administration of this sacrament, and the patient who certainly does not do so. The wider approach is therefore to be preferred."[40]

A further indication of this is the fact that the majority of theologians accept the revivescence of the sacrament of extreme unction when there was an obstacle to its original celebration.[41] In other words, the grace of the sacrament would later be conferred by Christ at the moment when the obstacle has disappeared—in this case, when there *is* actual danger of death.[42]

The second objection to our proposal concerns the young.

Would not the presentation of this sacrament as a consecration of infirm old age, have the effect of discouraging young patients in danger of death, from asking to receive it?

This objection would carry weight if the anointing of the sick were declared to be *exclusively* the sacrament of the old. But while accentuating for our own purposes here the relevance of this sacrament to old age, it is by no means our intention to suggest that this sacrament is otherwise than designed for *all* baptized persons who have reached the age of reason and who are in danger of death through physical illness. On the contrary, consider the effect which the sight of the aged sick communally receiving the anointing of the sick and offering their sickness to God for the world, would have on the young. Would it not encourage the young also to seek, at need, this anointing which strengthens the weak?

But—and here we come to the third objection—how will lay patients, young and old, be encouraged to ask to receive the anointing of the sick when, in the course of these communal celebrations, they see few or none of their aged priests among those receiving it?

We have here a difficulty, not of a doctrinal, but of a pastoral and psychological kind, and much more concrete than are the preceding ones. Many priests do, of course, die without receiving this sacrament. Does not the seeking and public reception of this anointing amount to an open and humble admission that one is feeble and in danger of death? And, whether one is priest or layman, does not such an admission constitute a blow to one's self-esteem? Furthermore, in our post-conciliar era, would not a priest who publicly received this sacrament seem to be proclaiming that he ought to resign his office — of parish priest, for example?[43]

Some, it must be admitted, would so interpret the action of such a priest. Nevertheless, it would be easy and highly useful if this priest could make use of the occasion to explain to those present the difference between serious illness with danger of death, and inability to work or to discharge a pastoral function. Those who request this anointing admit that they are sick people, but not necessarily that they should take to their beds or that they should retire from the work they still have the energy to cope with. They request this sacrament precisely in the hope that its curing of their spiritual weakness might well have happy repercussions on their physical health to enable them to continue to serve society and to promote its development. Furthermore, priests so anointed by their fellow-priests, would be, for the People of God, a very fine example both of priestly mutual aid and of faith in the power of the Risen Christ as exercised through this sacrament. One may add that such priests could more effectually recommend to others the reception of this sacrament; for, by the humility they have shown in receiving it, do they not in a sense merit the reward of seeing their recommendation accepted?

These, then, are our answers to the difficulties raised. But there is another difficulty, more subtle than the others. We have unhesitatingly claimed that the anointing of the sick involves a sacramental consecration of the condition of serious illness. But how can we claim this? Are we not contradicting the explicit teaching of Saint Thomas Aquinas, the Doctor *par excellence* of the Church?

Saint Thomas says that, unlike the purpose of the anointing which occurs during the consecration of an altar, that of the sacrament of the sick is not to consecrate the sick; this sacrament can be repeated and does not leave a mark or character on the soul.[44] Why is this so? Only a sacrament which deputes a person with a view to his receiving or discharging a sacred duty, impresses a character on the soul. This is the case with the sacraments of baptism, confirmation, holy orders, where the anointing has the effect of a consecration; only a medicinal anointing is involved in the sacrament we are discussing here. The anointing of the sick does not depute the Christian to discharge a sacred function or to receive a sacred gift.[45] Between the exterior sign of the anointing and the special grace of the sacrament (health of body and of soul, spiritual healing through physical healing),[46] comes the intermediary effect ("res et sacramentum") secured by the sacramental sign with a view to the special grace of the sacrament, and this intermediary effect is none other than a spiritual anointing, a certain interior devotion,[47] but not a character.

Such is the context of ideas within which Saint Thomas Aquinas rejects the notion that this sacrament involves a consecration of the sick. This rejection was inevitable within the meaning of his terms in the passages referred to here: there is no consecration where there is no character imprinted on the soul.[48] To claim that this anointing consecrates a sick person would imply that it can be received once only.

Elsewhere,[49] however, Saint Thomas Aquinas takes a wider view of consecration — a view that does not demand the presence of a sacramental "character" as the *sine qua non* of consecration — when he says that a nun's solemn profession *consecrates* her to God. Similarly, we can say that, through the anointing of the sick, the risen Christ consecrates to Himself the condition of dangerous infirmity [50] of a Christian already consecrated by baptism, and perhaps also by confirmation and by holy orders.

Similarly,[51] as Canon Martimort points out, the Church's former practice of conferring this sacrament once only in the course of the same illness,[52] would imply that the effect of interior devotion can lead to a reviviscence of the sacrament in a case where the recipient afterwards commits a mortal sin;[53] it is therefore not suppressed by that sin. In this sense, Martimort explicitly says, we can speak about a consecration of the condition of infirmity through this sacrament.[54]

Msgr. Theas says the same thing: "This sacrament was therefore instituted, it seems, to sanctify those in this particular state of life in the Church and in the world. Its purpose is to enable them to be more effectually a force in the life of the Church and in the life of the world."[55]

As does marriage, sickness constitutes an enduring condition — even though both may in certain cases last for only a short time. If, following Pius XI, Vatican II could say of married couples that they are "strengthened and as it were consecrated (*veluti consecrantur*) by a special sacrament in order that they may worthily discharge the duties of their state,"[56] one fails to see why a similar claim cannot be made for the sick and for the sacrament which sanctifies their state. Its "objective" consecration is constituted by the special anointing of the interior devotion in which Saint Thomas Aquinas saw the "res et sacramentum" of the sacrament. This spiritual anointing, produced by the exterior anointing, disposes the soul to receive the sacramental grace of spiritual and physical healing, a particular type of sanctifying grace. Suffice it to say that this spiritual anointing which indirectly consecrates the infirm, is distinguished from the sacramental grace: think, for example, of an habitual "ordination" of the imagination, which suppresses the influence of terrifying and agonizing images, and so disposes the person to a greater openness to the sacramental grace.[57]

In other words, it is not the person as such that the anointing of the sick immediately consecrates, but rather his state of sickness. This consecration disappears with the ending of that state; or more precisely, it disappears when there is no longer the danger of death which brought it into existence. It is therefore a sickness entailing danger of death which this sacrament consecrates, which it inserts in the mystery of Christ the Redeemer, and which it removes from the influence of Satan and transfers to the service of the Kingdom of the beloved Son.[58]

It is true that this interior and spiritual anointing, which results from the exterior anointing and is intended for the spiritual and physical healing of the sick person, does not depute the Christian to a sacred function or prepare him specifically for the reception of any other sacrament; but it does depute him to a sacred suffering for the Church and for the world, and it disposes him to receive with better dispositions, when he is in danger of death, the Eucharistic Viaticum.[59] In this respect, one might be inclined to say that this anointing constitutes a quasi-character in the sacramental sense; without it, one could not explain the reviviscence of this sacrament.

The sacrificial purpose, in favor of the Church, of the anointing of the sick, has been, as we have already said, explicitly emphasized by Vatican II: "The Church urges the sick to contribute to the common good of the People of God, by freely uniting their sufferings with the passion and death of Christ."[60] This text, which immediately follows a statement about the sacrament of the sick, is sufficient indication that the Church does not confer this sacrament in order to dispense the patient from dying [61] by physically curing him, but much rather to direct him, through an eventual temporary healing of his mortal body, towards a perfect sacrificial self-consecration in union with the death of Christ: "And for their sake I consecrate myself, that they also may be consecrated in truth" (Jn. 17, 19).

The sacramental consecration of the anointing of the sick orientates them towards the final reception of the Eucharist that we call Viaticum, the supreme sacramental association with the redemptive death of Christ for the salvation of the world. Through the spiritual healing effected by this anointing, the anointed patient is strengthened to overcome the selfishness to which his death-shadowed illness inclines him, by integrating himself more than ever with the sacrifice of Christ and of the Church for the Church and for the world, in the Eucharist. Whereas his illness tends to make him self-centered to the exclusion of society and even of the Church, this anointing aims at inserting him more deeply in both.[62] Without it, he would not be as well disposed to receive the Eucharistic Christ, to eat His flesh and to drink His blood for the life of the world.

In providing that "a continuous rite shall be prepared according to which the sick man is anointed after he has made his confession and before he receives Viaticum,"[63] Vatican II is not merely concerned about establishing a logical order; it is implying the redemptive purpose of the anointing of the sick, since this sacrament is orientated towards the supreme mystery of universal salvation — the Eucharist. In dependence on the Eucharistic Christ, the anointing of the sick is a mystery of love, not only vertical but also horizontal; and to it the general statement of Vatican II about all the sacraments applies: "Through the sacraments, there is communicated and nourished that charity toward God and man which is the soul of the entire apostolate."[64] This anointing orientates the sick man towards the Eucharistic oblation of his illness, an oblation which consecrates the world to God.[65]

In effect, the whole cosmos is the extension of the body of the sick person who is in danger of death. Through this weakened body, anointed by the Risen Christ in order that His sick member may more easily pass from this world to the Father, the consecration of the universe, the priestly garment of Christ, continues. Far from being anointed merely to secure an individual and temporary healing, which anyhow would leave its mortality unaffected, the body of the sick person is consecrated in order, through a death in conformity with that of Christ, to draw with it the rest of the baptized and even all mankind towards complete definitive healing of soul and body in the beatific vision and in the glorious resurrection. Through and in his sick body, it is the whole creation "subjected to futility' which is "groaning in travail" waiting for the redemption of this body (cf. Rom. 8, 20-23). The anointing of the patient is an advance sign and almost a promise of his glorious resurrection[66] and of the resurrection of the heavens and the earth in him.[67] It has therefore a cosmic significance: it is the sick universe which this anointing penetrates and transfigures, restoring it to the service of the human body against which it had revolted. The consecration of oil[68] frees it to some extent from "futility," and sets it free "from its bondage to decay" so as already to introduce it partly into "the glorious liberty of the children of God" (Rom. 8, 20).

We can say, therefore, that the anointing of the sick represents an important stage of their "trans-secularization," of their passage from this life to the life to come,[69] and through them, of the transsecularization of the world which is the extension of their bodies. And in this way we re-discover, in a new and deeper way, the role of this ignored sacrament in the full development of the person, of the world and of the Church. Its *raison d'être* is to place at the service of this full and universal development, the whole "ending of life,"[70] which is infirm old age in danger of death, in order that this mysterious and inestimable anointing may transfigure it into eternal youth in the glorious resurrection. For is it not the special function of this anointing to render great assistance to all the infirm in danger of death, so that they may patiently accept all the temporal ills inflicted by God the Savior, in order to make satisfaction to the Father through Christ Jesus?[71] Does it not thus place "the passivities of diminishment" at the service of personal, universal, and ecclesial development? Does it not therefore make old age and mortal sickness a mystery of *satispassion*,[72] completing the satisfaction made in the prime of life; and is it not, as it were, the permanent revelation of the compassion of the whole Church, to Christ crucified[73] and with Him, for the divinization of the world?

Let us conclude our reflections on the sacrament of "the third age" by drawing them together into a prayer of consecration[74] which the infirm, both old and young, could recite together after having received it:

"Lord Jesus, we believe that you have instituted this anointing and that You give it to us to strengthen and comfort our infirmities, our old age, and our death. We thank You for having come to give us this anointing which You have received from the Father to spread upon us, while taking possession of us in the power of Your Spirit.[75]

"You have come to anoint with holy oil our infirmities and our old age. We accept them from Your pierced hands.[76] We unite them with the infirmity and weakness of Your Passion. We offer them to You for the sanctification and for the eternal salvation of the youth of the world, as well as for the renewal and for the eternal youthfulness of Your Church.

"Heal our bodies and our souls, wounded by our sins and our sufferings. You have not suppressed suffering, but you have taken it on Yourself[77] in order to give us the courage to endure our own. We are not alone or separated or abandoned or useless: having been anointed by You, and through and with You, we are saving the world.[78] We accept our own diminishment in order that it may grow.

"Convinced, Lord, that to remain in this body is to live in exile from You, we prefer to leave it in order to be with You (2 Cor. 5, 6-8). An Angel from Heaven comforted You in

Your agony. Passion of Christ, strengthen us at the hour of death. Lord Jesus, grant that we may rest in Your pierced side. Unite our death with Your death in order to make it, for the world, a way to the Father. And may we awaken in the light of Your glory."

NOTES

[1] DS, 1695-1696. On this text of Saint James, see A. d'Alès, DBS, 3 (1938), 262-272: art. "Extrême-Onction"; and also Teofilo da Orbiso, *Verbum Domini,* 31 (1953), 71-82: *De oratione, extrema-unctione et confessione.*

[2] A careful distinction must be made between "danger of death" and "at the point of death." In this connection, see *Sacrosanctum Concilium* of Vatican II (par. 73): *"Extreme unction,* which may also and more fittingly be called *anointing of the sick,* is not a sacrament for those only who are at the point of death. Hence, as soon as any one of the faithful begins to be in danger of death from sickness or old age, the appropriate time for him to receive this sacrament has certainly already arrived."

[3] Saint Thomas Aquinas, *Summa con. Gen.,* IV, 73: "spiritualis medicina contra peccatum."

[4] DS, 1695: Christ instituted the sacrament while entrusting to Saint James the mission to promulgate it.

[5] DS, 1696: here the Council of Trent is clearly drawing on Saint Thomas Aquinas (*Summa con. Gen.,* IV 73).

[6] DS, 1696: "magnam in eo (sc. aegrotante) divinae misericordiae fiduciam excitando, quo infirmus sublevatus et morbi incommoda ac labores levius fert, et tentationibus daemonis . . . facilius resistit."

[7] Saint Thomas Aquinas, ST, Sup., 30. lc.

[8] Cf. Saint Thomas Aquinas, *Summa con. Gen.,* IV. 73: "hoc sacramentum est ultimum et quodammodo consummativum totius spiritualis curationis, quo homo quasi ad participandam gloriam praeparatur; unde et extrema unctio praeparatur." This explanation of Saint Thomas is exact only if it is qualified, as we have done, with the phrase: "without thereby derogating from the power of Holy Viaticum." However, Saint Thomas does not ignore this (ST. III. 65. 3). It would be more exact to use the term "extreme unction" to signify the last of the anointings, and not the last sacramental rite before death. In this connection, see P. De Letter S.J., *Sacramentum Mundi,* vol. I (1968), pp 37-40: art. "Anointing of the Sick."

[9] We presuppose, of course, the intention to receive the sacrament, and we are speaking only about the baptized.

[10] It could not, of course, prevent death. Even when the anointing of the sick results in improvement of the patient's health, this is ultimately to prepare him for a more Christian death. Anyhow, the sacrament seeks to effect a *spiritual* healing, as Father de Letter S.J. clearly emphasizes: "spiritual healing . . . either temporary victory

over illness in restored bodily health or definitive victory in a Christian death: immediate for the departing soul (after eventual cleansing) and delayed for the body till the glorious resurrection. This victory consists in overcoming the spiritual disability and the hindrance to living the life of grace which illness entails" (*Sacramentum Mundi,* vol. I, 1968, pp. 38-40: art. "Anointing of the Sick"). However, can one rule out that the sacrament of the anointing of the sick will snatch from death those whom it physically heals shortly before the end of human history, when Christ will come "to judge *the living* and the dead," as the Creed says following 1 Th. 4, 15-17? It does not seem so.

[11] This expression, used by Saint Thomas Aquinas, splendidly sums up his theology of the anointing of the sick (cf. our notes 2, 4, 6 and 7); admirably synthesized in the *Summa con. Gen.,* IV, 73. The expression occurs in ST, III. 65. 1: "spei respondet extrema-unctio."

[12] These terms, in the opinion of A. M. Roguet O.P., are not synonyms: see *Maison-Dieu,* no. 77 (1964), p. 149.

[13] LG, 11. The exhortation in question here is that of the Council itself and not an allusion to a liturgical prayer, because it does not seem that the liturgy of the anointing of the sick contains such an exhortation, and, for our part, we should like to see the new revised rite of this sacrament (cf. *Sacrosanctum Concilium,* 75) explicitly implementing this exhortation. But the conciliar exhortation merely adapts to the particular case of the anointing of the sick the general New Testament exhortation to compassion towards Christ crucified, or more accurately, with Him, by citing the Pauline texts which express this. It must also be observed that this conciliar exhortation is seen by Vatican II as inseparable from the prayer of the whole Church for the sick: "The whole Church commends those who are ill to the suffering and glorified Lord" (LG, 11). Saint Thomas Aquinas had already interpreted in this sense the text of Saint James (5, 14-15: "Let him call for the elders of the church. . . . The prayer of faith will save the sick man"): "Quia tamen hoc sacramentum perfectae curationis effectum habet, et in eo requiritur copia gratiae, competit huic sacramento . . . quod oratio totius Ecclesiae ad effectum hujus sacramenti coadjuvet" (*Summa con. Gen.,* IV. 73 *sub fine*). In this light, one better understands why the form itself of the sacrament, and that (it seems) of its divine institution ("let them pray over him"), is deprecative rather than indicative: the efficaciousness of the prayer of the minister (s) of the sacrament is not independent of the prayer of the whole Church (as is also the case with the celebration of the Eucharist, according to the mediaeval tradition: there the priest does *mysterio* what the people do *voto;* cf. Y. M. J. Congar O.P., *Jalons pour une théologie du laicat,* Paris, 1953, pp. 280-281; 288).

[14] Cf. B. de Margerie S.J.: *Le Christ pour le Monde or Christ for the World,* chap. XI.

[15] Z. Alszéghy S.J., "L'effeto corporale dell'Estrema Unzione," *Gregorianum,* 38 (1957), 403-405.

[16] Cf. J. Betz, *Encyclopédie de la Foi,* Paris, 1966, vol. 3, pp. 228-229, art. "Onction des Malades." This sacrament effects, to use this author's well chosen phrase, a "sanatio in radice" of the sickness, inas-

much, one might add, as the physical infirmity is a fruit of the sin against which is directed the sacramental grace of the anointing (cf. Jas. 5, 15; Saint Thomas Aquinas, *Summa con. Gen.*, IV, 73: ex peccato derivatur infirmitas corporalis . . . ; spiritualis sanatio ex anima derivatur ad corpus, quando fuerit opportunum, per extremam unctionem; *ibid.* IV, 58). This point of view is well stressed by Father De Letter: "Because of the interdependence between body and soul in the psychophysical unity of man, the spiritual strengthening of the soul which results from the sacramental grace, reacts on the body and can thus have an influence on its healing (*op.cit.* in our note 8).

[17] Vatican II, *Sacrosanctum Concilium,* 73: note the significance of the phrase, *"begins* to be in danger of death." The danger of death, which conditions in every case the liceity and certainly even the validity of the celebration of this sacrament — according to the Church's ordinary magisterium since the Middle Ages — in no way implies the absence of any hope of cure, since such a hope can co-exist with the danger of death.

[18] Except perhaps in the 1917 Code of Canon Law, art. 940; Vatican II does not go beyond this; we think that these two texts should be interpreted, not in the light of the excessively narrow statement of L. Godefroy (DTC, V, 2 col., 2019): "old age can be equated with dangerous illness when it involves the probability of death from one day to the next," but rather in the light of F. Cappello S.J. (*De Extrema Unctione,* Rome, 1949, p. 158, par. 231): "Old age is in itself a serious infirmity. Therefore the sacrament of extreme unction is validly and licitly conferred because of old age *(propter senium)*. On this point, there is no difficulty or difference among the theologians. All agree about this, and this is confirmed by the immemorial custom of the Church. . . . The reason for this is that, as Cicero says, 'senectus ipsa morbus est': old age is itself a disease. Physical strength diminishes, the senses become less effective, weaknesses increase, the physiological condition of the body gets daily worse, to the point at which old age signifies not only a danger of death, but also its certainty." All the commentators on the 1917 Code do not view the matter so liberally however. So, for example, Bachofen: "Some signs of approaching dissolution, such as fainting or sinking spells, should appear before extreme unction is given" (*A Commentary on the New Code of Canon Law,* London, 1925, vol. IV, p. 402). This is not surprising, since Bachofen has not grasped the fact that old age itself is a rious illness.

[19] In this connection, see the bibliographies given in the big Larousse at the end of the volumes containing "gérontologie" and "vieillesse"; the publications of the international congresses of gerontology, notably of the 1960 congress: *Ageing around the World,* vol. 1: "Social and psychological aspects of ageing," N.Y., 1962 (952 pages); M. A. McBride, *New Catholic Encyclopedia,* Washington, vol. I, pp. 198-200, art. "Aged, care of the."

[20] Father Teilhard de Chardin S.J., *Milieu Divin,* part 2, section 3.

[21] A desire which Schilleceeckx calls "spiritual extreme unction" (*Le Christ, Sacrament de la Rencontre de Dieu,* Paris, 1960 p. 175).

Extreme Unction was administered to Father Teilhard immediately after his physical death (see Cuenot, *Teilhard de Chardin,* Baltimore, 1965, p. 388).

[22] In this connection, see F. Lepargneur O.P., "Situation du malade en anthropologie chrétienne," *Revue de l'Université d'Ottawa,* 37 (1967), 440-446; 452-454; 460-462.

[23] Rahner-Vorgrimler, *Theological Dictionary,* N.Y., 1965, p. 24: "Sickness has become a saving situation, which, regardless of how the sickness may end, will lead to salvation."

[24] *Ibid.*

[25] Karl Rahner, *Inquiries,* N.Y., 1964, pp. 294-298.

[26] Cf. Saint Thomas Aquinas, ST, I. II. 114. 10, 3 and 4.

[27] Saint Thomas Aquinas, *De Spe Theologica,* Quaestio unica, 1. 4c.

[28] Saint Thomas Aquinas, ST, I. II 114. 10: "Tantum dat Deus viris justis de bonis temporalibus, et etiam de malis, quantum eis expedit ad perveniendum ad vitam aeternam." Inasmuch as they lead to eternal life by facilitating the practice of the virtues, temporal evils, it must be said, become in a sense benefits. One can and indeed should hope for them, that is, desire them with trust in God and expect them through the fidelity of divine Providence of God's plan of salvation for us.

[29] Msgr. Théas, *Notitiae,* 6 (1970), 22-34.

[30] In this way, the anointing of the sick ceases to be associated with a highly imminent death, and sickness with danger of death no longer suggests the idea of being bed-ridden or being unable to do any work.

[31] *Sacrosanctum Concilium,* par. 27.

[32] In the archdiocese of Dubuque, Iowa. The text presenting this experiment is by Father Spaight. It consists of two sermons (polycopied).

[33] It is thus that we think it possible to show the organic connection between the doctrine of Vatican II (cf. note 13) on the ecclesial mission inseparable from the anointing of the sick, and the text (as well as the context) of the Epistle of Saint James which promulgates this sacrament.

[34] "Danger of death cannot be measured by mere age or by any other general rule, for it depends above all else on the conditions and the resistance of the organism" (E. Doronzo O.M.I., *De Extrema Unctione,* Milwaukee, 1955, vol. II, p. 665).

[35] Canon 1254, 2. Elsewhere (can. 523), however, the Code distinguishes between serious illness and danger of death. One cannot therefore make too much here of canon 1254, 2.

[36] See note 34.

[37] E.G., C. A. Bachofen O.S.B., *A Commentary on the New Code of Canon Law,* London, 1925, vol. IV, p. 402. But this text was published prior to the reform of the ritual: see note 38.

[38] Cf. Doronzo, *op.cit.* (note 34), vol. II, p. 560 (in connection with the modification of the Ritual, tit. 5, c. 1, n. 5).

[39] Benedict XIV. *De Synodo diocesana,* VIII. 5. 2.

[40] Théas, *Notitiae,* no. 50, t. 6 (1970), p. 27. We admit that there is a legitimate doubt concerning the question of age (cf. Canon 941).

[41] Cf. Capello, *De Extrema-Unctione,* Rome, 1949, par. 310-314.

[42] *Ibid.,* par. 230, p. 157; this line of reasoning is valid only for theologians who hold that an actual danger of death does not constitute a condition for the validity of the conferring of the sacrament. This is the position of a growing minority; it is not our position. And since there can be no revivescence of an invalid sacrament, we must conclude that the sacrament should be repeated when there is definite danger of death from sickness.

[43] Cf. Vatican II, *Christus Dominus,* par. 31 *sub fine.*

[44] Saint Thomas Aquinas, STS, 33. 1; 30. 3.

[45] *Ibid.,* 30. 3. 2 and 3.

[46] *Ibid.,* 33. 1, *sed contra* and *corpus.*

[47] *Ibid.,* 30. 3. 3; Father Gardeil (commentator on Saint Thomas Aquinas: *L'Extrême-Onction,* Paris, 1967, p. 123) rightly observes that "this state of a certain duration" offers some analogy with the indelible "mark" of the three non-repeatable sacraments. But he confuses it (p. 12, *ibid.*) with "the state of complete consecration to God" to which it should lead, just as the "res et sacramentum" produces the "res" of the sacrament.

[48] Cf. the text cited in note 44.

[49] Saint Thomas Aquinas, ST, II. II. 88. 11.

[50] The expression "status infirmitatis" is used several times by Saint Thomas Aquinas in STS, 33. 2. It enables him to distinguish different states of infirmity in the course of the same illness and so to justify the repetition of the sacrament.

[51] A. G. Martimort, *Les signes de la nouvelle Alliance* (English translation, Collegeville, U.S.A., 1963, p. 275). Martimort speaks about the *present custom* that prevails in the Church. Since this book has been written, the apostolic constitution *Sacram Unctionem Infirmorum,* of 30 November 1972, provides that "this sacrament may be repeated if the patient, after having received the anointing of the sick, recovers but relapses, or if, during the same illness, *the danger of death* becomes serious." The controversy in question has therefore been decided.

[52] Cf. Cappello, *op.cit.,* note 41, par. 309. The author points out that there can be periods during a prolonged illness when it ceases for a time to be serious; a recurrence of the danger of death makes it lawful to repeat the anointing of the sick. Applying this principle to old age, he considers that the repetition of the sacrament is more readily admissible in this case.

[53] We presuppose, of course, that this is followed by confession or an act of perfect contrition.

[54] Text cited in note 51.

[55] Théas, *op.cit.,* (note 40) p. 27.

[56] GS, 48.

[57] Doronzo, *op. cit.,* t. II, pp. 274-275. We note with this author (p. 275) the need to ascribe a permanent effect to this anointing, distinct from the sacramental grace, in order to explain the reviviscence of the sacrament; this permanent effect is precisely the "res et sacramentum."

[58] Cf. P. Beillevert, *Catholicisme,* Paris, 1952, t. III, col. 64-65, art. "Consécration."

[59] Cf. Saint Thomas Aquinas, ST, III. 65. 3: "per extremam unctionem praeparatur homo ad digne sumendum corpus Christi." In fact, this text does not contradict what Saint Thomas had written in what today we call the "Supplement" (30.3): the anointing does not depute to the reception of another sacrament. It disposes and prepares for it, but this is not the same thing. But if this text is read in its immediate context: "omnia alia sacramenta ordinari videntur ad hoc sacramentum (sc. Eucharistiae) sicut ad finem" — one sees that Saint Thomas has clarified in the *Summa Theologica* a point which perhaps he had not yet come to appreciate when he was writing his Commentary on the Sentences which today is included in the *Supplement:* namely, that the anointing of the sick is orientated towards the Eucharist as its purpose. It purifies with a view to the reception of the Eucharist.

[60] LG, 11.

[61] The message of Vatican II to the sick: we shall return to this.

[62] Cf. Théas: "The communal character adds . . . the reintegration of the suffering members of the community with their brethren" (*Notitae,* 6, 1970, p. 30). Properly speaking, it is only through being the occasion of special temptations that sickness tends to make people cut themselves away from the Church.

[63] *Sacrosanctum Concilium,* par. 74. (This new rite has, in fact, been promulgated in 1973).

[64] LG, 33.

[65] LG, 34.

[66] Inasmuch as it is a sign (though not an infallible sign) of predestination.

[67] Cf. this beautiful text of Saint Ambrose (*De Fide Resurrectionis,* latter half): "Resurrexit in eo mundus, resurrexit in eo coelum, resurrexit in eo terra. Erit enim coelum novum et terra nova."

[68] If all agree in speaking about a consecration of oil, it is very difficult to see why one should refuse to speak about a consecration of sickness by means of the consecrated oil. Cf. Saint Thomas Aquinas, STS, 29. 5, where the word "consecration" has the same meaning as the word "sanctification," in connection with the anointing of the scik.

[69] On the idea of trans-secularization, see B. de Margerie S.J., "Le Christ, la sécularisation et la con sécration du monde," in NRT, 91 (1969), 379-380 and 392.

[70] DS, 1964; cf. 1698: "sacramentum exeuntium": in a sense, the whole of old age is "exitus vitae" (1694).

[71] DS, 1693.

[72] Theologians use this word to designate the sufferings of the souls in Purgatory, who make satisfaction but no longer merit. We are not using the word with this full sense here: we use it as emphasizing the "passivity" of the sick person.

[73] LG, 11: "The Church exhorts them (namely, those on whom she confers this anointing) to contribute to the welfare of the whole People of God by freely associating themselves with the passion and death of Christ."

[74] We offer this text in the hope that it might be useful to the authors of a future rite of the communal anointing of the sick: cf. SC, 74.

[75] "The anointing of Christ, which He Himself has received from the Father in order to bestow it on us, is essentially an investiture of the Spirit of God, in order to teach the Christian the unique value of this death and to enable him to die his own death in the Lord" (F. Bourassa S.J., *Science et Esprit,* 20, 1968, 40; cf. pp. 49-50: extract from a remarkable article on the sacramental grace of the anointing of the sick which, for this author, is "the healing of man, in the sense that such healing reaches, and even directly reaches, the body itself, but does so with a view to the good of the person *as a person*—i.e. to the salvation and eternal health of the whole man": *Sciences eccl.,* 19, 1967, 45).

[76] Cf. 2 Cor. 13, 4: "For Christ was crucified in weakness ("ex asthéneias," the noun corresponding to the verb "asthénei" used in Jas. 5, 14), but lives by the power of God. For we are weak in him, but . . . we shall live with him by the power of God."

[77] Message of Vatican II to the sick: "Christ has not suppressed suffering; He has not even willed to unveil to us its whole mystery; He has taken it on Himself, and this is enough to make us understand all its value."

[78] *Ibid.*: "Take courage, you who must suffer in obscurity: you are the chosen ones of the Kingdom of God . . . you are the brethren of the suffering Christ, and with Him, if you so will, you are saving the world. This is the Christian science of suffering, the only one which gives peace. Know that you are not alone, or separated, or abandoned, or useless: you are called by God to be His living and transparent likeness" (AAS, 58, 1966, 16-17).

N.B. On the problems raised by concelebration by several priests in the administration of the anointing of the sick, see Doronzo (*op.cit,* in note 34), t.II, pp. 774-799; and Capello (*op.cit.,* in note 41) pars. 127-133: according to the moralists, the unity between matter and form would not be kept if more than the space of the recital of a *Pater Noster* separated the anointing and the prayer of the priest; in that case, the sacrament would be invalid. In this connection, see H. Jone O.F.M.Cap., *Moral Theology,* Westminster, Maryland (U.S.A.), 1953, par. 444.

chapter six

The Eucharist: Sacrament of Growth in Love and Social Development

AT first sight, it might seem highly unlikely that the Eucharist has been an influence on economic and social development. Has it not been frequently and insistently repeated that industrial civilization found its most fruitful soil in the Protestant countries, at a time when (more than today) the Eucharistic Sacrifice and (less frequently)[1] the Real Presence were being rejected, — and that this civilization found a largely barren soil in the Catholic lands?

The Catholic, however, sees his life as a unit which he seeks constantly to unify more and more perfectly. That life has two main poles, at two very different levels: his daily work and his weekly or even daily Communion, and he will not be easily persuaded that these two are not closely linked. He will not concede without question that his receiving the Bread of Life has no influence on the labor by which he earns his daily bread. He perceives in an obscure way that there is an intimate relationship between these two; and he relies on the theologians to bring this fact into clearer focus for him.

We shall therefore attempt to show how the Eucharist, as the sacrament of fraternal charity, divinizes and facilitates, even at the natural level, the dialog between those whom it unites among themselves, and, through that dialogue, the productive work and the sharing of its output.

It is in the light of Biblical doctrine, of classic theology, of conciliar declarations, and of the social encyclicals, that we can grasp more clearly the indirect but real influence which the Eucharist exerts on the social and economic life of those who receive It. Such a study, so attractive in the context of the growth of the Third World, demands a method which never confuses, while at the same time never separates, the natural domain and the supernatural order, what is human and what is divine, in a universe which, in its totality, is the extension of the sacred Humanity, inseparably and inconfusibly united with the Word of Life.

A. *The Eucharist, sacrament of the dialog of friendship.*

Ours is a "culture" so infested with noise, with propaganda, with slogans of every kind, a "culture" so little concerned with truth and so obsessed with making money, that it is hagridden with suspicion and distrust; and yet, a world in which the majority of people hunger for what they find most difficult to secure — an authentic self-communing and a real dialog with others and with God.

Such is the atmosphere in which many people, even Christians, live, and it is there that the Eucharistic dialog of friendship has its place. It is in the Eucharist that they recover the ability to enter into dialog with others and especially with God, and even to hold a fruitful monolog with themselves.

"He who eats my flesh and drinks my blood abides in me and I in him" (Jn. 6, 56); "we who are many are one body, for we all partake of the one bread" (1 Cor. 10, 17). The Catholic tradition has understood and expressed what was hidden in the inexhaustible splendor of these words of Jesus and of Paul. The special effect of the Eucharist, Its specific sacramental grace, is to increase the communicant's twofold supernatural love of God and of men; to promote the increasingly effective exercise — through acts which become more and more intense, generous, and pure — of the "horizontal" fraternal love and of a true love of self, which are the concrete expression of the pure "vertical" love of God, loved for Himself and above all His gifts.[2]

Intersubjective dialog, the expression of fraternal love, is at once a prerequisite,[3] a demand, and a result of the Eucharistic Communion, which in turn is the culminating point of the dialog between God and man, of the message of the divine Love and of the answer which it awakens in the human heart. The "horizontal" dialog proclaims to the world the mysterious reality of the "vertical" dialog which is its source. The breaking of the divine Bread commands and facilitates a new[4] breaking of the human heart and of the human word, the reconciling contrition and the word of fraternal collaboration which stimulate the sharing of the earthly bread.

This dialog of the Eucharistic guests arouses, perfects, and in a sense consecrates, the dialog between fellow-workers, between man and man in everyday life. Without such a dialog, how could there be a workers' participation in the running of an industry, a sharing by citizens in the responsibility of decision-making, a cooperation of all men in the building up of the world community and of its political body? All these are salient points in the socio-economic program of John XXIII.[5]

We limit ourselves here to an analysis of the dialog within a factory, a dialog which — as the neo-capitalist concern with "human relations" recognizes — conditions its good economic functioning, and still more, transforms it into a community of people. "All this implies that the workers have their say in and make their own contribution to the efficient running and development of the enterprise. . . . Obviously, any firm which is concerned for the human dignity of its workers must maintain a necessary and efficient unity of direction. But it must not treat those employees who spend their days in service with the firm as though they were mere cogs in the machinery, denying them any opportunity of expressing their wishes or bringing their experience to bear on the work in hand, and keeping them entirely passive in regard to decisions that regulate their activity."[6]

What John XXIII is saying here emerges very clearly. Even if workers, as Pius XII had already claimed, do not have a natural right to co-management of the business enterprise, they have the natural and inalienable right to be heard, and therefore to have a say "in regard to decisions that regulate their activity." The latter phrase implies a narrower concept than that of "co-management," but it is already one of considerable scope; for to this right there is a corresponding "duty to claim it as an expression of their human dignity." This is the path which leads to "a better knowledge of the true God, transcendent and personal," as John XXIII said in *Pacem in Terris*.[7]

It is within the framework of this right and of this duty to have a say in the running of the enterprise, that the workers exercise their natural right, not to co-management, but to co-responsibility.[8] The management should recognize this right and duty of the workers to have their share in co-responsibility. If the employers are unwilling to listen to the workers, or if the workers make no effort to understand the problems of their employers, how can there be any fruitful dialog between them?

Workers and employers can sincerely talk and listen to one another, only if together they acknowledge "the existence of a moral order which is transcendent, absolute, universal, and equally binding upon all." Otherwise, "both sides speak of 'justice' and 'the demands of justice,' but these words frequently take on different or opposite meanings according to which side uses them."[9]

Now, in fact, as a consequence of original sin and of actual sins, God has so counfounded the language of men that one no longer understands what the other is saying (cf. Gen. 11, 7) and that therefore they have "ceased to build the city" of the earth (cf. Gen. 11, 8) — i.e. to fulfil their mission.

But the Word of God became human word in order to re-establish dialog among men, by curing, particularly through the Eucharistic language,[10] the deafness, the dumbness, the blindness of the ears, the tongue, and the eyes of the heart (cf. Eph. 1, 18). The sacramental communion with the incarnate Word re-establishes and completes the dialog without which the earthly city cannot be built. As Vatican II says: "The union of all peoples in a universal faith was to be achieved by the Church of the New Covenant, a Church which speaks all tongues, which lovingly understands and accepts all tongues, and thus overcomes the divisiveness of Babel" (*Ad Gentes*, par. 4).

Other things being equal, however, who better than the communicants — "members of the same body, and partakers of the promise in Christ Jesus through the gospel" (Eph. 3, 6) — can give full and living reality, within the business enterprise and throughout the world, to all the stages of the human dialog as described by Paul VI: communion of life and of customs; willingness to listen to others; readiness to acknowledge what is true in the attitudes of others; a sincere effort made to convey with "clarity, meekness, trust, and prudence," the truths, even of a merely natural kind, concerning personal and social rights, and to do so without the least trace of "arrogance, barbed words, or offensive bitterness?"[11]

If either party lacks these dispositions, how could there be effective communication between them? And are not these attitudes the only ones capable of rising above the clashes inherent in liberal capitalism and in the Marxist class war (both contrary to Christianity) and of securing the dialog of human solidarity and of Christian brotherhood?[12]

But what must be done in order that "the tongue . . . a fire . . . a restless evil, full of deadly poison" with which "we bless the Lord and Father . . . and curse men, who are made in the likeness of God" (Jas. 3, 6-9) — and the tongue which speaks out of the abundance of an "evil treasure" (cf. Mt. 12, 34-35) — may be transformed into an instrument for the dialog which the incarnate Word seeks to establish, through us, with our contemporaries?

While it is true that, as Saint James tells us (3, 8), "no human being can tame the tongue," all things are possible to him who believes in the active real Presence of Christ in the Eucharist, and who receives Christ in this sacrament. For in the Eucharist, sacrament of the dialog of friendship, Christ is the "live coal" taken "off the altar," which touches the impure lips of men, lips soiled with social injustice, takes away their "iniquities" and disposes them to bring blessings to others in a fraternal dialog (cf. Is. 6, 5-7).

In one's own life and in the sinful and saintly history of redeemed mankind, it is through the Eucharist that man achieves the fullness of self-realization as a social being; for, as the encyclical *Mater et Magistra* says: "Individual human beings are the foundation, the cause and the end of every social institution. That is necessarily so, for men are by nature social beings. This fact must be recognized, as also the fact that they are raised in the plan of Providence to an order of reality which is above nature."[13]

In effect, one cannot think about the individual man, freely raised to the supernatural order, except in his relationship to Christ the perfect Man: "The Son of God made man," wrote Pius XII in 1955, "is the only solid foundation of mankind, even as regards secular and social life. By assuming human nature, He has confirmed its dignity as the basis and the fundamental norm of the moral order."[14]

The incarnate Son of God is, then, the very basis of man's social life. But where can modern man encounter the Word made flesh? In the poor and in the priest, but above all in the Eucharist which joins them, and which is thus the only solid foundation of men's social life, and of that dialog between them through which history is shaped. In culpably rejecting the Bread of the dialog of friendship, man alienates and degrades himself, and ceases to be the purpose of human institutions, to become their instrument and means; because he thereby diminishes, not to say destroys, his capacity to listen as a brother and to answer as a brother.

Was it not for this reason that Saint John, at the end of his long life, presented the Eucharistic Christ as the mediator of the mutual communion between Christians? Let us look again at this inspired text:

"[We] proclaim to you the eternal life which was with the Father and was made manifest to us . . . so that you may have fellowship with us; and our fellowship (koinônia) is with the Father and with his Son Jesus Christ. . . . If we say we have fellowship with him while we walk in darkness [that is of hate], we lie and do not live according to the truth; but if we walk in the light . . . we have fellowship with one another, and the blood of Christ his Son cleanses us from all sin" (1 Jn. 1, 2-7).

Some exegetes hold that the First Epistle of Saint John is a Eucharistic catechesis and that the word "koinônia" could here have cultic and Eucharistic overtones.[15] This is very probably true, particularly when one takes into account that John was writing long after Paul, with a knowledge of Paul's writings and of his use of the word "koinônia" in a Eucharistic context (1 Cor. 10, 16-17).

The present significance of the Johannine text is, therefore, this: the blood of the Eucharistic "koinônia" with Christ cleanses from sins against the fraternal "koinônia," and re-establishes this "mutual fellowship" which today we call "the dialog."[16] Through the dialog, the horizontal communion of the faithful with one another is re-established, as is also their vertical communion with the members of the apostolic college, continued in the episcopal college ("fellowship with us"), and even that of the whole Church with the Father and with the Word of life ("fellowship with the Father").

As Father Hamer writes, "the word *koinônia* in the New Testament signifies a way of life (of being and of acting) and a relationship with God and with men, characterizing the Christian community. While therefore this word is not synonymous with *Church* in the sense of 'social group,' it nevertheless signifies the situation in which Christians are to one another, in their shared dependence on Christ and on the Spirit. We are at the very heart of the mystery of the Church"[17] — which is the mystery of the Eucharistic dialog.[18]

A brilliant passage by Saint Bonaventure will help us to synthesize our ideas on the Eucharist, sacrament of the dialog: "Communion is threefold. The first is purely spiritual: communion according to interior love. The second is physical: communion according to external relations. The third comes between these two: communion according to the Sacrament of the Altar. . . . Thus, there is a triple communion: spiritual, sacramental and physical."[19]

Sacramental Communion — which persupposses a minimum of spiritual communion, through the state of grace, with all other Christians and with all men of good will, and physical communion with some — tends towards the perfection of this physical communion in the division of possessions, and towards the fullness of this spiritual communion in interior love, by means of "the dialog."

Since the Eucharist, inasmuch as It is Christ the Savior Himself, is the most powerful agent of sanctification, It is also the inexhaustible source of the most complete and most constantly renewed dialog.

But if it is to be given its fullness, this dialog demands the mediation of a transitive action — of work, of production in common.

B. *The Eucharist, sacrament of productive work done in common.*

In effect, men in general enter into a dialog only in order that together they may build the world; and Christians do so only in order, together, to build the Church, the Reign of God, through the celebration of the Eucharist.

The Eucharist, which is conditioned by the socialized work of man and by his production, indirectly conditions this work, and therefore, more indirectly still, conditions this production. Here we have the two terms of a dialectical relationship: we must investigate these terms, while showing that they do not belong at the same level.

Biblical history is the Eucharistic history of mankind.

From the outset, the history of ancient Israel is a preparation for the Eucharist, the latter being instituted in the fullness of time — of these latter days which are to continue, illuminated by the Eucharistic sun, center of the new Israel, until their trans-Eucharistic consummation, when, the consecrated species having ceased to exist, God will be "everything to every one" (1 Cor. 15, 28).

In the past, the Eucharist has been conditioned by the Jewish Passover, a synthesis between the pastoral economy of the ancient Israelites and the agrarian economy of the Canaanites, a synthesis integrated in the "economy" (as the word is used by the Greek Fathers — i.e. dispensation) of the cult which God has revealed.

"If we leave etymology aside, the Passover is seen to be a rite practiced by shepherds. It is the kind of sacrifice which nomads or semi-nomads offer, and no other sacrifice in all Israelite ritual is more like the sacrifices of the ancient Arabs: there is no priest, no altar, and the use of blood is most important. The Passover was the spring-time sacrifice of a young animal in order to secure fecundity and prosperity for the flock. . . . It may have been a feast celebrated when the tribe struck camp before setting out for the spring pastures, but this is not the whole explanation: it was, in a more general way, an offering for the welfare of the flock, like the old Arab feast which fell in the month of Rajab, the first month of Spring. The other details of the Passover stress still more that it was essentially a feast for nomads: the victim was roasted over a fire without any kitchen utensils; it was eaten with unleavened bread (which is still the normal bread of Bedouins today) and with bitter herbs (which does not mean vegetables grown in the garden, but the desert plants which Bedouins pick to season their food). The ritual prescribed that those eating it should have their belts already fastened, sandals on their feet (as if they were going to make a long journey on foot), and a shepherd's stick in one hand. . . . The Passover was the Israelite version of the spring-time feast which all the Semitic nomads, kept, but in Israel it acquired a particular meaning. . . . One springtime there had been a startling intervention of God: he had brought Israel out of Egypt, and this divine intervention marked the beginning of Israel's history as a people, as God's Chosen People."[20]

A sacrifice, then, of semi-nomads; for, already, at the time of their entry into the land of Canaan, the Hebrews were no longer pure nomads, as some would suppose. Since the era of the Patriarchs, in Egypt and in the desert, they had gone in for cultivation, at least in a desultory way, in accordance with the practice of semi-nomads, who sow cereals when they are to spend an extended period in a region favorable to such crops. But such limited cultivation is something quite different from full range cultivation, not only of cereals but also of fruit trees and of the vine.

In the course of several generations, and through necessity, the Hebrews became settled farmers. Their mentors in this development were those same Cannanites who were, as the case might be, their slaves or fellow-citizens, or proprietors in their own right. This passage from a semi-nomadic to an agricultural life style was a profound transformation which took place in the era of the Judges. Though initially they had found it repugnant, the Israelites were won over more and more to the agricultural way of life. This development entailed serious injury to the Mosaic religion, since the mass of the people were constantly tempted to ignore the way of life presented by Moses under the inspiration of God.

However, there was no lack of faithful Israelites who regarded the agricultural life as good and conducive to the good life, but saw all this as the gift of Yahweh. In modern terms, we might say that they saw the divine conditioning of the economic conditioning itself! Did not God say to the People of Israel: "I will give to your land the early rain and the later rain, that you may gather in your corn, and your wine, and your oil" (Deut. 11, 14)? One could add other Scriptural texts to the same effect.[21]

It is more important to emphasize, however, that the Old Testament is validating the transformation — or, as we would say, the humanization — of nature by labor,[22] by viticulture in particular, at the same time as it stresses the gifts of God which make agriculture possible. God is not only the Creator: He is also the Providence that guides the Israelites, and even the Master who, through the Canaanites, teaches them the agricultural way of life.[23]

There is one point we have not yet properly focused and considered. The Word of God willed that first there should be a pre-determined degree of development (of cultural development of the Greeks, political development of the Romans, religious development of the Jews), in the "fullness of time" (Gal. 4, 4), before He inserted into human history;

and similarly, He has made the Eucharist, which is the extension of the Incarnation, dependent on the development, in Israel and throughout the Mediterranean world, from a pastoral and nomadic economy to that of sedentary agriculture. How would it have been possible to institute the Eucharist, in the form willed by Jesus, except within a world where human labor had previously transformed the wheat into bread and the grapes into wine, by methods already considerably developed and complex?

A comparison of the already cited Biblical texts with the description of the Rechabites in Jeremiah, provides a negative proof that the institution of the Eucharist was dependent as regards its willed form on the existence of an agrarian civilization. At least six centuries after the conquest of Canaan and six centuries before the birth of Christ, they obstinately preferred tents and the nomadic life to houses and the settled life of viticulture. Jeremiah "set before the sons of the house of the Rechamites pots full of wine and cups" and said to them: "Drink the wine"; and they answered: "We will not drink wine, because Jonadab, the son of Rechab, our father, commanded us, saying: You shall drink no wine, neither you nor your children, for ever. Neither shall you build houses, nor sow seed, nor plant vineyards, nor have any; but you shall dwell in tents all your days, that you may live many days upon the face of the earth, to which you are strangers" (Jer. 35, 5-7).

What must be noted is that the life style of the Rechabites was in no way a carry-over from the nomadic period of Israel, but a reaction begun in about 840 B.C. by Jonadab, a convinced Yahwist, enemy of the cult of Baal (cf. 4 Kings 10, 15-24)—a reaction[24] in favor of nomadism, subsequent to the difficulties which the true religion encountered in the agrarian economy. It was all a little like the situation under the Vichy régime, when some people were urging a return to the land through hostility to the industrial civilization!

Yahweh highly praised the fidelity of the Rechabites to the commands of Jonadab, even after 250 years, though

He had ordered Jeremiah to lead them into the Temple and to offer them wine (Jer. 35, 18-19 and 35, 2); nevertheless, it was no part of the divine plan that such a reaction should become general, for this would have made impossible both the cultural ceremonies of the Old Testament (e.g. the libations of wine mentioned in Ex. 29, 40 and Num. 15, 5. 10) and the Eucharistic Sacrifice of the New Covenant.

It is God Himself who shows us, through the religious history of "Israel according to the flesh" (1 Cor. 10, 18), that the Bread of Heaven and the Chalice of the New Covenant with "the Israel of God" (Gal. 6, 16) are dependent on earthly bread and wine. God Himself teaches us that the humanization of nature by the work of man is the constantly renewed precondition for the divinization of the workers through the Eucharist.[25] The institution of the Eucharist presupposes, through the sacred history of Israel, the experience of a human communion based on the transformation and the humanization of nature by work. Communion in work is the condition for the appearance of the matter of the sacrament.

The bread and the wine, products of the agricultural labor (today partly mechanized and industrialized) of human society, in becoming the matter of the sacrifice of the Whole Christ and the condition of its supernatural unity, manifest, to the "enlightened eyes of the heart" (Eph. 1, 18), that virtuous and vigorous collaboration in the building of the earthly city is a condition for heavenly citizenship and for entry into "the city which has foundations, whose builder and maker is God" (Heb. 11, 10).

The Eucharist is the sign *par excellence* of this activity of Christ as architect of His Church with the collaboration of His baptized members: "I shall build my church" (Mt. 16, 18).[26] It signifies, while it mediatizes, the growth of supernatural love among Christians—a love which is itself the origin, not purely and simply of their work,[27] but of a more generous and therefore[28] more rational work for the earthly city and for the indispensable growth of its production and even of its productivity.

In the Eucharist, the Church efficaciously sacrifices herself, not only for the salvation of immortal souls and for the glorious resurrection of mortal bodies, but also for the peace, for the well-being and for the development of the earthly city. Since the Eucharist is the visible sign which effects the invisible growth of love among the members of the same social and mystical body and in regard to all those who are not yet of that body, it is, *ispo facto*, the sign which indirectly mediatizes the productive work of so many men, if not as to its actual existence, at least in the dynamism and the fullness of its effectuality.

At first sight, does not such a statement surprise us and upset our customary way of looking at things? De we not distinguish so throughly in our minds between the spiritual and the temporal that we are likely to regard them as entirely separate from ane another? Are we not inclined to forget that, in the ultimate analysis, both economic and social development are dependent upon the same Providence of God who gives Himself to us in the Eucharist?

However, the statement in question is so entirely right that it is scarcely possible to deny it without thereby rejecting several aspects of the Church's doctrines concerning development and grace.

In fact, it is the Church herself that affirms the influence of the spiritual life on the temporal order. Pope John XXIII writes: "To search for spiritual perfection and eternal salvation in the conduct of human affairs and institutions is not to rob these of the power to achieve their immediate, specific ends, but to enhance this power."[29] In other words, when the Christian, in his work to increase production, opens himself to the Eucharist, the supreme value and ultimate end as well as the preeminent means of all his activity, the specific and immediate efficiency of this work is increased. A man is a unified being: his spiritual life enlightens his mind and strengthens his will, and thus reacts on his earthly activity. Grace urges him to take action towards the discharge of his professional duty—and we shall shortly consider the link between this and development.

This positive reason is completed by a thesis of a seemingly negative kind. "Without the strengthening grace of our Savior, no one can observe for long all the precepts of the natural law, or, consequently, acquire solid and perfect virtues."[30] This principle applies also in the socio-economic domain, wherein human relationships demand the fulfilment of the natural law and consequently the exercise of the acquired and the infused virtues.

Now, what in concrete terms is signified by this principle? It implies clearly that, in the divine plan for the redemption of a humanity called and even re-called to the supernatural life, the man who, ignoring the actual graces which invite him to pray, rejects the gift of sanctifying grace and of supernatural love, thereby injures himself and maims the integrity of his authentic human nature and of his ethical dynamism. The man who does not pray is not and cannot be fully man; the refusal to pray is synonymous with the rejection of the graces without which no one can for long observe, in its fullness, the natural law, or therefore persevere in justice and in love towards others. Other things being equal, how could such a one work and produce with as much efficiency as does his praying, supernaturally just and loving fellow-worker? Thus, if public opinion in the developed countries is to understand the need to help other countries in the throes of development, time, though indispensable, is not enough; a help which goes beyond man is also needed. Only grace can act on the human will in order to destroy the past and still present injustice of the rich countries, and to orientate their citizens towards that true growth which is never at the expense of others, but for their benefit. "The development of nations is, and will continue to be, closely connected with the apostolate and with the preaching of the Gospel":[31] closely connected, in other words, with an abundant outpouring of the grace whose principal source is the Eucharist.

For this supreme sacrament kindles in the soul a loving determination to do divine will— and this is its special fruit. How could it be denied that the foremost temporal duty of men today, a duty deeply rooted in their professional work, is that of collaborating actively in the socio-economic betterment[32] of developing countries, in Africa, in Asia, in Latin America? The spiritual light and ardor emanating from the Eucharistic Christ are directed, therefore, towards the fulfilment of professional duty as polarized by concern for the development of the Third World. In other words, Christ the Developer, present and active in the Holy Eucharist, is directing the minds and energies of His recipients towards the development of the whole man and of every man, towards a betterment of the human situation in all its aspects, not merely in its socio-economic ones.[33]

Other things being equal, the sacramental grace of Communion and especially of daily Communion, provides the most powerful and most efficacious impetus towards an intelligent and generous work capable of saving whole peoples from famine, from ignorance, from misery, and from disease. In giving Himself to us, Christ, Victim for our salvation, makes us hear the distress call of men, a call which is an extension of His own. The Eucharistic Christ, who "is working still" (Jn. 5, 17), acts within the communicant in order that he may deploy "his activity as a loyal response to God's commandment, as a collaboration in His salvific work, and as a personal contribution to the fulfilment of His providential plan within human history . . . and that he may live this dedication as a synthesis of scientific technical and professional effort with the highest spiritual values."[34]

What more efficaciously than the receiving and eating (cf. Jn. 6, 54) of the Savior in Communion and especially in daily communion, could strengthen in mutual love the workers who are collaborating in the salvific action of God the Father (an action whose acme is the Mass) for the realization of His "providential plan within human history" (development and peace) through a synthesis of temporal activities and of spiritual values?

The Eucharist, whose matter is so dependent on man's work, presents Itself, therefore, in its sacramental grace and its efficaciousness, as the sacrament of productive work for the benefit of society. It is the visible sign which, mediately and indirectly, represents, demands, gives, effects, and conditions the work done through love of God and of men, in union with men and for their development. Let us dwell on this statement.

The Eucharist is *a representative sign of productive work.* The matter of the Eucharistic sacrifice represents a temporal production already effected today within the framework of the three sectors of the economy: agriculture gives the wheat and the grapes; industry gives the machinery for transforming these into bread and wine; the service industries see to their distribution. By its matter, the Eucharist is therefore the representative sign of work done for society. As Paul VI eloquently said: "When work is done in common, when hope, hardship, ambition, and joy are shared, it brings together and firmly unites the wills, minds, and hearts of men: in its accomplishment, men find themselves to be brothers."[35]

But the matter of the bread and of the wine also represents a nourishment sufficient to ward off death and to sustain life by conquering hunger—and consequently it represents a growth in the production, not of luxury goods, but of goods to meet basic human needs.

Furthermore, by the conditions for its reception, the Eucharist is *the sign of the recognition of the obligation to work.* As the sacrament of the intensification of fraternal love, the Eucharist received by the Christian imposes on him the duty to work, directly or indirectly, to ensure that his brethren get the earthly bread of mortal life.[36] "By this we know love, that he laid down his life for us; and we ought to lay down our lives for the brethren" (1 Jn. 3, 16). And surely one of the most beautiful ways of laying down one's life for one's brethern is to work in order to save them from death. By approaching the holy table, the communicant recognizes that this signifies the acceptance of an obligatory divine invitation to productive work for the benefit of society. "In the sweat of your face shall you eat bread" (Gen. 3, 19): not only the bread of mortal life, but also the Bread of Eternal Life. "Do not labor for the food which perishes but for the food which endures to eternal life" (Jn. 6, 27).

In the third place, the Eucharist is *the efficacious sign of efficacious work.* We know that every sacrament causes by signifying, and produces the grace which it signifies. But, beyond this, it also carries a mediate and indirect efficaciousness to which we have already alluded. The love whose growth is fostered by the Eucharist, is very specially exercised in the fulfilment of professional duty, this being one of the special purposes of this sacrament. By increasing mutual love—which is the source of renewed, ample, lasting, selfless, and efficacious efforts in the socio-economic domain—the Eucharist indirectly but really increases production and productivity.[37] Through this sacrament, the sacred Humanity of the Word-Creator "mediatizes" the growth of production, of which His divine Person, conjointly with the Father and Their Spirit, is the First Cause. Through the Eucharist, the statement of Jesus takes on today a new meaning in the temporal order: "My Father is working still, and I am working" through the Christians who abide in me thanks to Communion (cf. Jn. 5, 17; 6, 56). It is Christ Himself who, through the "Eucharistized" workers continues His work of completing the Creation and the Redemption.[38]

Finally, conditioned by human labor, the Eucharist is *the sign which conditions*, not just the work of man, but *a certain splendor, fullness, and blossoming of human labor.* Without a rich Eucharistic life, without (where possible) daily Communion, many Christians would not have the moral and spiritual strength, the necessary love, to develop their "technical and scientific skills," their professional aptitudes, or to invest their money in enterprises which yield less but are more useful to society. Now, all this conditions socio-economic development, which is an integral part of man's whole development. Love drawn from the Eucharist is the bond of perfection (Col. 3, 14); it ensures the inter-relationship of virtues, governs and transfigures the acts of the acquired and infused moral virtues by subordinating them to the Final End, and it thus becomes the basis and the root of social justice itself, the "mother" of that public-spirited generosity which leads a man to invest in useful enterprises promoting human development rather than in more lucrative but less useful ones.[39]

In certain respects, but not necessarily in all, the communicant, and especially the daily communicant, will find that he can understand more clearly and implement more readily the idea of John XXIII: "Increase in production and productive efficiency is sound policy, and indeed a vital necessity."[40] But, within the same limits, he is also more apt than are many others to direct production towards the service of man. "Economic development must be kept under the control of mankind."[41]

In the divine plan, the Eucharist is therefore the sacrament of work done with a view to the general good of the whole world and the development of each and every person.[42]

No one would question the grandeur of such a vision; but several difficulties may suggest themselves.

In the first place, is not the growth of production and of socio-economic development a comparatively recent phenomenon, post-dating the institution of the Eucharist by some seventeen or eighteen centuries? And did it not occur predominantly in the Protestant countries, where the majority of the population had for long rejected the Catholic doctrine concerning the mode and the efficaciousness (*ex opere operato*) of the Real Presence of Christ in the Eucharist?

This objection carries little weight. We are making no claim whatever that the Eucharistic life is the direct and immediate cause of productivity, but rather of the supernatural dynamism which causes a man to do his work in a more efficacious way. The inequality of God's natural gifts—geographical conditions, climate, natural resources, intelligence, culture—is sufficient to explain certain time lags in the emergence of an industrial civilization or its slower development in various countries.[43] It is only with the qualification, "other things being equal," that we have claimed a special situation, in the economic domain, for the communicant. Just as the providential plan makes the existence of the Eucharist dependent on the availability of bread and wine, so too this plan may make the fullness of its indirect efficaciousness in economic and social matters depend on the simultaneous presence of various factors of which God is as much the Creator as He is of the bread and the wine.

Furthermore, we in no way deny that the Calvinist or Lutheran Protestant, when he takes part in the Lord's Supper as celebrated in his church and contemplates the sacrifice of Christ which it commemorates, can gain on this occasion greater sacrificial love for God and men, and a greater determination to work for them. Vatican II teaches that, while "the lack of the sacrament of orders" means that such Protestant celebrations "have not preserved the genuine and total reality of the Eucharistic mystery, nevertheless, when they commemorate the Lord's death and resurrection in the Holy Supper, they profess that it signifies life in communion with Christ and they await His coming in glory."[44]

Let us also recall, with Vatican II, that "the Spirit of Christ has not refrained from using these separated Christian Churches as means of salvation which derive their efficacy from the very fullness of grace and truth entrusted to the Catholic Church."[45] From this text, we can conclude that the social value of the Lord's Supper as celebrated in the "reformed" Churches, was itself due, in a sense, to the Eucharist as celebrated in the Catholic Church—to the Eucharist which is Christ full of grace and truth, Christ the fullness of Revelation, Christ the mediator and the preeminent means of salvation.

At a deeper level, in every age of history, the supernatural generosity active in the progress of successive civilizations, and notably of the industrial civilization, derived secretly from the Cross of Christ. And even as regards progress after the Pasch of the Lord, this generosity was welling up from a renewal of the sacrificial Lord's Supper, without which the Cross would remain "a sealed spring," and was serving to illuminate and to strengthen, even in their secular preoccupations, those who were notionally rejecting the Eucharistic Sacrifice with which, through their good faith, they were unconsciously united to the point of being integrated with it. Is not the Mass, in effect, the sacrament of the sacrifice of all mankind,[46] at least of all those who are willing, however implicitly, to insert themselves in the Pasch of Christ?[47]

Finally, the Eucharist is the sacrament of man's work as a member of society, inasmuch as both presuppose the medium of human language. Man cannot transform nature by his work if he does not speak and if he does not use his language to transfigure while taming nature.[48] This itself already leads us to grasp the fact that without the truly human-divine words of the Eucharistic consecration, the sacrificial transubstantiation of the bread and the wine into the body and blood of the Redeemer of the universe could not occur. Without these words, the significative function of the consecrated species would not even be perceived. The human, but not purely human, language, which utters the words: "This is my body . . . This is my blood" (Mk. 14, 22-24), has a formal and decisive value for the constitution of the sacramental sign.[49] The Eucharist brings together the language of work and the work of language.[50]

But the Christian's use of the sacramental sign does not dispense from further verbal and real mediations in order that it may be fully significative in the eyes of others, whether Christians or otherwise. If such people are to perceive that I am offering myself as a victim, in union with Christ, for the whole Church and for all mankind, when I receive Holy Communion, they need not only to know that I am "devouring" (to use the original meaning of the verb "trôgô," occurring four times in John 6, 54-59) the flesh of the Savior, the bread consecrated by the words: "This is my body which is for you" (1 Cor. 11, 24), but they also need to view my oblation through a way of life whose ultimate meaning, for them, is determined by the word of Christ heard through mine. To grasp what I am doing when I receive the consecrated bread, the bread of unity, they need to see me sharing with others whatever I possess.

C. *The Eucharist sacrament of the just distribution or redistribution of the goods of the earth.*

It is not without a very profound reason that the Church, from her very beginnings, has called the Mass "the Breaking of the (consecrated) Bread" (1 Cor. 10, 16; 11, 23; Acts, 2, 42), a designation still current in the twelfth century. To focus the relevance of this designation in the socio-economic context of our own era, and to appreciate how good it would be to bring it back into currency, let us remind ourselves of an obligation laid down by the social doctrine of the Church.

Having pointed out that "the public conscience has been affected in recent years by the urgent needs of supporting the economic development and social progress of those countries which are still struggling against poverty and economic disabilities", Pope John XXIII goes on to say: "However, it is no less necessary—and justice itself demands—that the riches produced be evenly distributed among all members of the political community. This means that everything must be done to ensure that social progress keeps pace with economic progress."[51]

It is very true that increased production and just distribution condition one another: the producers of the national and world revenue will no longer even wish to produce if they are denied an increasing share in that revenue. Without such a share, how could they consume more? And would not a production without a corresponding consumption by the masses, tumble into that pernicious void which creates crises and wars?

The era of development presupposes, therefore, a redistribution of the national and world revenue, a redistribution admirably symbolized and indirectly caused by the breaking of the Eucharistic bread, the efficacious sign of the breaking of earthly bread and of the goods of the earth. The intensity of the Eucharistic life will bring economic progress and social progress into the same rhythm of linked development.

One after another, the inspired writers of the New Testament, Paul, Luke, and John, show us how Christ and His disciples have always understood that the communion of the faithful in the eating of the Eucharist goes hand in hand with certain earthly and visible presuppositions and consequences as regards the possession, use, and sharing of the goods of the earth. In the light of this Biblical tradition, let us see how the Eucharist offers us the basis for the demands and counsels uttered by the Church in regard to social justice. We shall take these texts in their historical order.

Let us recall some facts. Before the Breaking of the Eucharistic Bread, the early Christians used to celebrate together the "agapè"—i.e. a meal designed to manifest and to strengthen the bonds of love among the members of the same ecclesial community, a small group lost in the immensity of the pagan masses. While it was not a sacrificial meal,[25] the agapè modeled itself on that of the Last Supper, which had preceded the institution and the celebration of the Eucharistic Sacrifice. Here are the Apostle's words:

"When you meet together (in the same place),[53] it is not the Lord's Supper that you eat. For in eating, each one goes ahead with his own meal, and one is hungry and another is drunk. What! Do you not have houses to eat and drink in? Or do you despise the church of God and humiliate those who have nothing?"

After having described the institution of the Eucharist and dealt with the diseases and deaths occasioned by the receiving of Communion "in an unworthy manner,"[54] Paul adds:

"So then, my brethren, when you come together to eat, wait for one another—and if any be hungry, let him eat at home—lest you come together to be condemned" (1 Cor. 11, 20-34).

In this text, Paul makes the following points: "We have here (1) a general right to eat before attending the assembly; (2) a general obligation at the assembly to be in a fit condition to celebrate the Lord's Supper; (3) an admonition to await the arrival of the others before eating one's own supper;

(4) a noting of the impossibility, if the above admonition is ignored, for these other members of the community to take part in the meal, since they have nothing to eat; (5) a concession made to the hungry about eating some food before leaving home. Through the implementing of these points, the Christian assembly will become again the Lord's Supper, when, each one having brought his or her supper and all having arrived, care is taken to ensure that none of the brethren is without food."[55]

This summary usefully emphasizes what was a central concern of Paul in his First Epistle to the Corinthians: namely, to contrast the affluence of the rich with the penury of the poor. The first humiliate the second. The whole community of the faithful, as Saint John Chrysostom comments, are slighted if the rich set themselves apart in order to hold their own private meals in the sight of all, in the sight of the poor who regard themselves as unworthy of being invited. All make themselves unworthy to celebrate the holy mysteries which should follow the agapè, because they have all sinned against charity—the rich by sating themselves to the detriment of their brethren, the poor through envy and anger.[56]

Twenty centries have passed; by and large, the agapè is a thing of the past. But the Eucharistic Communion continues and should be a sacrificial feast of fraternal love. Who will deny, however, that certain communicants are really hungry—i.e. do not receive a proper wage or salary, while others, affluent in money and resources, "humiliate" their brethren who have nothing, and thus despise the whole Church at the very moment when they themselves are receiving the sacrament of her unity? (Is not this the exact opposite of what Jesus recommended in the parable concerning the choice of guests for the banquet: cf. Lk. 14, 12-14)

This is the lesson which Paul gives to the Christians of Corinth and to all Christians: the communicant who does not recognize Christ in his poor co-communicant, does not really "discern" the Body of the Lord, the Bread of unity and of love, from ordinary bread; he therefore communicates unworthily and is therefore "guilty of profaning the body and blood of the Lord," by leaving his Eucharistic brother a prey to hunger and thirst for the bread and wine of the world. The lesson becomes even clearer when placed in the context of some verses from the previous chapter of this epistle: "The bread which we break, is it not a participation in the body of Christ? Because there is one bread, we who are many are one body, for we all partake of the one bread" (1 Cor. 10, 16-17). In this text ("ton arton hôn *klômen*, ouki *koinônia* tou somatos tou Xristou"), the Eucharistic communion in the Body of the Risen Lord is presented as a shared *breaking* of the consecrated Bread ("klômen") and is designated by the same word ("koinônia") which Saint Paul uses for the sharing of earthly possessions and of the bread of this world among the guests at this sacred table of the word and of the Body of Christ.[57] In effect, shortly before this, Paul had written to the Romans (15, 26-27): "For Macedonia and Achaia have been pleased to make some contribution (koinônian poièsastai) for the poor among the saints at Jerusalem . . . for, if the Gentiles have come to share in their spiritual blessings, they ought also to be of (sacred) service to them in material blessings."[58] A few years later, Paul wrote to the Corinthians about the same collection: "(The poor of Jerusalem) give glory to God for your sympathetic generosity to them and to all" (2 Cor. 9, 13—Jerusalem Bible).

The profound and permanent meaning of the Pauline idea emerges clearly, therefore. If the Mass was called, right up to the twelfth century, "the Breaking of the Bread," and if the rite thus named was kept up throughout this whole period, we twentieth-century Christians should understand that, as brethren "seated at the same heavenly table in order to receive the immortal remedy in the breaking of the one bread",[59] and not just seated side by side solitarily eating similar but diverse bread, we should also break and share among ourselves the same earthly bread which we make together, thus realizing a total and authentic communion—spiritual and temporal, but always incarnated in the one and universal ecclesial communion. To break the Bread of Heaven and refuse to break the bread of earth, would be a sacrilegious absurdity. If the Communion is not total, it is no longer adoration; it is a crucifying again of the Body of Christ (cf. 1 Cor. 11, 27 and Heb. 6, 6; 10, 27).

The same theme of total communion was clearly implied by Paul's disciple, Luke, in his description of that church of Jerusalem which his master was actively assisting. "And they devoted themselves to the apostles' teaching and fellowship, to the breaking of bread (*tè koinônia, tè klasei*: grammatically, the latter phrase seems to be in apposition to the former, to 'fellowship,' to the *koinônia*) and to the prayers. . . . And all who believed were together and had all things in common; and they sold their possessions and goods and distributed them to all, as any had need" (Acts, 2, 42-46). The phrase "had all things in common" translates the Greek "apanta koina": the latter's kinship with the word "koinonia" is obvious.

From this passage, we can deduce that Luke intended to teach that the Eucharistic Communion is, by its very nature, a breaking of the one Bread and signifies a further communion of redistribution in the use of temporal things. A little later in Acts, Luke implies a clear preference of the Jerusalem Christian community for collective ownership, as distinct from private ownership, when there was no longer question of things for lasting and personal usage (such as one's house): "Now the company of those who believed were of one heart and soul, and no one said that any of the things which he possessed was *his own*, but they had everything in *common* (*idion*, *koina*, in Greek). . . . There was not a needy person among them, for as many as were possessors of land or houses sold them, and brought the proceeds of what was sold and laid them at the apostles' feet; and distribution was made to each as any had need" (Acts 4, 32-35).

We know, of course, that with Luke the word "all" (*pas*, *apas*) "does not carry its strictly literal meaning, but signifies the majority of people or the major part of a thing."[60] And we also see from the context (Acts 4, 36-37; 5, 4; 12, 12; 21,

16; Jas. 2, 1-9; 5, 1-5) that many of the Christians of Jerusalem had kept their personal possessions and houses. This does not hinder our grasping the point that Luke is seeking to emphasize: the mutual love and concord of the "cor unum," the "unanimity" (cf. Phil. 2, 2 and 2, 20) of the "anima una," rooted in the *koinônia* of the Breaking of Bread, was mirrored in the language (exclusion of *mine* in favor of *ours*) and in the ready sharing of possessions regarded not so much as *his* or *her* but as at the general disposal of all.[61]

It has become a commonplace objection that the situation described by Luke is a formula for economic bankruptcy. In relation to the early Church, this statement is an oversimplification. In reality, from the outset, the majority of its members shared a common poverty, whose later aggravation, generously mitigated by the collections made in the Pauline churches, was predominantly the result of Jewish persecutions and social injustices inflicted by the rich who, for the most part, did not belong to the Church. This point has been well established by Father Allo.[62]

There are solid reasons, therefore, for regarding as rooted in the word of God and in the public Revelation of the New Testament, the following statements which link the Eucharistic doctrine with the social doctrines of the Church. The special sacramental grace of the Eucharist renders efficacious and demands "the right of every man to use material goods for his own sustenance — a right which is prior to every other economic right, even that of private property . . . (which latter) is also admittedly a natural one."[63] In other words, the sacramental grace of the Bread of eternal Life efficaciously guarantees respect for the priority of the natural right to temporal life over the right to private property. In the second place, this sacramental grace does not impose, but makes it an obligation to regard as possible and desirable, the modifying of 'the wage-contract by applying to it elements taken from the contract of partnership, so that wage-earners and other employees participate in the ownership or the management, or in some way share in the profits."[64]

The example of the Christian community of Jerusalem was divinely inspired and designed for the edification of the pilgrim Church throughout her journey through human history. It still helps us to understand how the sacramental grace of the Eucharist elevates, rectifies, ennobles, and supernaturalizes the social life of man, the development of which is "at one an effect and a cause of the growing intervention of the State . . . and also the result and the expression of a natural, wellnigh irresistible urge in man to combine with his fellows for the attainment of aims and objectives which are beyond the means or the capabilities of single individuals."[65] Was not precisely the same direction taken by the experiment of the early Christians as co-owners of a common fund which made it possible to help the poor of the community? And have we not here an encouragement, eloquent even if indirect, offered to modern "cooperative enterprises" which John XXIII says should be safeguarded and encouraged.[66]

All natural right to the use of my possessions takes precedence over my ownership right in their regard. My possessions are yours as to their use. To me you are much more than a paid employee; you are my associate, my companion — just as to you I am your employer, but even more so your associate. Consequently, we shall join forces as associates in the property and the profits which are the fruits of our work together.

As co-guests united in body and blood in and through the Body and Blood of our Savior, we are co-owners — not only privately, but publicly too — of the domains of the State and even of the whole world: all is ours, because we are Christ's and Christ is God's (cf. 1 Cor. 3, 22-23); and is not God the supreme Owner to whom we as mere administrators must render an account? Receiving together this Owner and this supreme Gift in the Eucharist, each of us is less tempted to think that he has any right to exclusively private ownership of anything, and more inclined to allow the other to share the personal ownership of his possessions, as well as to recognize that what is at once *yours* and *everyone's* is still also, in a certain sense, *mine*. This is because, in the final analysis, I am yours and you are mine, in the Body and the Blood of Him who died 'to gather us into one (cf. Jn. 11, 52; 17. 23). Cannot I say to you, as He did to His Father: All I have is yours and all you have is mine" (Jn. 17, 10—Jerusalem Bible). Since neither of us has anything for his own exclusive use, we have all things in common (cf. 11 Cor. 6, 10), because together we have Christ who is not divided (cf. 1 Cor. 1, 13), but neither of us has exclusive possession of Him.

It thus becomes clear that the fervor itself of the Eucharistic life orientates the communicants towards various forms of collective ownership — forms whose nature places them between individual private property and public ownership.[67]

D. *The Eucharist, historic sacrament of the eschatological socialization.*

Jesus Christ, our paschal Lamb, our Good Shepherd, celebrated for the last time the agro-pastoral rite of the old economy at the very moment when He was instituting the new Pasch of the new economy, for the salvation of all the sheep of His flock and in order to merit for them the good works which are themselves meritorious of eternal life.

As the matter of the new Sacrifice, He used the fruits of an agriculture which His ancestors had learned from the Canaanites. The Israelites, in obedience to a divine command, had integrated these fruits into their cultus.

Today — the period of the public Revelation having been definitively completed — it might at first sight seem that the Church can no longer substantially adapt the cultus of the new and eternal Covenant by creating rites which would correspond to the secondary sectors (industrial) and the tertiary sectors (services) of modern civilization, in somewhat the same way as the Church of the old economy integrated in its cultus the elements of the pastoral and nomadic civilization of the Arabs and, later on, those of the agrarian civilization of the Canaanites. Automation could raise an analogous problem.

It is true that the Church can change in no way the substance of the sacraments instituted by Christ, or even the materiality of the rites which owe their origin to Him.[68] But she has created the sacramentals of the industrial era and she can create yet more[69] and insert them in a palpable way into the Mass or into other ceremonies.

It was in this direction that Pius XII wanted to direct our thoughts when he wrote in 1953:

"Technical progress comes from God; therefore it can and should lead to God. . . . The believer will include the works of modern technology among the motives for praise of God as proclaimed by the Angels of Bethlehem: 'Glory to God in the highest' (Lk. 2, 14). Side by side with the gold, frankincense, and myrrh offered by the Magi to the Infant-God, he will very naturally place the achievements of modern technology. . . . It is as though one presented to God the work which He Himself commanded: Fill the earth and subdue it (Gn. 1, 28)."[70]

No doubt, the creative imagination of the revisers of the liturgy will show itself to be fruitful in this domain. In the twentieth century, the Paschal mystery should convey, as palpably and visibly as possible, the industrial and technical civilization of our age to the Father, by recapitulating it in Christ Jesus.

On deeper reflection, however, it becomes evident that in reality this industrial and technical civilization, and even its tertiary sector, are already integrated in the preparation of the fixed Paschal rite of the new and eternal Covenant. In effect, the agricultural production of the bread and wine is already industrialized by the use of machinery, and the distribution of the matter of the Eucharistic sacrifice is inseparable from the complex system of the services of a socialized economy. In the world at large, the "Eucharistic species" result from the integrated efforts of the three sectors of production constituting "a single world economy" of which the national economies are 'integral parts."[71] Each Mass presupposes, offers, "consecrates,"[72] and aims to save by divinizing, the unified work of all mankind. In every Mass is renewed the recapitulation, temporal and historical, of all the sacrifices of mankind, united, unknown to themselves, with the Sacrifice of Jesus and with the agrarian or pastoral rites which leave their mark, verbal or real, on the supreme and definitive rite instituted by the sovereign Priest at the Last Supper.

A present recapitulation of the past history of mankind, the Eucharist is also, in its totality, an anticipation of and a yearning towards the future consummation of that history. It is the Bread for the journey, the Food of the pilgrims of eternity, the Viaticum which draws us towards the perfect eschatological communion of the Kingdom, in the new earth — our earth renewed by the Parousia of the Mediator (cf. Rev. 21, 1). In the mystery of the Eucharistic transubstantiation, we have the commencement and the pledge of the disappearance of the old world and the renewal of the universe (cf. Rev. 21, 1; 21, 4-5), of the perfect descent of the heavenly Jerusalem, "the dwelling of God with men," of a God who "will wipe away every tear from their eyes," and through whom "death shall be no more, neither shall there be mourning nor crying nor pain any more" — for "the former things" will pass away with the substance of the bread and of the wine (cf. Rev. 21, 3-4). Through the Eucharist, the world anticipates its own consummation and already begins to dry the tears still occasioned by the disorders inherent in the widespread use of "the former things" (Rev. 21, 4; cf. 1 Cor. 7, 28; Lk. 14, 18-20; Gen. 3, 17).

Thanks to the Eucharist of the pilgrimage, there will no longer be, in the transfigured cosmos of the new earth, production or consumption of perishable things, or discoursive dialog, or exclusively personal property, or even the sacramental Eucharist; all will enjoy forever, in a single act of intelligence and will, the indefectible fruit of the works they have accomplished in a state of grace and under the irradiation of the sacramental grace of the Eucharist.

The *koinônia* of passing things and of contrite hearts — a *koinônia* begun in this first and transitory world by the Breaking of the consecrated Bread — will reach its perfection in the renewed world. Together, all will possess, in a perfect communion, all natural and supernatural goods; all will possess one another in the total respect and the complete transparence of oblative love. Jesus said: "The righteous will shine like the sun in the kingdom of their Father" (Mt. 13, 43) — in other words, each of them, according to his degree of supernatural charity, will be an illuminating and burning sun of love in relation to innumerable other living, intelligent, singing, loved, and loving suns.[73]

In the light of this eschatological inter-communion, earthly participation in the Eucharist shows the transitory and perishable character of property and of work, and inevitably involves a twofold engagement: to fight against every form of the exploitation of man by man, whether communist or socialist, capitalist or liberal; and to fight for all the legitimate forms of socialization in co-responsibility.[74]

By the mere fact that he goes to the table of the sacrificial feast, the communicant says in effect to the others who have been invited: "I love you even unto death. I will give my life, and how much more therefore my temporal goods, for your eternal salvation (cf. 1 Jn. 3, 16-17). We are one body in Christ, and individual members one of another (Rm. 12, 5). Let us speak together, then, before we take decisions together, that these may be co-decisions. Let us work together to alleviate the hunger of the world. Let us make a better distribution of our possessions and our incomes. Let us join together. Together let us be co-owners, when this does not injure the intimacy of our own homes".[75]

Although the Eucharistic Communion does not immediately and wholly suppress the inequitable distribution of goods, or banish hunger and the various injustices of human existence, it is completely directed towards that result and will secure it at the moment when the sacramental species disappear. Meantime, it is through Communion, above all through daily Communion, that God wills to give to twentieth-century Christians the great benefit of a free, liberating, and personalizing socialization, for the good of all mankind. Through the daily gift of Himself to the builders of the earthly city, Christ wills to be, more and more, the common Good of the Church [76] and of humanity.

"Let us rejoice and exult and give him the glory, for the marriage of the Lamb has come. . . . Blessed are those who are invited to the marriage supper of the Lamb" (Rev. 19, 7 and 9). Blessed are the priests and the Christians who — in the light of the Bible and of the social encyclicals as directed on situations local, national, and worldwide — suffuse the socio-economic life of mankind with the sacramental grace of the Eucharist, our daily and "supersubstantial" Bread (cf. Mt. 7, 11) with a view to the development of every man and of all men.

E. *Conclusions: The Eucharist, source of earnest actions for the peace and development of the world.*

Paul VI ended his encyclical of Easter, 1967, with this question, or rather this ardent invitation: "For, if the new name for peace is development, who would not wish to labor for it with all his powers?"[77]

We have attempted to show how the whole sacramental life of the Church constitutes a magnificent and powerful contribution to the total development of all mankind. This is especially true of the Eucharistic mystery, the *raison d'être* of the whole sacramental economy. The Eucharistic Christ who gives Himself to Christians in Communion is, through them, the great architect of peace.

If peace, according to Saint Augustine, is the conciliation of wills in their earthly activities with a view to improving human life,[78] it is also, according to the Angelic Doctor, an act proper to that love whose efficacious sign and center is the Eucharist.[79]

Christ, present and active in the Eucharist, is therefore the foundation, not only of social life in general, but, very specially, of the world peace of which He is the source, the supreme agent, the final goal. To receive Holy Communion is both to become a single victim with Jesus our Peace (Eph. 2, 14) for the peace of the world, and to dispose oneself to act more efficaciously, in Him and through Him, with a view to bringing peace to hearts and minds, and even to transforming human institutions at the local, national, and world levels. The communicant cannot but share in the action of Christ ("for he is our peace, who has made us both one": Eph. 2, 14), for He "came and preached peace" (Eph. 2, 17) to those who are far off and to those who are near. All activity, humble and selfless, for the development and the peace of the world, finds its stimulus and its lever in the Eucharistic life.

To ask today for "our daily bread," the bread of earth and the Bread of Heaven, is necessarily to ask for the peace which is conditioned by both and which conditions the first. It is to seek the strength to work for development and peace, to act individually and collectively for peace, with the knowledge that each and every one of us will be judged by God on his efforts to promote social and world peace in favor of human development.

"The arrival of the atom bomb is the coming to mankind of an awareness of death, the growth of concrete humanity to its adult stature. Mankind finds itself in a sense compelled to reach the age of reason or to perish."[80]

But what must mankind do to reach the age of reason? What, especially, are the courses of action open to Christians, and to men of good will of whatever religious horizons? How can they fight against the closely linked threats of war and of underdevelopment?

They can join together in order to spread genuine facts as distinct from official ones. Such association would provide the necessary mediation for individual consciences; without association of alerted consciences, many others would remain dormant.[81]

They can give "form, consistency, and strength" — in the measure to which this is dependent on them — to the institutions of the world community";[82] for they know the vainness of the balance of terror and the insufficiency of the juridical institutions whose directors might not be animated by a constantly renewed spirit of humble devotion to the common good of the world, but they also know that this spirit must be incarnated in institutions, without which it would remain impractical and ineffacious.

Everywhere, they can and should take their place in the vanguard of concrete and progressive initiatives in favor of disarmament, in measures to promote the placing of atomic weapons under international control, and then controlled atomic disarmament through the submission of modern arms to an international institution of world security.[83]

What a vast field of action and generous aspirations, impregnated with true — because complete — realism, does not this offer to technicians, soldiers, diplomats, and politicians worthy of the name!

But, it may be objected, all these modes of action are beyond the reach of the average Christian and the ordinary man. Certainly, if we meant that such people could exercise an immediate influence in this domain. However, cannot they promote all these objectives within the framework of the national (political, trade union, cultural) organizations of which they are members, and through these organizations support international campaigns against hunger, ignorance, racism,[84] or campaigns aimed at the structural reform of existent international organizations? Is not action at local or national level a necessary mediation for universal action?

In the final analysis, the ordinary man, the ordinary Christian, is a decisive element through local bodies for the formation and the development of world public opinion, whose influence on the natural States is incalculable.

It is through him that concrete reality could still be given to the suggestion put forward by Paul VI in Bombay on 4 December 1964, and later developed in his encyclical, *Populorum Progressio:*

'At Bombay we called for the establishment of a great World Fund, to be made up of part of the money spent on arms, to relieve the most destitute of this world. What is true of the immediate struggle against want, holds good also when there is question of development. Only world-wide collaboration, of which a common fund would be both means and symbol, will succeed in overcoming vain rivalries and in establishing a fruitful and peaceful exchange between peoples."[85]

The indispensable use of all these concrete means by all men of good will, will be facilitated in the measure to which Christians, stimulated by the sacramental grace of the Eucharist, sacrament of interpersonal and world peace and reconciliation, become the first to use them, and involve others by their example.

Such activity for peace and development would contribute to the temporal and even eternal salvation of the work of mankind. The work of the inhuman man who rejects at once and deliberately the selfless effort for peace and for development, the grace of Christ, and supernatural charity, remains eternally barren, since it produces no fruit of glory and does not merit the vision of the eternal and triune Worker. Since it is of this world, such work withers, even before it is thrown into the inextinguishable fire (cf. Jn. 15, 6).

But Christ came into the world to save, not souls only, but bodies too, and therefore the works, even the temporal works, of men, His brethren. Christ is the Savior of human work because He snatches the activity of men from the dominion of Satan and makes it anew supernaturally fruitful.

The exhortations of John XXIII apply even to the ill-paid work or work done with outmoded tools by workers of the under-developed countries, provided it is also done with proper care and the required supernatural intention:

"We most earnestly beg all our sons the world over, clergy and laity, to be deeply conscious of the dignity, the nobility, which is theirs through being grafted on to Christ as shoots on a vine: 'I am the vine; you are the branches" (Jn. 15, 5). They are thus called to a share in His own divine life; and since they are united in mind and spirit with the divine Redeemer even when they are engaged in the affairs of the world, their work becomes a continuation of His work, penetrated with redemptive power. 'He that abides in me, and I in him, the same bears much fruit' (*ibid.*). Thus is man's work exalted and ennobled — so highly exalted that it leads to his own personal perfection of soul, and helps to extend to others the fruits of Redemption all over the world. It becomes a means whereby the Christian way of life can leaven this civilization in which we live and work — leaven it with the ferment of the Gospel."[86]

In other words, the Redeemer has not diminished the innumerable worker-victims of the "inhuman conditions" linked with underdevelopment, to being merely objects of His redemptive work. He associates them with Himself, as much as they themselves desire, as subjects of the co-redemptive (and not merely redeemed) history of the human race. In a sense very different from what Marx had in mind, it is thanks to Christ and in Christ that Christian workers, through the intimate offering up of their exterior works in union with the Eucharistic mystery, become more and more the Messianic people,[87] the collective Messiah, incorporated with the personal Messiah and, through Him, saving the developed and rich nations by meriting for them the poverty of spirit which conditions the temporal salvation of the Third World.

Only that work remains alienated which is not offered up and which is not integrated, implicitly or explicitly, in the Eucharistic mystery. In contrast, by offering up the consecrated Bread to the Father in the Spirit, the Messianic people incorporated with the Son are seeking, through Him, the "daily bread" for the human masses — i.e., the strength to work and to help others to work for the industrialization,[88] for the development, and for the peace of the world. "The new name for peace is development."

It is within the framework of this Eucharist-industrialization synthesis that, in the modern Church, the redemption of work and the work of Redemption are renewed. Thus is verified, and will continue increasingly to be verified, what John XXIII so pointedly said: "Christianity links earth and heaven."[89]

Nevertheless, the peace and development fostered by the Christian, filled with love for all mankind through the flesh and the blood of the Son of man, remain uncertain, fragile, and ephemeral, just as was the mortal life formerly assumed by Christ Himself.

The value of Saint Augustine's emphasis[90] on the mortal character of the life and of the nature of men who work for the imperfect peace of the earthly city, has been to remind us that such peace can only be a foretaste of the perfect peace of which the body of the Risen Lord is the immortal pledge.

The supreme act of man as raised to the supernatural order is not the transformation of nature, or its industrialization, or the pacification of society, or even the reflexive knowledge of his own spiritual and immortal freedom. It is an act which exceeds all his natural powers, an act received from Him who is its immediate, immanent, and transcendent Object, the passive act of the beatifying vision of the Revealer finally unveiled, the loving intuition of His eternal generation as Son and as Word of the Father, and of Their common and active breathing of the Spirit of Love.

This free gift is at once the ineffable reward and the conquest of him who, divinized by the grace of the Eucharist, received if possible daily,[91] has humanized nature and man himself through his work and through his action for peace. Man is inseparably a socio-political animal and a religious animal, destined to the enjoyment of the uncreated society of the divine Persons, through the conquest of the cosmos by an external work united to the immanent work of faith (cf. Jn. 6, 29) — the "creation" of human society and the building up of the Church (Eph. 4, 16).[92]

Through work, through socialization and through the sacramental life, which perfects the creation, man is brought more and more into relation with the Absolute. Through them, he constantly grows in dependence upon the uncreated Being, and in independence as regards each of the other creatures. Through them, he merits with increasing intensity eternal repose in the contemplation of the supreme "production": not that of the universe grown from nothing, "ex nihilo," but the immanent speech of the uncreated Word in Whom God expresses to Himself the knowledge He has of His eternal Goodness and of the goodness of all the creatures that share in that Goodness, the generation of the Son, not from nothing but from Himself, and the uncreated breathing of the Spirit of Love in whom Father and Son embrace one another in a common love of their common lovability and of the lovability of the world.[93]

Just as the intimate processions of the divine Persons constitute the *raison d'être* of the "external procession" which is the creation, so too is the face-to-face and loving contemplation of the uncreated production of the divine Persons of the Son and of the Spirit the ultimate *raison d'être* of the sacramental life, as well as of the created production, through human labor, of the earthly cities orientated towards their own unifying completion in one sole universal City.[94]

F. *Appendix: Collective private property and the irradiation of the Eucharist.*

The sacramental grace of the Eucharist has the effect of promoting usage-in-common and even common ownership of the goods of this world, at the same time as it respects, through love of the human person, the right to personal ownership, including ownership of the means of production.

In order to appreciate how Eucharistic charity orientates towards collective private ownership, let us consider the historic antecedents to the current ideas of the Church on this subject.

Aristotle, reacting against Plato's exclusive preferences for collective ownership, recommended private ownership both individual and collective.

It is useful to recall the Aristotelian doctrine of "koinônia" and its consequences as regards ownership, in order to secure a better understanding of the New Testament vision of the same "koinônia." In Aristotle's view, "koinônia" of ideas, of sentiments, and of ideals is the fruit of a selfless and mutual friendship of benevolence; but it is also accompanied by an active "koinônia" which seeks to promote the common good through action in common. Aristotle does not rule out that the united groups could be owners, together.[95]

This was precisely the situation with the fishermen of Galilee. Peter and John were "koinônoi" (Lk. 5, 10). As Daniel-Rops points out,[96] the fishermen had to form crews in order to acquire the necessary boats and nets, as well as to fish effectively. The crews were generally six or eight men under a "skipper," such as Simon Peter or Zebedee. They also united in order to share out the benefit of their catches (cf. Lk. 5, 7: metokhoi: sharers), and perhaps even to form "real co-operatives" for sales purposes. It may well be, therefore, that the socio-economic pattern of the professional life of some of the Apostles served in some way to determine the pattern of collective ownership in the Church of Jerusalem, and the communion which reigned there at every level among the first Christians.

In this community, however, private ownership was not suppressed. On the contrary, the heresy of the Apostolic Brethren in the third century, by simultaneously condemning marriage and private ownership, showed the concrete link between these two institutions. Family life, and consequently the common good, demands a minimum of personal private property.[97]

In the *Summa Theologica*, Saint Thomas Aquinas strikes a balance between private and collective ownership — a fact which certain commentators appear to have missed.

On the one hand, he lists the disadvantages of collective ownership, especially of the undivided kind,[98] by comparison with individual ownership; on the other hand, following an inspiration no longer Aristotelian but Biblical, he emphasizes the measures which the Old Alliance provided against the concentration of economic power and property in the hands of a few, to the detriment of the many: equal division of the land among all, temporary alienation with periodical redistribution within the framework of a jubilee year more ideal than historically observed.[99] The Angelic Doctor thus shows that, in his view, not only collective ownership, but also the individual ownership necessary, not for all, but for heads of families,[100] are open to abuses.

Shortly after the death of Saint Thomas Aquinas, the Church condemned as heretical the proposition of certain medieval Franciscans denying that Christ and His Apostles were owners, either individually or collectively.[101] In conformity with the Gospel, therefore, the Church presents Christ as a poor owner, in the service of the poor (cf. Jn. 12,

6; 13, 29), and as a preacher living on the alms which He distributed (cf. Lk. 8, 3; Jn. 13, 29).

Today, the same Church teaches that individual private property is in greater conformity with the natural law when it concerns domestic possessions: "among all the goods which can be objects of individual private ownership, none is in greater conformity with nature than the ground-plot or the house where the family lives and from which, wholly or in part, it derives its resources."[102] It emerges from this declaration of Pius XII that private possession of other goods is less in conformity with the demands of the natural law. This familial horizon of private ownership includes, according to John XXIII, "tools and equipment (in the case of craftsmen and owners of family farms), and shares in medium and large business concerns," this being perfectly compatible with the rejection of "any possibility of the concentration of undue economic power" in the hands of a few people.[103]

The tendency to socialization, in the rich and complex sense in which John XXIII uses this word,[104] finds its application not only, or even especially, in the expansion of public ownership,[105] but also, as he explicitly says, in the diffusion of a private ownership physically undivided and collective, but juridically individual and private, of the means of production:

"The small and average-sized undertakings in agriculture, in the arts and crafts, in commerce and industry, should be safeguarded and fostered by granting them the benefits of the larger firms by means of co-operative unions; while in the larger concerns there should be the possibility of moderating the contract of work by one of partnership."

This extract [106] in *Mater et Magistra* is a passage from a radio message of Pius XII in 1944. It seems to indicate that, in the view of both popes, a contract of work which borrows some elements from the contract of partnership is the best means of avoiding "the concentration of undue economic power in the hands of a few,"[107] and also of securing "the widest possible distribution of private property in terms of durable consumer goods, houses, land, tools, and equipment, and shares in medium and large business concerns."[108]

It may even be said that the suggestions of Pius XII and of John XXIII, which apply also to agriculture, as explicitly mentioned, open the way to a partial solution of the problem of rural ownership in the many developing countries, such as those of Latin America: the "latifundios," of which Vatican II forsees the division, the expropriation (whenever the common good requires it) "which must be reckoned in equity after all the circumstances have been weighed,"[109] could, on the contrary, conserve their economic unity, and at the same time, when transformed into personal enterprises, belong juridically to a number of shareholders, their cultivators, co-owners with the original owner. The experiment has already been made.

To meet the abuse created by an ownership so private that it deprives others, there is no need to urge nationalization and public ownership as the only or even the special solution. A better course is to develop various forms of co-ownership, and to eliminate to the utmost the anonymity of shareholders. It is necessary to promote a certain type of collective, non-public ownership of a more human and controllable kind, of which cooperatives of production provide a model.[110]

Vatican II, moreover, points in the same direction with its recommendation that "it is very important to facilitate the access of both individuals and groups to some control over material goods." Does it not say that "private ownership or some other kind of dominion over material goods . . . constitutes a kind of prerequisite for civil liberties"?[111]

Between individuals and the State, there are intermediary groups whose concrete existence often conditions the effective exercise of personal freedom within the State. If individual private ownership constitutes an "indispensable zone of personal and familial antonomy,"[112] its exercise is in fact dependent on the real existence of groups exercising their right of private ownership in a collective way, at least in a very great number of cases. And one may well regard the sacramental grace of the Eucharist as directed towards the satisfaction of this personal and social necessity.

NOTES

[1] The Lutheran doctrine professes "consubstantiation," admitting the simultaneous real presence of the body of Christ and of the bread. In contrast, the doctrine of the Catholic Church (transubstantiation) holds that the substance of the bread disappears at the moment of consecration, to give place to the substance of the body of Christ.

[2] Cf. Saint Thomas Aquinas, ST, III. 79. 4; also cf. Gasque, "Rôle social de l'Eucharistie", *Eucharistia,* Paris, 1934, pp. 415-433.

[3] The Eucharist is normally a sacrament of the living, which must be received in the state of grace; it is only *per accidens* that it restores rather than increases sanctifying grace.

[4] Adjective used for the same reason as holds for the comment in note 3.

[5] PT, 73-74 and 145; cf. ST. I. II. 105. 1.

[6] MM, 92 (C.T.S. translation).

[7] PT, 44-45.

[8] John XXIII puts forth this idea very strongly: "Every man has, of his very nature, a need to express himself in his work and thereby to perfect his own being." Consequently, the economic system must not "compromise human dignity, lessen a man's sense of responsibility or rob him of any opportunity for exercising personal iniative" (MM 82-83: C.T.S. translation).

[9] MM, 205-206.

[10] The Eucharist, as a sacrament, is a sign, and therefore, in the broad sense, a language.

[11] ES, part 3, *passim.*

[12] MM, 23.

[13] MM, 219 (C.T.S. translation): GS, 63.

[14] Pius XII, Radio message of Christmas 1955, AAS, 48 (1956), 34. The human nature of Christ, it too, is "intrinsically social."

[15] Cf. A. Hamann O.F.M., DSAM, t. IV (1961), 1562-1563: art "Eucharistie."

[16] This is not to say that every "dialog" is "communion" in the sense of complete communion. But can real dialog exist without a certain initial communion?

[17] J. Hamer O.P., *L'Eglise est une communion,* Paris 1962, p. 178.

[18] In effect, the Eucharist carries at its fullest the dialog of Revelation between God and mankind, the latter answering in faith.

[19] Saint Bonaventure, IV Sent., dist 18, par. 2, art. 1, q. 1, contra 1. Cited by Hamer, *op cit.*, p 188.

[20] R. de Vaux O.P., *Institutions de l'A.T.,* Paris 1958, t. II, pp. 383-407, especially 389-390 and 394 (English translation: "Ancient Israel: Its Life and Institutions": translated by John McHugh: Dartmann, Longman and Todd: pp. 489-493).

[21] Cf. X. Léon-Dufour, *Vocabulaire de Théologie biblique,* Paris 1962; articles "vin," "vigne": Desnoyers, *Histoire du peuple hebreu*, Bruges 1922, t. I, pp. 82-83.

[22] Cf. GS, 67. 2: "Work comes immediately from the person. In a sense, the person stamps the things of nature with his seal and

subdues them to his will" (Abbott, p. 275). In *Rerum Novarum,* Leo XIII was already saying things analogous to this.

[23] Cf. Desnoyers, *op.cit.* (note 19), t. I, pp. 20-21, 77 sq., 105-109, 360 sq. As the later enemies of Israel, the Canaanites were at once an instrument of divine punishment and of human progress.

[24] R. de Vaux O.P.: *op.cit.* (t. I, pp. 32-33).

[25] Cf, Paul VI, ES, DC, 61 (1964), 1076: "The bread which is the product of knowledge, of technique, and especially of work, becomes sacred for the table and for the altar"; GS, 38. 2.

[26] Cf. LG, 17: "the priest alone can complete the building up of the Body in the Eucharistic Sacrifice" (*sacerdotis tamen est aedificationem Corporis sacrificio eucharistici perficere"*): Abbott, p. 36. But above all, Mt. 16, 18 must be collated with Eph. 4, 11-12, which envisages all Christians through its reference to certain types by way of examples.

[27] Clearly, a man devoid of charity can work very well and even better than many Christians, if his natural gifts are superior to theirs.

[28] An intelligent generosity will dispose towards more rational work.

[29] MM, 257 (C.T.S. translation).

[30] Paul VI: *Summi Dei Verbum,* AAS, 55 (1963), 191; ST, I. II. 709. 4.

[31] Cardinal Feltin, DC, 58 (1961), 176.

[32] Cf. PP, 25 and 32; GS, 64; MM, 172 and 148.

[33] GS, 64: "The fundamental purpose of this productivity must not be the mere multiplication of products. . . . Rather, it must be the service of man, and indeed of the whole man" (Abbott, p. 273).

[34] PT, see DC, 60 (1963), 539-540.

[35] PP, 27.

[36] Saint Thomas Aquinas contrasts, in one of his Biblical commentaries, earthly bread called "the bread of death" (it cannot prevent death) with the Bread of Life which is the Eucharist: Cf. p. 56, n. 106.

[37] It could even be said that the Eucharist, by acting on the will, exercises an indirect influence on its faculty to produce or productivity and, in dependence on the latter, on production. Note that the distinction between production and productivity is explicitly made in GS, 66-67.

[38] PP, 28.

[39] By pouring love into hearts, the Eucharist influences the whole moral life: cf. ST II. II. 23. 8, c. 1. 2. 3; 8. 3. 3. Cf. Pius XI, QA, par. 56.

[40] MM, 168 (CT.S. translation).

[41] 65. 1.

[42] Cf. B. de Margerie S.J., *Reinhold Niebuhr, théologien de la communauté mondiale,* Bruges-Paris, 1969, pp. 388-395.

[43] A point developed by A. Fanfani: "Catholicism, Protestantism, and Capitalism" (trans. N.Y. 1935, chapters V to VII).

[44] UR, par. 22 (Abbott 364).

[45] UR, par. 3 (Abbott 346).

[46] A viewpoint dear to Y. de Montcheuil S.J., in the Augustinian line (cf. Saint Augustine, *De Civitate Dei.* 10. 5 and 10. 20).

[47] GS. 22. 5.

[48] Only human collaboration, mediatized by language, permits the domestication of nature.

[49] ST, III. 60. 6.

[50] Cf. note 42.

[51] MM, 168 (C.T.S. translation).

[52] From this viewpoint, there is scarcely any difference, for a Protestant theologian, between agapes and the Lord's Supper.

[53] The author is here using the French translation by Allo: Paris, 1935 (Gabalda).

[54] Here Saint Paul seems to be speaking of less worthy Communions, and not purely and simply of unworthy Communions: cf. R. Cornêly S.J., *Commentarius in I Cor.* (II. 29-30), Paris, 1909, p. 351; cf. p. 333.

[55] Dom H. Leclercq, *Dictionnaire d'Archéologie chrétienne et de Liturgie,* t. I (1924), col. 785: art. "Agape." See also C. Bernas, *New Catholic Encyclopedia,* I (1967), 193.

[56] Cited by Cornély, *op.cit.* (note 51) p. 353. We do not pretend to take up any position as regards the discussion whether the agapès took place before or after the Eucharist. See Allo, *op.cit.* (note 50), p. 289 sq.; L. Thomas, DBS, 1 (1928), 154-173. Our only purpose is to derive the social conclusions which result from the Pauline text.

[57] On the meaning of "koinônia" in Biblical Greek, see J. Hamer O.P., *L'Eglise est une Communion,* Paris, 1962, pp. 173-178.

[58] "Sacred service" translates the Greek "leitourgêsai."

[59] Pius XII, *Mediator Dei,* AAS, 39 (1947), 565.

[60] Cf. Jacquier, *Actes des Apôtres,* Paris, 1926,[2], pp. 156-158. The imperfect tenses of Acts 2, 44-45 show that the sales were not general but occurred according to the needs of the community and in the measure of these needs.

[61] Cf. Knabenbauer S.J., *Commentarius in Actus Apostolorum,* Paris, 1928[2], in Act 2, 45 and 4, 32-37, pp. 65-91.

[62] Allo, *Seconde Epitre aux Corinthiens,* Paris, 1937, pp. 204-206.

[63] MM, 43; PP, 22-24; cf. ST, II. II. 66. 2: the universal right to usage forms part of the primary natural law; the right to ownership forms part of the secondary natural law.

[64] MM, 32, 79: this would give concrete expression to the astonishing statement of Leo XIII: "All the goods of nature, all the treasures of grace, belong in common and indiscriminately to all mankind" *(Rerum Novarum).*

[65] MM, 60.

[66] MM, 85, 89, 150, 167.

[67] See our appendix on this subject.

[68] DS, 1728, 3857.

[69] Vatican II, SC, 63 and 79.

[70] Pius XII, radio message of Christmas 1953, AAS, 46 (1954), 7. In this connection, the new Offertory prayers of the Mass in the Latin rite point towards a consecration of the working day, symbolized by the bread and by the wine, which are presented in these prayers as at once the fruits of manual work, of the earth and of the vine.

[71] PT, 130.

[72] LG, 34.

[73] This commentary on Mt. 13, 43 derives from a sermon of Saint Robert Bellarmine.

[74] In this connection, see a text of Pius XII: " . . . as if, for two thousand years, the awarness of *the collective responsibility of all for all* did not exist and continue to exist in the soul of the Church" (AAS, 33, 1941, 215).

[75] Cf. ST, II. II. 26. 5. 3: after having written, in the corpus of the article, that ("when there is question of the salvation of our neighbor's soul, we should give precedence to this over our own body," Saint Thomas adds: "It is not necessary, in the name of charity, to risk one's life for the neighbor's salvation, but if one does so, one's charity is perfect." Now, the Eucharist makes us tend towards the perfection of charity.

[76] Saint Thomas Aquians, *in libr. IV Sent.,* dist. 49, 4. 3. 4.

[77] PP, 87.

[78] Saint Augustine, *De Civitate Dei,* XIX, 17. 13-15: peace is "de rebus ad mortalem vitam pertinentibus humanarum quaedam compositio voluntatum"; see also XIX, 17. 57 of the same work.

[79] ST, II. II. 29. . 1; cf. J. Comblin, *Théologie de la Paix,* t. II, pp. 253-273.

[80] P. Antoine S.J.: "Signification spirituelle de l'événement atomique" *Etudes,* May 1964, p. 580.

[81] Cf. J. Comblin, *Théologie de la Paix,* t. II, pp. 364-367.

[82] R. Bosc S.J., *Sociologie de la Paix,* Paris, 1965, p. 229.

[83] *Ibid.,* pp. 183-184.

[84] *Ibid.,* p. 222.

[85] PP, 51.

[86] MM, 69 (CTS 259).

[87] Cf. LG, 9. 2: "The Messianic people . . . is used by Christ as an instrument for the redemption of all" (Abbott P. 26). Of course, the non-proletarians are associated with these proletarians in the Messianic people.

[88] Cf. MM, 5.

[89] MM, 3.

[90] Cf. note 78. Comblin (*op.cit.,* t. II, p. 69) defines peace as follows in the light of Saint Augustine: "An agreement of all concerning a stable social order with a view to organizing the temporal activities of men in unity."

[91] Cf. B. de Margerie S.J., *Le Christ pour le Monde* or *Christ for the World* (Chicago, 1974), (Paris, 1971), chap. 16, sect. C: the reader will find there a discussion concerning the existential decision of daily Communion as macro-decision in the service of development and in response to the evangelical counsel *par excellence.*

[92] Cf. B. de Margerie S.J., *Reinhold Niebuhr, théologien de la* communauté mondiale, Paris-Bruges, 1969, third part, ch. 11, pars. 2 and 3.

[93] Cf. ST I. 37. 2. 3; 34. 3; 27. 5. 2 which I synthesize here. The expression "production of a divine Person" was used several times by Saint Thomas: ST, I. 30. 2. 4; 42. 2 etc.

[94] Cf. ST, I. 45. 6; 1. 45. 7. 3.

[95] Aristotle: Nicomachean Ethics.

[96] Daniel Rops, *Vie quotidienne en Palestine au temps de Jésus,* Paris, 1961, p. 290.

[97] On this heresy, see the article in DTC. On the link between marriage and property, see Pius XI, QA, pars. 62 and 68.

[98] ST, II. II. 66. 2.

[99] ST, I. II. 105. 2c and ad 3; cf. Lev. 25.

[100] Cf. J. Y. Calvez S.J., "Actualité de la Propriéte privée", *Revue de l'Action Populaire,* 1962, p. 1173, note 9.

[101] DS, 930.

[102] Pius XII, radio message of 1st June 1941: AAS, 33 (1941), 213. Pius XII adds: "Nature itself has intimately linked private ownership with the existence of human society and its true civilization, but in a particular way with the existence and development of the family." (See also John XXIII, MM, 45).

[103] MM, 34.

[104] Cf. note 65 of the present chapter.

[105] Cf. GS, 71. 4.

[106] MM, 84 (CTS translation).

[107] Text cited at note 103.

[108] MM, 116.

[109] GS, 71. 6.

[110] A reflection by L. J. de Mesquita, *As enciclicas sociais de Joao XXIII,* Rio de Janeiro, 1963[2], citing Father Haring. We may add, for clarity, that the co-owner in a collective ownership must be able to alienate his part of it; otherwise, he would be real master of nothing.

[111] GS, 71. 1-4.

[112] *Ibid.*

appendix

Encyclical
Populorum Progressio
of Pope Paul VI

ENCYCLICAL LETTER

DEVELOPMENT OF PEOPLES

(This encyclical letter, addressed to bishops, priests, religious, the faithful and all men of good will, and bearing the Latin title "Populorum Progressio," was made public Mar. 28, 1967. The following translation was released by NC News Service.

The encyclical represents a theoretical extension and practical application of social teaching stated in previous encyclicals and, more recently and solemnly, in the second part of the "Pastoral Constitution on the Church in the Modern World" which was promulgated by the Second Vatican Council. Like other recent encyclicals, it was addressed to all men of good will.)

1. Development of Peoples

The development of peoples has the Church's close attention, particularly the development of those peoples who are striving to escape from hunger, misery, endemic diseases and ignorance; of those who are looking for a wider share in the benefits of civilization and a more active improvement of their human qualities; of those who are aiming purposefully at their complete fulfillment. Following on the Second Vatican Ecumenical Council, a renewed consciousness of the demands of the Gospel makes it her duty to put herself at the service of all, to help them grasp their serious problem in all its dimensions, and to convince them that solidarity in action at this turning point in human history is a matter of urgency.

2. Social Teaching of the Popes

Our predecessors in their great encyclicals — Leo XIII in "Rerum Novarum"(1), Pius XI in "Quadragesimo Anno" (2) and John XXIII in "Mater et Magistra (3) and "Pacem in Terris" (4) — not to mention the messages of Pius XII (5) to the world, did not fail in the duty of their office of shedding the light of the Gospel on the social questions of their times.

3. The Principal Fact

Today the principal fact that we must all recognize is that the social question has become world-wide. John XXIII stated this in unambiguous terms (6), and the council echoed him in its "Pastoral Constitution on the Church in the Modern World" (7). This teaching is important and its application urgent. Today the peoples in hunger are making a dramatic appeal to the peoples blessed with abundance. The Church shudders at this cry of anguish and calls each one to give a loving response of charity to this brother's cry for help.

4. Our Journeys

Before we became Pope, two journeys — to Latin America in 1960 and to Africa in 1962 — brought us into direct contact with the acute problems pressing on continents full of life and hope. Then on becoming Father of all we made further journeys, to the Holy Land and India, and were able to see and virtually touch the very serious difficulties besetting peoples of long-standing civilizations who are at grips with the problem of development. While the Second Vatican Ecumenical Council was being held in Rome, providential circumstances permitted us to address in person the General Assembly of the United Nations, and we pleaded the cause of poor peoples before this distinguished body.

5. Justice and Peace

Then quite recently, in our desire to carry out the wishes of the council and give specific expression to the Holy See's contribution to this great cause of peoples in development, we considered it our duty to set up a pontifical commission in the Church's central administration, charged with "bringing to the whole of God's People the full knowledge of the part expected of them at the present time, so as to further the progress of poorer peoples, to encourage social justice among nations, to offer to less developed nations the means whereby they can further their own progress" (8). Its name, which is also its program, is Justice and Peace. We think that this can and should bring together men of good will with our Catholic sons and our Christian brothers. So it is to all that we address this solemn appeal for concrete action toward man's complete development and the development of all mankind.

PART I

FOR MAN'S COMPLETE DEVELOPMENT

I. THE DATA OF THE PROBLEM

6. Men's Aspirations

Freedom from misery; the greater assurance of finding subsistence, health and fixed employment; an increased share of responsibility without oppression of any kind and in security from situations that do violence to their dignity as men; better education — in brief, to seek to do more, know more and have more in order to be more: that is what men aspire to now when a greater number of them are condemned to live in conditions that make this lawful desire illusory. Besides, peoples who have recently gained national independence experience the need to add to this political freedom a fitting autonomous growth, social as well as economic, in order to assure their citizens of a full human enhancement and to take their rightful place with other nations.

7. Colonization and Colonialism

Though insufficient for the immensity and urgency of the task, the means inherited from the past are not lacking. It must certainly be recognized that colonizing powers have often furthered their own interests, power or glory, and that their departure has sometimes left a precarious economy, bound up, for instance, with the production of one kind of crop whose market prices are subject to sudden and considerable variation. Yet, while recognizing the damage done by a certain type of colonialism and its consequences, one must at the same time acknowledge the qualities and achievement of colonizers who brought their science and technical knowledge and left beneficial results of their presence in so many underprivileged regions. The structures established by them persist, however incomplete they may be; they diminished ignorance and sickness, brought the benefits of communications, and improved living conditions.

8. Imbalance Becoming Greater

Yet, once this is admitted, it remains only too true that the resultant situation is manifestly inadequate for facing the hard reality of modern economics. Left to itself, it works rather to widen the differences in the world's levels of life, not to diminish them; rich peoples enjoy rapid growth whereas the poor develop slowly. The imbalance is on the increase; some produce a surplus of foodstuffs, others cruelly lack them and see their exports made uncertain.

9. Increasing Awareness

At the same time, social conflicts have taken on world dimensions. The acute disquiet which has taken hold of the poor classes in countries that are becoming industrialized, is now embracing those whose economy is almost exclusively agrarian; farming people, too, are becoming aware of their "undeserved hardship"(9). There is also the scandal of glaring inequalities not merely in the enjoyment of possessions but even more in the exercise of power. While a small restricted group enjoys a refined civilization in certain regions, the remainder of the population, poor and scattered, is "deprived of nearly all possibility of personal initiative and of responsibility, and oftentimes even its living and working conditions are unworthy of the human person"(10).

10. Conflict of Civilizations

Furthermore, the conflict between traditional civilizations and the new elements of industrial civilization breaks down structures which do not adapt themselves to new conditions. Their framework, sometimes rigid, was the indispensable prop to personal and family life; older people remain attached to it, the young escape from it, as from a useless barrier, to turn eagerly to new forms of life in society. The conflict of the generations is made more serious by a tragic dilemma: whether to retain ancestral institutions and convictions and renounce progress, or to admit techniques and civilizations from outside and reject along with the traditions of the past all their human richness. In effect, the moral, spiritual and religious supports of the past too often give way without securing in return any guarantee of a place in the new world.

11. Conclusion

In this confusion the temptation becomes stronger to risk being swept away toward types of messianism which give promises but create illusions. The resulting dangers are patent: violent popular reactions, agitation toward insurrection, and a drifting toward totalitarian ideologies. Such are the data of the problem. Its seriousness is evident to all.

II. THE CHURCH AND DEVELOPMENT

12. Work of the Missionaries

True to the teaching and example of her divine Founder, who cited the preaching of the Gospel to the poor as a sign of His mission(11), the Church has never failed to foster the human progress of the nations to which she brings faith in Christ. Her missionaries have built not only churches but also hostels and hospitals, schools and universities. Teaching the local populations the means of deriving the best advantages from their natural resources, missionaries have often protected them from the greed of foreigners. Without doubt their work, inasmuch as it was human, was not perfect, and sometimes the announcement of the authentic Gospel message was infiltrated by many ways of thinking and acting which were characteristic of their home country. But the missionaries were also able to develop and foster local institutions. In many a region they were among the pioneers in material progress as well as in cultural advancement. Let it suffice to recall the example of Father Charles de Foucauld, whose charity earned him the title "Universal Brother," and who edited an invaluable dictionary of the Tuareg language. We ought to pay tribute to these pioneers who have been too often forgotten but who were urged on by the love of Christ, just as we honor their imitators and successors who today still continue to put themselves at the generous and unselfish service of those to whom they announce the Gospel.

13. Church and World

However, local and individual undertakings are no longer enough. The present situation of the world demands concerted action based on a clear vision of all economic, social, cultural, and spiritual aspects. Experienced in human affairs, the Church, without attempting to interfere in any way in the politics of states, "seeks but a solitary goal: to carry forward the work of Christ Himself under the lead of the befriending Spirit. And Christ entered this world to give witness to the truth, to rescue and not to sit in judgment, to serve and not to be served"(12). Founded to establish on earth the kingdom of heaven and not to conquer any earthly power, the Church clearly states that the two realms are distinct, just as the two powers, ecclesiastical and civil, are supreme, each in its own domain(13). But, since the Church lives in history, she ought to "scrutinize the signs of the times and interpret them in the light of the Gospel"(14). Sharing the noblest aspirations of men and suffering when she sees them not satisfied, she wishes to help them attain their full flowering, and that is why she offers men what she possesses as her characteristic attribute: a global vision of man and of the human race.

14. Christian Vision of Development

Development cannot be limited to mere economic growth. In order to be authentic, it must be complete; integral, that is, it has to promote the good of every man and of the whole man. As an eminent specialist has very rightly and emphatically declared: "We do not believe in separating the economic from the human, nor development from the civilizations in which it exists. What we hold important is man, each man and each group of men, and we even include the whole of humanity"(15).

15. The Vocation to Self-Fulfillment

In the design of God, every man is called upon to develop and fulfill himself, for every life is a vocation. At birth, everyone is granted, in germ, a set of aptitudes and qualities for him to bring to fruition. Their coming to maturity, which will be the result of education received from the environment and personal efforts, will allow each man to direct himself toward the destiny intended for him by his Creator. Endowed with intelligence and freedom, he is responsible for his fulfillment as he is for his salvation. He is aided, or sometimes impeded, by those who educate him and those with whom he lives, but each one remains, whatever be these influences affecting him, the principal agent of his own success or failure. By the unaided effort of his own intelligence and his will, each man can grow in humanity, can enhance his personal worth, can become more a person.

16. Personal Responsibility

However, this self-fulfillment is not something optional. Just as the whole of creation is ordained to its Creator, so spiritual beings should of their own accord orientate their lives to God, the first truth and the supreme good. Thus it is that human fulfillment constitutes, as it were, a summary of our duties. But there is much more: this harmonious enrichment of nature by personal and responsible effort is ordered to a further perfection. By reason of his union with Christ, the source of life, man attains to new fulfillment of himself, to a transcendent humanism which gives him his greatest possible perfection; this is the highest goal of personal development.

17. And Communal Responsibility

But each man is a member of society. He is part of the whole of mankind. It is not just certain individuals, but all men, who are called to this fullness of development. Civilizations are born, develop and die. But humanity is advancing along the path of history like the waves of a rising tide encroaching gradually on the shore. We have inherited from past generations, and we have benefitted from the work of our contemporaries; for this reason we have obligations toward all, and we cannot refuse to interest ourselves in those who will come after us to enlarge the human family. The reality of human solidarity, which is a benefit for us, also imposes a duty.

18. Scale of Values

This personal and communal development would be threatened if the true scale of values were undermined. The desire for necessities is legitimate, and work undertaken to obtain them is a duty: "If any man will not work, neither let him eat"(16). But the acquiring of temporal goods can lead to greed, to the insatiable desire for more, and can make increased power a tempting objective. Individuals, families and nations can be overcome by avarice, be they poor or rich, and all can fall victim to a stifling materialism.

19. The Ambivalence of Growth

Increased possession is not the ultimate goal of nations nor of individuals. All growth is ambivalent. It is essential if man is to develop as a man, but in a way it imprisons man if he considers it the supreme good, and it restricts his vision. Then we see hearts harden and minds close, and men no longer gather together in friendship but out of self-interest, which soon leads to oppositions and disunity. The exclusive pursuit of possessions thus becomes an obstacle to individual fulfillment and to man's true greatness. Both for nations and for individual men, avarice is the most evident form of moral underdevelopment.

20. Toward a More Human Condition

If further development calls for the work of more and more technicians, even more necessary is the deep thought and reflection of wise men in search of a new humanism which will enable modern man to find himself anew by embracing the higher values of love and friendship, of prayer and contemplation(17). This is what will permit the fullness of authentic development, a development which is for each and all the transition from less human conditions to those which are more human.

21. The Ideal To Be Pursued

Less human conditions: the lack of material necessities for those who are without the minimum essential for life, the moral deficiencies of those who are mutilated by selfishness. Less human conditions: oppressive social structures, whether due to the abuses of ownership or to the abuses of power, to the exploitation of workers or to unjust transactions. Conditions that are more human: the passage from misery toward the possession of necessities, victory over social scourges, the growth of knowledge, the acquisition of culture. Additional conditions that are more human: increased esteem for the dignity of others, the turning toward the spirit of poverty (18), cooperation for the common good, the will and desire for peace. Conditions that are still more human: the acknowledgment by man of supreme values, and of God their source and their finality. Conditions that, finally and above all, are more human: faith, a gift of God accepted by the good will of man, and unity in the charity of Christ, who calls us all to share as sons in the life of the living God, the Father of all men.

III. ACTION TO BE UNDERTAKEN

22. The Universal Purpose of Created Things

"Fill the earth and subdue it" (19): the Bible, from the first page on, teaches us that the whole of creation is for man, that it is his responsibility to develop it by intelligent effort and by means of his labor to perfect it, so to speak, for his use. If the world is made to furnish each individual with the means of livelihood and the instruments for his growth and progress, each man has therefore the right to find in the world what is necessary for himself. The recent council reminded us of this: "God intended the earth and all that it contains for the use of every human being and people. Thus, as all men follow justice and unite in charity, created goods should abound for them on a reasonable basis"(20). All other rights whatsoever, including those of property and of free commerce, are to be subordinated to this principle. They should not hinder but on the contrary favor its application. It is a grave and urgent social duty to redirect them to their primary finality.

23. Property

"If someone who has the riches of this world sees his brother in need and closes his heart to him, how does the love of God abide in him?"(21) It is well known how strong were the words used by the Fathers of the Church to describe the proper attitude of persons who possess anything towards persons in need. To quote St. Ambrose: "You are not making a gift of your possessions to the poor person. You are handing over to him what is his. For what has been given in common for the use of all, you have arrogated to yourself. The world is given to all, and not only to the rich" (22). That is, private property does not constitute for anyone an absolute and unconditioned right. No one is justified in keeping for his exclusive use what he does not need, when others lack necessities. In a word, "according to the traditional doctrine as found in the Fathers of the Church and the great theologians, the right to property must never be exercised to the detriment of the common good." If there should arise a conflict "between acquired private rights and primary community exigencies," it is the responsibility of public authorities "to look for a solution, with the active participation of individuals and social groups"(23).

24. Use of Revenue

If certain landed estates impede the general prosperity because they are extensive, unused or poorly used, or because they bring hardship to peoples or are detrimental to the interests of the country, the common good sometimes demands their expropriation. While giving a clear statement on this(24), the council recalled no less clearly that the available revenue is not to be used in accordance with mere whim, and that no place must be given to selfish speculation. Consequently, it is unacceptable that citizens with abundant incomes from the resources and activity of their country should transfer a considerable part of this income abroad purely for their own advantage, without care for the manifest wrong they inflict on their country by doing this(25).

25. Industrialization

The introduction of industry is a necessity for economic growth and human progress; it is also a sign of development and contributes to it. By persistent work and use of his intelligence man gradually wrests nature's secrets from her and finds a better application for her riches. As his self-mastery increases, he develops a taste for research and discovery, an ability to take a calculated risk, boldness in enterprises, generosity in what he does, and a sense of responsibility.

26. Liberal Capitalism

But it is unfortunate that on these new conditions of society a system has been constructed which considers profit as the key motive for economic progress, com petition as the supreme law of economics, and private ownership of the means of production as an absolute right that has no limits and carries no corresponding social obligation. This unchecked liberalism leads to dictatorship rightly denounced by Pius XI as producing "the international imperialism of money"(26). One cannot condemn such abuses too strongly by solemnly recalling once again that the economy is at the service of man(27). But, if it is true that a type of capitalism has been the source of excessive suffering, injustices and fratricidal conflicts whose effects still persist, it would also be wrong to attribute to industrialization itself evils that belong to the woeful system which accompanied it. On the contrary, one must recognize in all justice the irreplaceable contribution made by the organization of labor and of industry to what development has accomplished.

27. Work

Similarly with work; while it can sometimes be given exaggerated significance, it is for all something willed and blessed by God. Man created to His image "must cooperate with his Creator in the perfecting of creation and communicate to the earth the spiritual imprint he himself has received"(28). God, who has endowed man with intelligence, imagination and sensitivity, has also given him the means of completing his work in a certain way; whether he be artist or craftsman, engaged in management, industry or agriculture, everyone who works is a creator. Bent over a material that resists his efforts, a man by his work gives his imprint to it, acquiring, as he does so, perseverance, skill and a spirit of invention. Further, when work is done in common, when hope, hardship, ambition and joy are shared, it brings together and firmly unites the wills, minds and hearts of men. In its accomplishment, men find themselves to be brothers(29).

28. Contrary Effects of Work

Work, of course, can have contrary effects, for it promises money, pleasure and power, invites some to selfishness, others to revolt; it also develops professional awareness, sense of duty and charity to one's neighbor. When it is more scientific and better organized, there is a risk of its dehumanizing those who perform it, by making them its servants, for work is human only if it remains intelligent and free. John XXIII gave a reminder of the urgency of giving everyone who works his proper dignity by making him a true sharer in the work he does with others: "Every effort should be made that the enterprise become a community of persons in the dealings, activities and standing of all its members"(30). Man's labor means much more still for the Christian: the mission of sharing in the creation of the supernatural world(31) which remains incomplete until we all come to build up together that perfect Man of whom St. Paul speaks, "who realizes the fullness of Christ"(32).

29. Urgency of the Task To Be Done

We must make haste; too many are suffering, and the distance is growing that separates the progress of some and the stagnation, not to say the regression, of others. Yet the work required should advance smoothly if there is not to be the risk of losing indispensable equilibrium. A hasty agrarian reform can fail. Industrialization, if introduced suddenly, can displace structures still necessary, and can produce hardships in society which would be a setback in terms of human values.

30. Temptation to Violence

There are certainly situations whose injustice cries to heaven. When whole populations destitute of necessities live in a state of dependence barring them from all initiative and responsibility, and all opportunity to advance culturally and share in social and political life, recourse to violence, as a means to right these wrongs to human dignity, is a grave temptation.

31. Revolution

We know, however, that a revolutionary uprising — save where there is manifest, long-standing tyranny which would do great damage to fundamental personal rights and dangerous harm to the common good of the country — produces new injustices, throws more elements out of balance and brings on new disasters. A real evil should not be fought against at the cost of greater misery.

32. Reform

We want to be clearly understood: the present situation must be faced with courage, and the injustices linked with it must be fought against and overcome. Development demands bold transformations, innovations that go deep. Urgent reforms should be undertaken without delay. It is for each one to take his share in them with generosity, particularly those whose education, position and opportunities afford them wide scope for action. May they show an example, and give of their own possessions as several of our brothers in the episcopacy have done(33). In so doing, they will live up to men's expectations and be faithful to the Spirit of God, since it is "the ferment of the Gospel which has aroused and continues to arouse in man's heart the irresistible requirements of his dignity"(34).

33. Programs and Planning

Individual initiative alone and the mere free play of competition could never assure successful development. One must avoid the risk of increasing still more the wealth of the rich and the dominion of the strong, while leaving the poor in their misery and adding to the servitude of the oppressed. Hence, programs are necessary in order "to encourage, stimulate, coordinate, supplement and integrate"(35) the activity of individuals and of intermediary bodies. It pertains to the public authorities to choose, even to lay down, the objectives to be pursued, the ends to be achieved, and the means for attaining these, and it is for them to stimulate all the forces engaged in this common activity. But let them take care to associate private initiative and intermediary bodies with this work. They will thus avoid the danger of complete collectivization or of arbitrary planning, which, by denying liberty, would prevent the exercise of the fundamental rights of the human person.

34. At Man's Service

This is true since every program made to increase production has, in the last analysis, no other raison d'etre than the service of man. Such programs should reduce inequalities, fight discriminations, free man from various types of servitude and enable him to be the instrument of his own material betterment, of his moral progress and of his spiritual growth. To speak of development, is in effect to show as much concern for social progress as for economic growth. It is not sufficient to increase overall wealth for it to be distributed equitably. It is not sufficient to promote technology to render the world a more human place in which to live. The mistakes of their predecessors should warn those on the road to development of the dangers to be avoided in this field. Tomorrow's technocracy can beget evils no less redoubtable than those due to the liberalism of yesterday. Economics and technology have no meaning unless they are related to the good of man, whom they should serve. And man is only truly man in as far as, master of his own acts and judge of their worth, he is author of his own advancement, in keeping with the nature which was given to him by his Creator and whose possibilities and exigencies he himself freely assumes.

35. Efforts To Achieve Literacy

It can even be affirmed that economic growth depends in the first place upon social progress; thus, basic education is the primary object of any plan of development. Indeed, hunger for education is no less debasing than hunger for food; an illiterate is a person with an undernourished mind. To be able to read and write, to acquire a professional formation, means to recover confidence in oneself and to discover that one can progress along with the others. As we said in our message to the UNESCO Congress held in 1965 at Teheran, for man literacy is "a fundamental factor of social integration, as well as of personal enrichment, and for society it is a privileged instrument of economic progress and of development"(36). We also rejoice at the good work accomplished in this field by private initiative, by the public authorities and by international organizations; these are the primary agents of development, because they render man capable of acting for himself.

36. The Family

But man finds his true identity only in his social milieu, where the family plays a fundamental role. The family's influence may have been excessive, at some periods of history and in some places, when it was exercised to the detriment of the fundamental rights of the individual. The long-standing social frameworks, often too rigid and badly organized, existing in developing countries, are, nevertheless, still necessary for a time; yet their excessive hold should be gradually relaxed. But the natural family, monogamous and stable as the divine plan conceived it(37) and as Christianity sanctified it, must remain the place where "the various generations come together and help one another to grow wiser and to harmonize personal rights with the other requirements of social life"(38).

37. Demography

It is true that too frequently an accelerated demographic increase adds its own difficulties to the problems of development; the size of the population increases more rapidly than available resources, and things are found to have reached apparently an impasse. From that moment the temptation is great to check the demographic increase by means of radical measures. It is certain that public authorities can intervene, within the limit of their competence, by favoring the availability of appropriate information and by adopting suitable measures, provided that these be in conformity with the moral law and that they respect the rightful freedom of married couples. Where the inalienable right to marriage and procreation is lacking, human dignity has ceased to exist. Finally, it is for the parents to decide, with full knowledge of the matter, on the number of their children, taking into account their responsibilities toward God, themselves, the children they have already brought into the world, and the community to which they belong. In all this they must follow the demands of their own conscience enlightened by God's law authentically interpreted, and sustained by confidence in Him(39).

38. Professional Organizations

In the task of development, man, who finds his life's primary environment in the family, is often aided by professional organizations. If it is their objective to promote the interests of their members, their responsibility is also great with regard to the educative task which at the same time they can and ought to accomplish. By means of the information they provide and the formation they propose, they can do much to give to all a sense of the common good and of the consequent obligations that fall upon each person.

39. Legitimate Pluralism

All social action involves a doctrine. The Christian cannot admit that which is based upon a materialistic and atheistic philosophy, which respects neither the religious orientation of life to its final end nor human freedom and dignity. But, provided that these values are safeguarded, a pluralism of professional organizations and trade unions is admissible, and from certain points of view useful, if thereby liberty is protected and emulation stimulated. And we most willingly pay homage to all those who labor in them to give unselfish service to their brothers.

40. Promotion of Culture

In addition to professional organizations, there are also institutions which are at work. Their role is no less important for the success of development. "The future of the world stands in peril," the council gravely affirms, "unless wiser men are forthcoming." And it adds: "Many nations, poorer in economic goods, are quite rich in wisdom and able to offer noteworthy advantages to others" (40). Rich or poor, each country possesses a civilization handed down by their ancestors: institutions called for by life in this world, and higher manifestations of the life of the spirit, manifestations of an artistic intellectual and religious character. When the latter possess true human values, it would be grave error to sacrifice them to the former. A people that would act in this way would thereby lose the best of its patrimony; in order to live, it would be sacrificing its reasons for living. Christ's teaching also applies to people: "What does it profit a man to gain the whole world if he suffers the loss of his soul"(41).

41. Materialism: Source of Temptation

Less well-off peoples can never be sufficiently on their guard against this temptation which comes to them from wealthy nations. For these nations all too often set an example of success in a highly technical and culturally developed civilization; they also provide the model for a way of acting that is principally aimed at the conquest of material prosperity. Not that material prosperity of itself precludes the activity of the human spirit. On the contrary, the human spirit, "increasingly free of its bondage to creatures, can be more easily drawn to the worship and contemplation of the Creator"(42). However, "modern civilization itself often complicates the approach to God, not for any essential reason but because it is excessively engrossed in earthly affairs"(43). Developing nations must know how to discriminate among those things that are held out to them; they must be able to assess critically and eliminate those deceptive goods which would only bring about a lowering of the human ideal, and to accept those values that are sound and beneficial, in order to develop them alongside their own, in accordance with their own genius.

42. Conclusion

What must be aimed at is complete humanism(44). And what is that if not the fully-rounded development of the whole man and of all men? A humanism closed in on itself, and not open to the values of the spirit and to God who is their source, could achieve apparent success. True, man can organize the world apart from God, but "without God man can organize it in the end only to man's detriment. An isolated humanism is an inhuman humanism"(45). There is no true humanism but that which is open to the Absolute and is conscious of a vocation which gives human life its true meaning. Far from being the ultimate measure of all things, man can only realize himself by reaching beyond himself. As Pascal has said so well: "Man infinitely surpasses man"(46).

PART II

THE DEVELOPMENT OF THE HUMAN RACE IN THE SPIRIT OF SOLIDARITY

43. Introduction

There can be no progress toward the complete development of man without the simultaneous development of all humanity in the spirit of solidarity. As we said at Bombay: "Man must meet man, nation meet nation, as brothers and sisters, as children of God. In this mutual understanding and friendship, in this sacred communion, we must also begin to work together to build the common future of the human race"(47). We also suggested a search for concrete and practical ways of organization and cooperation, so that all available resources be pooled and thus a true communion among all nations be achieved.

44. Brotherhood of Peoples

This duty is the concern especially of better-off nations. Their obligations stem from a brotherhood that is at once human and supernatural, and take on a threefold aspect: the duty of human solidarity — and the aid that the rich nations must give to developing countries; the duty of social justice — the rectification of inequitable trade relations between powerful nations and weak nations; the duty of universal charity — the effort to bring about a world that is more human toward all men, where all will be able to give and receive, without one group making progress at the expense of the other. The question is urgent, for on it depends the future of the civilization of the world.

I. AID FOR THE WEAK

45. War against Hunger

"If a brother or a sister be naked," says St. James, "if they lack their daily nourishment, and one of you says to them: 'Go in peace, be warmed and be filled,' without giving them what is necessary for the body, what good does it do?"(48) Today no one can be ignorant any longer of the fact that in whole continents countless men and women are ravished by hunger, countless numbers of children are undernourished, so that many of them die in infancy, while the physical growth and mental development of many others are retarded and as a result whole regions are condemned to the most depressing despondency.

46. Today

Anguished appeals have already been sounded in the past: that of John XXIII was warmly received(49). We ourselves repeated it in our Christmas Message of

1963(50), and again in 1966 on behalf of India(51). The campaign against hunger being carried on by the Food and Agriculture Organization (FAO) and encouraged by the Holy See, has been generously supported. Our Caritas Internationalis is at work everywhere, and many Catholics, at the urging of our brothers in the episcopacy, contribute generously of their means and spend themselves without counting the cost in assisting those who are in want, continually widening the circle of those they look upon as neighbors.

47. Tomorrow

But neither all this nor the private and public funds that have been invested, nor the gifts and loans that have been made, can suffice. It is not just a matter of eliminating hunger, nor even of reducing poverty. The struggle against destitution, though urgent and necessary, is not enough. It is a question, rather, of building a world where every man, no matter what his race, religion or nationality, can live a fully human life, freed from servitude imposed on him by other men or by natural forces over which he has not sufficient control; a world where freedom is not an empty word and where the poor man Lazarus can sit down at the same table with the rich man(52). This demands great generosity, much sacrifice, and unceasing effort on the part of the rich man. Let each one examine his conscience, a conscience that conveys a new message for our times. Is he prepared to support out of his own pocket works and undertakings organized in favor of the most destitute? Is he ready to pay higher taxes so that the public authorities can intensify their efforts in favor of development? Is he ready to pay a higher price for imported goods so that the producer may be more justly rewarded? Or to leave his country, if necessary and if he is young, in order to assist in this development of the young nations?

48. Duty of Human Solidarity

The same duty of solidarity that rests on individuals exists also for nations: "Advanced nations have a very heavy obligation to help the developing peoples" (53). It is necessary to put this teaching of the council into effect. Although it is normal that a nation should be the first to benefit from the gifts that Providence has bestowed on it as the fruit of the labors of its people, still no country can claim on that account to keep its wealth for itself alone. Every nation must produce more and better quality goods to give to all its inhabitants a truly human standard of living, and also to contribute to the common development of the human race. Given the increasing needs of the underdeveloped countries, it should be considered quite normal for an advanced country to devote a part of its production to meet their needs, and to train teachers, engineers, technicians and scholars prepared to put their knowledge and their skill at the disposal of less fortunate peoples.

49. Superfluous Wealth

We must repeat once more that the superfluous wealth of rich countries should be placed at the service of poor nations. The rule which up to now held good for the benefit of those nearest to us, must today be applied to all the needy of this world. Besides, the rich will be the first to benefit as a result. Otherwise their continued greed will certainly call down upon them the judgment of God and the wrath of the poor, with consequences no one can foretell. If today's flourishing civilizations remain selfishly wrapped up in themselves, they could easily place their highest values in jeopardy, sacrificing their will to be great to the desire to possess more. To them we could apply also the parable of the rich man whose fields yielded an abundant harvest and who did not know where to store his harvest: "God said to him: 'Fool, this night do they demand your soul of you' "(54).

50. Planning

In order to be fully effective, these efforts ought not remain scattered or isolated, much less be in competition for reasons of power or prestige; the present situation calls for concerted planning. A planned program is, of course, better and more effective than occasional aid left to individual good will. It presupposes, as we said above, careful study, the selection of ends and the choice of means, as well as a reorganization of efforts to meet the needs of the present and the demands of the foreseeable future. More important, a concerted plan has advantages that go beyond the field of economic growth and social progress; for, in addition, it gives significance and value to the work undertaken. While shaping the world, it sets a higher value on man.

51. World Fund

But it is necessary to go still further. At Bombay we called for the establishment of a great World Fund, to be made up of part of the money spent on arms, to relieve the most destitute of this world(55). What is true of the immediate struggle against want, holds good also when there is a question of development. Only worldwide collaboration, of which a common fund would be both means and symbol, will succeed in overcoming vain rivalries and in establishing a fruitful and peaceful exchange between peoples.

52. Its Advantages

There is certainly no need to do away with bilateral and multilateral agreements: they allow ties of dependence and feelings of bitterness, left over from the era of colonialism, to yield place to the happier relationship of friendship based on a footing of constitutional and political equality. However, if they were to be fitted into the framework of worldwide collaboration, they would be beyond all suspicion, and as a result there would be less distrust on the part of the receiving nations. These would have less cause for fearing that, under the cloak of financial aid or technical assistance, there lurk certain manifestations of what has come to be called neo-colonialism, in the form of political pressures and economic suzerainty aimed at maintaining or acquiring complete dominance.

53. Its Urgency

Besides, who does not see that such a fund would make it easier to take measures to prevent certain wasteful expenditures, the result of fear or pride? When so many people are hungry, when so many families suffer from destitution, when so many remain steeped in ignorance, when so many schools, hospitals and homes worthy of the name remain to be built, all public or private squandering of wealth, all expenditure prompted by motives of national or personal ostentation, every exhausting armament race, becomes an intolerable scandal. We are conscious of our duty to denounce it. Would that those in authority listen to our words before it is too late!

54. Dialogue To Be Started

This means that it is absolutely necessary to create among all peoples that dialogue for whose establishment we expressed our hope in our first encyclical "Ecclesiam Suam"(56). This dialogue between those who contribute wealth and those who benefit from it, will provide the possibility of making an assessment of the contribution necessary, not only drawn up in terms of the generosity and the available wealth of the donor nations, but also conditioned by the real needs of the receiving countries and the use to which the financial assistance can be put. Developing countries will thus no longer risk being overwhelmed by debts whose repayment swallows up the greater part of their gains. Rates of interest and time for repayment of the loans could be so arranged as not to be too great a burden on either party, taking into account free gifts, interest-free or low-interest loans, and the time needed for liquidating the debts. Guarantees could be given to those who provide the capital that it will be put to use according to an agreed plan and with a reasonable measure of efficiency, since there is no question of encouraging parasites or the indolent. And the receiving countries could demand that there be no interference in their political life or subversion of their social structures. As sovereign states, they have the right to conduct their own affairs, to decide on their policies and to move freely toward the kind of society they choose. What must be brought about, therefore, is a system of cooperation freely undertaken, an effective and mutual sharing, carried out with equal dignity on either side, for the construction of a more human world.

55. Its Necessity

The task might seem impossible in those regions where the cares of day-to-day survival fill the entire existence of families incapable of planning the kind of work which would open the way to a future that is less desperate. These, however, are the men and women who must be helped, who must be persuaded to work for their own betterment and endeavor to acquire gradually the means to that end.

This common task will not succeed without concerted, constant and courageous efforts. But let everyone be convinced of this: the very life of poor nations, civil peace in developing countries, and world peace itself are at stake.

II. EQUITY IN TRADE RELATIONS

56. The efforts which are being made to assist developing nations on a financial and technical basis, though considerable, would be illusory if their benefits were to be partially nullified as a consequence of the trade relations existing between rich and poor countries. The confidence of these latter would be severely shaken if they had the impression that what was being given them with one hand was being taken away with the other.

57. Increasing Disproportion

Of course, highly industralized nations export for the most part manufactured goods, while countries with less developed economies have only food, fibers and other raw materials to sell. As a result of technical progress, the value of manufactured goods is rapidly increasing and they can always find an adequate market. On the other hand, raw materials produced by underdeveloped countries are subject to wide and sudden fluctuations in price, a state of affairs far removed from the progressively increasing value of industrial products. As a result, nations whose industrialization is limited are faced with serious difficulties when they have to rely on their exports to balance their economy and to carry out their plans for development. The poor nations remain ever poor while the rich ones become still richer.

58. Beyond Liberalism

In other words, the rule of free trade, taken by itself, is no longer able to govern international relations. Its advantages are certainly evident when the parties involved are not affected by any excessive inequalities of economic power; it is an incentive to progress and a reward for effort. That is why industrially developed countries see in it a law of justice. But the situation is no longer the same when economic conditions differ too widely from country to country; prices which are "freely" set in the market can produce unfair results. One must recognize that it is the fundamental principle of liberalism, as the rule for commercial exchange, which is questioned here.

59. Contractual Justice between Nations

The teaching of Leo XIII in "Rerum Novarum" is always valid: if the positions of the contracting parties are too unequal, the consent of the parties does not suffice to guarantee the justice of their contract, and the rule of free agreement remains subservient to the demands of the natural law(57). What was true of the just wage for the individual is also true of international contracts: an economy of exchange can no longer be based solely on the law of free competition, a law which, in its turn, too often creates an economic dictatorship. Freedom of trade is fair only if it is subject to the demands of social justice.

60. Measures To Be Taken

Moreover, this has been understood by the developed nations themselves, which are striving, by means of appropriate measures, to re-establish within their own economies a balance, which competition, if left to itself, tends to compromise. Thus it happens that these nations often support their agriculture at the price of sacrifices imposed on economically more favored sectors. Similarly, to maintain the commercial relations which are developing among themselves, especially within a common market, the financial, fiscal, and social policy of these nations tries to restore comparable opportunities to competing industries which are not equally prospering.

61. International Agreements

In this area, one cannot employ two systems of weights and measures. What holds for a national economy or among developed countries is valid also in commercial relations between rich nations and poor nations. Without abolishing the competitive market, it should be kept within the limits which make it just and moral, and therefore human. In trade between developed and underdeveloped economies, conditions are too disparate and the degrees of genuine freedom available are too unequal. In order that international trade be human and moral, social justice requires that it restore to the participants a certain equality of opportunity. This equality is a long-term objective, but to reach it we must begin now to create true equality in discussions and negotiations. Here again international agreements on a rather wide scale would be helpful; they would establish general norms for regulating certain prices, for guaranteeing certain types of production, for supporting certain new industries. Who is there who does not see that such a common effort aimed at increased justice in business relations between peoples would bestow on developing nations positive assistance, the effects of which would be not only immediate but lasting?

62. Obstacles To Overcome: Nationalism

Among still other obstacles which are opposed to the formation of a world which is more just and which is better organized toward a universal solidarity, we wish to speak of nationalism and racism. It is only natural that communities which have recently reached their political independence should be jealous of a national unity which is still fragile, and that they should strive to protect it. Likewise, it is to be expected that nations endowed with an ancient culture should be proud of the patrimony which their history has bequeathed to them. But these legitimate feelings should be ennobled by that universal charity which embraces the entire human family. Nationalism isolates people from their true good. It would be especially harmful where the weakness of national economies demands rather the pooling of efforts, of knowledge and of funds, in order to implement programs of development and to increase commercial and cultural exchange.

63. Racism

Racism is not the exclusive lot of young nations, where sometimes it hides beneath the rivalries of clans and political parties, with heavy losses for justice and at the risk of civil war. During the colonial period it often flared up between the colonists and the indigenous population, and stood in the way of mutually profitable understanding, often giving rise to bitterness in the wake of genuine injustices. It is still an obstacle to collaboration among disadvantaged nations and a cause of division and hatred within countries whenever individuals and families see the inviolable rights of the human person held in scorn, as they themselves are unjustly subjected to a regime of discrimination because of their race or their color.

64. Toward a Unified World

We are deeply distressed by such a situation which is laden with threats for the future. We are, nonetheless, hopeful: a more deeply felt need for collaboration, a heightened sense of unity, will finally triumph over misunderstandings and selfishness. We hope that the countries whose development is less advanced will be able to take advantage of their proximity in order to organize among themselves, on a broadened territorial basis, areas for concerted development, to draw up programs in common, to coordinate investments, to distribute the means of production, and to organize trade. We hope also that multilateral and international bodies, by means of the reorganization which is required, will discover the ways that will allow peoples which are still underdeveloped to break through the barriers which seem to enclose them and to discover for themselves, in full fidelity to their own proper genius, the means for their social and human progress.

65. Peoples as Artisans of Their Own Destiny

Such is the goal we must attain. World unity, ever more effective, should allow all peoples to become the artisans of their destiny. The past has too often been characterized by relationships of violence between nations. May the day dawn when international relations will be marked with the stamp of mutual respect and friendship, of inter-dependence in collaboration; and when the betterment of all will be seen as the responsibility of each individual. The younger or weaker nations ask to assume their active part in the construction of a better world, one which shows deeper respect for the rights and the vocation of the individual. This is a legitimate appeal. Everyone should hear it and respond to it.

III. UNIVERSAL CHARITY

66. The world is sick. Its illness consists less in the unproductive monopolization of resources by a small number of men than in the lack of brotherhood among individuals and peoples.

67. The Duty of Welcoming Others

We cannot insist too much on the duty of welcoming others — a duty springing from human solidarity and Christian charity — which is incumbent both on the families and the cultural organizations of the host countries. Centers of welcome and hostels must be multiplied, especially for youth. This must be done first to protect them from loneliness, the feeling of abandonment and distress, which undermines all moral resistance. This is also necessary to protect them from the unhealthy situation in which they find themselves, forced as they are to compare the extreme poverty of their homeland with the luxury and waste which often surround them. It should be done also to protect them against the subversive teachings and temptations to aggression which assail them, as they recall so much "unmerited misery"(58). Finally, and above all, this hospitality should aim to provide them, in the warm atmosphere of a brotherly welcome, with the example of wholesome living, an esteem for genuine and effective Christian charity, an esteem for spiritual values.

68. The Dramatic Situation of Young Students

It is painful to think of the numerous young people who come to more advanced countries to receive the science, the competence, and the culture which will make them more qualified to serve their homeland, and who certainly acquire there a formation of high quality, but who too often lose the esteem for the spiritual values which often were to be found, as a precious patrimony, in the civilizations where they had grown up.

69. Emigrant Workers

The same welcome is due to emigrant workers, who live in conditions which are often inhuman, and who economize on what they earn in order to send a little relief to their families living in misery in their native lands.

70. Social Sensitivity

Our second recommendation is for those whose business calls them to countries recently opened to industrialization: industrialists, merchants, leaders or representatives of larger enterprises. It happens that they are not lacking in social sensitivity in their own country. Why then do they return to the inhuman principles of individualism when they operate in less developed countries? Their advantaged situation should on the contrary move them to become the initiators of social progress and of human advancement in the area where their business calls them. Their very sense of organization should suggest to them the means for making intelligent use of the labor of the indigenous population, of forming qualified workers, of training engineers and staffs, of giving scope to their initiative, of introducing them progressively into higher positions, thus preparing them to share, in the near future, in the responsibilities of management. At least let justice always rule the relations between superiors and their subordinates. Let standard contracts with reciprocal obligations govern these relationships. Finally, let no one, whatever his status, be subjected unjustly to the arbitrariness of others.

71. Development Missions

We are happy that experts are being sent in larger and larger numbers on development missions by institutions, whether international or bilateral, or by private organizations. "They ought not conduct themselves in a lordly fashion, but as helpers and co-workers"(59). A people quickly perceives whether those who come to help them do so with or without affection, whether they come merely to apply their techniques or to recognize in man his full value. Their message is in danger of being rejected if it is not presented in the context of brotherly love.

72. Qualities Sought for in the Experts

Hence, necessary technical competence must be accompanied by authentic signs of disinterested love. Freed of all nationalistic pride and of every appearance of racism, experts should learn how to work in close collaboration with all. They realize that their competence does not confer on them a superiority in every field. The civilization which formed them contains, without doubt, elements of universal humanism, but it is not the only civilization nor does it enjoy a monopoly of valuable elements. Moreover, it cannot be imported without undergoing adaptations. The men on these missions will be intent on discovering, along with its history, the component elements of the cultural riches of the country receiving them. Mutual understanding will be established which will enrich both cultures.

73. Dialogue between Civilizations

Between civilizations, as between persons, sincere dialogue indeed creates brotherhood. The work of development will draw nations together in the attainment of goals pursued with a common effort if all, from governments and their representatives to the last expert, are inspired by brotherly love and moved by the sincere desire to build a civilization founded on world solidarity. A dialogue based on man, and not on commodities or technical skills, will then begin. It will be fruitful if it brings to the peoples who benefit from it the means of self-betterment and spiritual growth, if the technicians act as educators, and if the instruction imparted is characterized by so lofty a spiritual and moral tone that it guarantees not merely economic but human development. When aid programs have terminated, the relationships thus established will endure. Who does not see of what importance they will be for the peace of the world?

74. Appeal to Youth

Many young people have already responded with warmth and enthusiasm to the appeal of Pius XII for lay missionaries(60). Many also are those who have spontaneously put themselves at the disposition of official or private organizations which are collaborating with developing nations. We are pleased to learn that in certain nations "military service" can be partially accomplished by doing "social service," a "service pure and simple." We bless these undertakings and the good will which inspires them. May all those who wish to belong to Christ hear His appeal: "I was hungry and you gave me to eat, thirsty and you gave me to drink, a stranger and you took me in, naked and you clothed me, sick and you visited me, a prisoner and you came to see me"(61). No one can remain indifferent to the lot of his brothers who are still buried in wretchedness, and are victims of insecurity, slaves of ignorance. Like the heart of Christ, the heart of the Christian must sympathize with this misery: "I have pity on this multitude"(62).

75. Prayer and Action

The prayer of all ought to rise with fervor to the Almighty. Having become aware of such great misfortunes, the human race will apply itself with intelligence and steadfastness to abolish them. This prayer should be matched by the resolute commitment of each individual — according to the measure of his strength and possibilities — to the struggle against underdevelopment. May individuals, social groups, and nations join hands in brotherly fashion, the strong aiding the weak to grow, exerting all their competence, enthusiasm and disinterested love. More than any other, the individual who is animated by true charity labors skillfully to discover the causes of misery, to find the means to combat it, to overcome it resolutely. A creator of peace, he "will follow his path, lighting the lamps of joy and playing their brilliance and loveliness on the hearts of men across the surface of the globe, leading them to recognize, across all frontiers, the faces of their brothers, the faces of their friends"(63).

DEVELOPMENT IS THE NEW NAME FOR PEACE

76. Conclusion

Excessive economic, social and cultural inequalities among peoples arouse tensions and conflicts, and are a danger to peace. As we said to the Fathers of the council when we returned from our journey of peace to the United Nations: "The condition of the peoples in process of development ought to be the object of our consideration; or, better: Our charity for the poor in the world — and there are multitudes of them — must become more considerate, more active, more generous"(64). To wage war on misery and to struggle against injustice is to promote, along with improved conditions, the human and spiritual progress of all men, and therefore the common good of humanity. Peace cannot be limited to a mere absence of war, the result of an ever precarious balance of forces. No, peace is something that is built up day after day, in the pursuit of an order intended by God, which implies a more perfect form of justice among men(65).

77. End to Isolation

The peoples themselves have the prime responsibility to work for their own development. But they will not bring this about in isolation. Regional agreements among weak nations for mutual support, understandings of wider scope entered into for their help, more far-reaching agreements to establish programs for closer cooperation among groups of nations — these are the milestones on the road to development that leads to peace.

78. Toward an Effective World Authority

This international collaboration on a worldwide scale requires institutions that will prepare, coordinate and direct it, until finally there is established an order of justice which is universally recognized. With all our heart, we encourage these organizations which have undertaken this collaboration for the development of the peoples of the world, and our wish is that they grow in prestige and authority. "Your vocation," as we said to the representatives of the United Nations in New York, "is to bring not some people but all peoples to treat each other as brothers. . . . Who does not see the necessity of thus establishing progressively a world authority, capable of acting effectively in the juridical and political sectors?"(66)

79. A Well-Founded Hope for a Better World

Some would consider such hopes utopian. It may be that these persons are not realistic enough, and that they have not perceived the dynamism of a world which desires to live more fraternally — a world which, in spite of its ignorance, its mistakes and even its sins, its relapses into barbarism and its wanderings far from the road of salvation, is, even unaware, taking slow but sure steps toward its Creator. This road toward a greater humanity requires effort and sacrifice. But suffering itself, accepted for the love of our brethren, favors the progress of the entire human family. Christians know that union with the sacrifice of our Savior contributes to the building up of the Body of Christ in its plentitude, the assembled People of God(67).

80. Universal Solidarity

We are united in this progress toward God. We have desired to remind all men how crucial is the present moment, how urgent the work to be done. The hour for action has now sounded. At stake are the survival of so many innocent children and, for so many families overcome by misery, the access to conditions fit for human beings; at stake are the peace of the world and the future of civilization. It is time for all men and all peoples to face up to their responsibilities.

A FINAL APPEAL

81. Catholics

First, we appeal to all our sons. In countries undergoing development no less than in others, the laymen should take up as their own proper task the renewal of the temporal order. If the role of the hierarchy is to teach and to interpret authentically the norms of morality to be followed in this matter, it belongs to the laymen, without waiting passively for orders and directives, to take the initiative freely and to infuse a Christian spirit into the mentality, customs, laws and structures of the community in which they live(68). Changes are necessary, basic reforms are indispensable; the laymen should strive resolutely to permeate them with the spirit of the Gospel. We ask our Catholic sons who belong to the more favored nations to bring their talents and give their active participation to organizations, be they of an official or private nature, civil or religious, which are working to overcome the difficulties of the developing nations. They will certainly desire to be in the first ranks of those who collaborate to establish as fact and reality an international morality based on justice and equity.

82. Christians and Believers

We are sure that all Christians, our brethren, will wish to expand their common cooperative effort in order to help mankind vanquish selfishness, pride and rivalries, to overcome ambitions and injustices, to open up to all the road to a more human life, where each man will be loved and helped as his brother, as his neighbor. And, still deeply impressed by the memory of our unforgettable encounter in

Bombay with our non-Christian brethren, we invite them anew to work with all their heart and their intelligence toward this goal, that all the children of men may lead a life worthy of the children of God.

83. Men of Good Will

Finally, we turn to all men of good will who believe that the way to peace lies in the area of development. Delegates to international organizations, government officials, gentlemen of the press, educators: all of you, each in your own way, are the builders of a new world. We entreat Almighty God to enlighten your minds and strengthen your determination to alert public opinion and to involve the peoples of the world. Educators, it is your task to awaken in persons, from their earliest years, a love for the peoples who live in misery. Gentlemen of the press, it is up to you to place before our eyes the story of the efforts exerted to promote mutual assistance among peoples, as well as the spectacle of the miseries which men tend to forget in order to quiet their consciences. Thus, at least, the wealthy will know that the poor stand outside their doors waiting to receive some left-overs from their banquets.

84. Government Authorities

Government officials, it is your concern to mobilize your peoples to form a more effective world solidarity, and above all to make them accept the necessary taxes on their luxuries and their wasteful expenditures, in order to bring about development and to save the peace. Delegates to international organizations, it depends on you to see that the dangerous and futile rivalry of powers should give place to collaboration which is friendly, peaceful and free of vested interests, in order to achieve a responsible development of mankind, in which all men will have an opportunity to find their fulfillment.

85. Men of Learning

If it is true that the world is in trouble because of the lack of thinking, then we call upon men of reflection and of learning, Catholics, Christians, those who hold God in honor, who thirst for an absolute, for justice and for truth: we call upon all men of good will. Following Christ, we make bold to ask you earnestly: "Seek and you shall find"(69), open the paths which lead to mutual assistance among peoples, to a deepening of human knowledge, to an enlargement of heart, to a more brotherly way of living within a truly universal human society.

86. A Task for All

All of you who have heard the appeal of suffering peoples, all of you who are working to answer their cries: you are the apostles of a development which is good and genuine, which is not wealth that is self-centered and sought for its own sake, but rather an economy which is put at the service of man, the bread which is daily distributed to all, as a source of brotherhood and a sign of Providence.

87. Blessing

With a full heart we bless you, and we appeal to all men of good will to join you in a spirit of brotherhood. For, if the new name for peace is development, who would not wish to labor for it with all his powers? Yes, we ask you, all of you, to heed our cry of anguish, in the name of the Lord.

From the Vatican, on the Feast of Easter, the twenty-sixth day of March in the year one thousand nine hundred and sixty-seven.

PAUL PP. VI

FOOTNOTES

(1) Cf. "Acta Leonis XIII," Vol. XI (1892), pp. 97-140. (2) Cf. "Acta Apostolicae Sedis," 23 (1931), pp. 177-228. (3) Cf. AAS, 53 (1961), pp. 401-64. (4) Cf. AAS, 55 (1963), pp. 257-304. (5) Cf. in particular the radio message of June 1, 1941, for the 50th anniversary of "Rerum Novarum," in AAS, 33 (1941), pp. 195-205; Christmas radio message of 1942, in AAS, 35 (1943), pp. 9-24; address to a group of workers on the anniversary of "Rerum Novarum," May 14, 1953, in AAS, 45 (1953), pp. 402-8.

(6) Cf. Encyclical "Mater et Magistra," May 15, 1961, AAS, 53 (1961), p. 440. (7) "Gaudium et Spes" ("Pastoral Constitution on the Church in the Modern World"), Arts. 63-72, AAS, 58 (1966), pp. 1084-94. (8) Motu Proprio "Catholicam Christi Ecclesiam," Jan. 6,

1967, AAS, 59 (1967), p. 27. (9) Encyclical "Rerum Novarum," May 15, 1891, "Acta Leonis XIII," Vol. XI (1892), p. 98. (10) "Gaudium et Spes," Art. 63, n. 3.

(11) Cf. Luke 7:22. (12) "Gaudium et Spes," Art. 3, n. 2. (13) Cf. Encyclical "Immortale Dei," Nov. 1, 1885, "Acta Leonis XIII," Vol. V (1895), p. 127. (14) "Gaudium et Spes," Art. 4, n. 1. (15) L.-J. Lebret, O. P., "Dynamique Concrete du Developpement," Paris: Economie et Humanisme, Les Editiones Ouvrieres, 1961, p. 28.

(16) 2 Thess. 3:10. (17) Cf., e. g., J. Maritain, "Les Conditions Spirituelles du Progres et de la Paix," in "Recontre des Cultures a l'UNESCO sous le Signe du Concile Oecumenique Vatican II," Paris; Mame, 1966, p. 66. (18) Cf. Matt. 5:3. (19) Gen. 1:28. (20) "Gaudium et Spes," Art. 69, n. 1.

(21) 1 John 3:17. (22) De Nabuthe, C. 12, N. 53 (P. L. 14, 747); cf. J.-R. Palanque, "St. Ambroise et l'Empire Romain," Paris; De Boccard, 1933, pp. 336, ff. (23) Letter to the 52nd session of the French Social Weeks (Brest, 1965), in "L'Homme et la Revolution Urbaine," Lyons, "Chronique Sociale 1965," pp. 8, 9; cf. "L'Osservatore Romano," July 10, 1965; "Documentation Catholique," Vol. 62, Paris, 1965, Col. 1365. (24) "Gaudium et Spes," Art. 71, n. 6. (25) Cf. Ibid., Art. 65, n. 3.

(26) Encyclical "Quadragesimo Anno," May 15, 1931, AAS, 23 (1931), p. 212. (27) Cf., e. g., Colin Clark, "The Conditions of Economic Progress," 3rd ed., London: Macmillan and Co., and New York: St. Martin's Press, 1960, pp. 3-6. (28) Letter to the 51st session of the French Social Weeks (Lyons, 1964), in "Le Travail et les Travailleurs dans la Societe Contemporain," Lyons, "Chronique Sociale 1965," p. 6; cf. "L'Osservatore Romano," July 10, 1964; "Documentation Catholique," Vol. 61, Paris, 1964, Col. 931. (29) Cf., e. g., M.-D. Chenu, O. P., "Pour une Theologie du Travail," Paris: Editions du Seuil, 1955; Eng. transl., "The Theology of Work: An Exploration," Dublin: Gill and Son, 1963. (30) "Mater et Magistra," AAS, 53 (1961); N. 423.

(31) Cf., e. g., O. von Nell-Breuning, S. J., "Wirtschaft und Gesellschaft," Vol. I: Grundfragen, Freiburg: Herder, 1956, pp. 183-84. (32) Eph. 4:13. (33) Cf., e. g., Bishop Manuel Larrain Errazuriz of Talca, Chile, "Lettre Pastorale sur le Developpement et la Paix," Paris: Pax Christi, 1965. (34) "Gaudium et Spes," Art. 26, n. 4. (35) "Mater et Magistra," AAS, 53 (1961), p. 414.

(36) "L'Osservatore Romano," Sept. 11, 1965; "Documentation Catholique," Vol. 62, Paris, 1965, Col. 1674-75. (37) Matt. 19:16. (38) "Gaudium et Spes," Art. 52, n. 2. (39) Cf. Ibid., Arts. 50-51, and Note 14; Art. 87, nos. 2 and 3. (40) Ibid., Art. 15, n. 3.

(41) Matt. 16:26. (42) "Gaudium et Spes," Art. 57, n. 4. (43) Ibid., Art. 19, n. 2. (44) Cf., e. g., J. Maritain, "L'Humanisme Integral," Paris: Aubier, 1936; Eng. transl., "True Humanism," London: Geoffrey Bles, and New York: Charles Scribner's Sons, 1938. (45) H. de Lubac, S. J., "Le Drame de l'Humanisme Athee," 3rd ed., Paris: Spes, 1945, p. 10; Eng. transl., "The Drama of Atheistic Humanism," London: Sheed and Ward, 1949, p. VII.

(46) "Pensees," ed. Brunschvicq, N. 434; cf. M. Zundel, "L'Homme Passe l'Homme," Le Caire, Editions du Lien, 1944. (47) Address to the representatives of non-Christian religions, Dec. 3, 1964, AAS, 57 (1965), p. 132. (48) James 2:15-16. (49) Cf. "Mater et Magistra," AAS, 53 (1961), pp. 440, ff. (50) Cf. AAS, 56 (1964), pp. 57-58.

(51) Cf. "Encicliche e Discorsi di Paolo VI," Vol. IX, Rome, Ed. Paoline, 1966, pp. 132-36; "Documentation Catholique," Vol. 43, Paris, 1966, Col. 403-6. (52) Cf. Luke 16:19-31. (53) "Gaudium et Spes," Art. 86, n. 3. (54) Luke 12:20. (55) Message to the world, entrusted to journalists on Dec. 4, 1964, cf. AAS, 57 (1965), p. 135.

(56) Cf. AAS, 56 (1964), pp. 639, ff. (57) Cf. "Acta Leonis XIII," Vol. XI (1892), p. 131. (58) Cf. Ibid., p. 98. (59) "Gaudium et Spes," Art. 85, n. 2. (60) Cf. Encyclical "Fidei Donum," Apr. 21, 1957, AAS, 49 (1957), p. 246.

(61) Matt. 25:35-36. (62) Mark 8:2. (63) Address of John XXIII upon reception of the Balzan Prize for Peace, May 10, 1963, AAS, 55 (1963), p. 455. (64) AAS, 57 (1965), p. 896. (65) Cf. Encyclical "Pacem in Terris," Apr. 11, 1963, AAS, 55 (1963), p. 301.

(66) AAS, 57 (1965), p. 880. (67) Cf. Eph. 4:12; "Lumen Gentium" ("Dogmatic Constitution on the Church"), Art. 13. (68) Cf. "Apostolicam Actuositatem" ("Decree on the Apostolate of the Laity"), Arts. 7, 13, 24. (69) Luke 11:9.

Bibliography

Works of General Reference:

E.H. Schillebeeckx O.P., *Le Christ, sacrament de la rencontre de Dieu*, 1960.

K. Rahner, *Inquiries*, N.Y., 1964.

L.J. Lebret O.P., *Le drame du XXe siecle*, Paris, 1960.

M.D. Chenu O.P., *Pour une théologie du travail*, Paris, 1955.

Saint Thomas Aquinas: *Summa Theologica; Summa Contra Gentiles.*

Saint Ignatius Loyola: *Spiritual Exercises.*

R. Laurentin, *Dévoloppement et salut*, Paris, 1969.

B. de Margerie S.J.: *Reinhold Niebuhr, Théologien de la communauté mondiale*, Paris, Bruges, 1969.
Christ for the World, Chicago, 1974.

Paul VI: Encyclical *Populorum Progressio, 1967*.

John XXIII: Encyclical *Mater et Magistra* (1961).

F. Houtart, *The Church and the developing nations: some questions for theologians*, in the collection: *Theology of Renewal*, Montreal, 1968, v. II, pp. 358-383.

Works with particular relevance to the themes discussed in the various chapters:

Ch. I: *Baptism and Confirmation.*

K. Rahner S.J., *Est-il possible aujourd'hui de croire?* Tours, 1966.

Ch. II: *Marriage, World Population:*

Saint Augustine: *De bono conjugali; De civitate Dei.*
L. Lochet, "Les fins du mariage," NRT, 73 (1951) 453 ff., 562 ff.
A. Sauvy, *De Malthus a Mao-Tsé-Toung*, Paris, 1958.
R. Mols S.J., *Démographie et Paternité responsable*, NRT, 91 (1969) 298 ff, 399 ff.
G. Cottier O.P., *Régulation des Naissances et Développement démographique*, Bruges-Paris, 1969.
P. Beltrao S.J., "Problemi attuali della Pianificazione familiare," *Civiltà Cattolica*, no. 2871, 1970.
C. Clark, *Population Growth and Land Use*, London, 1968.
P. Chauchard, *Volonté et Sexualité*, Paris, 1969.
J. C. Ford S.J., et G. Kelly S.J., *Contemporary Moral Theology*, Westminister, Maryland, USA, 1963, vol. III.
F. Zimmermann, *Catholic Viewpoint on overpopulstion*, Garden City, 1961.
L. Ciccone C.M., "L.'Enciclica H.V.: Analisi e Commento," *Divus Thomas*, Piacenza, 72 (1969) and 73 (1970).

Ch. III: *The Priest:*

Y. M. J. Congar O.P., "Le sacerdoce du NT, dans Vatican II", *Le Prêtre*, US 68, Paris, 1968.
L. Lécuyer C.SSp. *Ibid.*, "Le Presbyterium."
B. de Margerie S.J.: "Population mondiale, célibat du clergé et evangélisation sacramentelle," *Revue de l'Université d'Ottawa*, 36 (1966), 86-106;
"La pénurie de clergé en Amerique latine: faut-il ordonner prêtres des hommes mariés?" NRT, 92 (May 1970).

Ch. IV: *Penance and Renewal in Development:*

B. de Margerie S.J.: "Mission du confesseur et conscience sociale" *Studia Moralia*, Rome, 1965, vol. II, pp. 227-291 (considerably revised).

Lebret et Suavet O.P., *Pour rajeunir l'examen de conscience*, Ed. Ouvrières, Paris, 1952.

A. Chanson, *Pour mieux confesser*, Arras, 1958.

Ch. V: *The Anointing of the Sick:*

F. Cappello S.J., *De extrema unctione*, Rome, 1949.

J. Betz, *Encyclopédie de la Foi*, Paris, 1966, vol. 3, art. "Onction des Malades."

Mgr. Théas, "Rapport sur la célébration de l'Onction des Infirmes à Lourdes," *Notitiae*, 6 (1970) 22-24.

E. Doronzo O.M.I., *De Extrema Unctione*, Milwaukee (USA) 1955, 2 vols.

G. Martimort, *Les signes de la Nouvelle Alliance.*

F. Lepargneur O.P., "Situation du malade en anthropologie crétienne," RUO 37 (1967) 440-462.

F. Bourassa S.J., "La grâce sacramentelle de l'onction des infirmes, *Sciences ecclés.*, 19 (1967) and *Science et Esprit*, 20 (1968).

Ch. VI: *The Eucharist:*

B. de Margerie S.J., *A Ingreja em estaso de diálogo*, Manhumirim, Brazil, 1965, 303-353 (used here with considerable revision).

R. de Vaux O.P., *Institutions de l'A.T.*, Paris, 1958, 2 vols. Desnoyers, *Histoire du peuple hébreu*, Bruges, 1922, 3 vols.

J. Hamer O.P., *L'Eglise est une communion*, Paris 1962.

A. Hamann O.F.M., DSAM vol. IV (1961), art. "Eucharistie."

Allo O.P., *Seconde Epitre aux Corinthens*, Paris, 1937.

Index of Biblical References

Index of Quotations From St. Thomas

Analytical Index